Coaching for Systems and Teacher Change

Coaching for Systems and Teacher Change

by

Jennifer D. Pierce, Ph.D.
American Institutes for Research
Arlington, Virginia

and

Kimberly St. Martin, Ph.D.
Michigan's MTSS Technical Assistance Center
Lansing

Baltimore • London • Sydney

Paul H. Brookes Publishing Co.
Post Office Box 10624
Baltimore, Maryland 21285-0624
USA
www.brookespublishing.com

Typeset by Absolute Service, Inc., Towson, Maryland.
Manufactured in the United States of America by
Kase Printing, Inc., Hudson, New Hampshire.

Photo of Jennifer D. Pierce by Jamiya Wilson © Jamiya Wilson. Photo of Kimberly St. Martin © Lifetouch.

Front cover stock art and other stock art © iStock.

Library of Congress Cataloging-in-Publication Data
Names: Pierce, Jennifer D., author. | St. Martin, Kimberly, author.
Title: Coaching for systems and teacher change / Jennifer D. Pierce and Kimberly St. Martin.
Description: Baltimore: Paul H. Brookes Publishing Co., 2022. | Includes bibliographical references and index.
Identifiers: LCCN 2022000633 (print) | LCCN 2022000634 (ebook) | ISBN 9781681254227 (paperback) |
     ISBN 9781681254234 (epub) | ISBN 9781681254241 (pdf)
Subjects: LCSH: Mentoring in education. | Teachers—In-service learning. | Teachers—Professional relationships. |
     Effective teaching.
Classification: LCC LB1731.4 .P55 2022 (print) | LCC LB1731.4 (ebook) |
     DDC 371.102—dc23/eng/20220215
LC record available at https://lccn.loc.gov/2022000633
LC ebook record available at https://lccn.loc.gov/2022000634

British Library Cataloguing in Publication data are available from the British Library.

2026   2025   2024   2023   2022

10   9   8   7   6   5   4   3   2   1

Contents

Section II   Strategies and Resources for More Effective Coaching

Section III Implementing an Effective Coaching Framework

Appendices

About the Downloads

Purchasers of this book may download, print, and/or photocopy the Appendices for professional or educational use.

To access the materials that come with this book:

1. Go to the Brookes Publishing Download Hub: http://downloads.brookespublishing.com

2. Register to create an account (or log in with an existing account).

3. Filter or search for the book title *Coaching for Systems and Teacher Change.*

A complete list of resources available online follows, including blank templates that appear in the print book.

Chapter 1

Chapter 2

Chapter 3

Chapter 4

About the Authors

Jennifer D. Pierce, Ph.D., Senior Technical Assistant Consultant/Researcher, American Institutes for Research (AIR), Arlington, VA

Dr. Pierce is Senior Technical Assistant Consultant/Researcher for American Institutes for Research (AIR) and has experience working as a teacher, coach, and building- and district-level leader. She also has served in higher education as an adjunct instructor. Her areas of expertise center on supporting the implementation of evidence-based interventions by teachers and schools, including teacher and systems coaching models to reduce the research-to-practice gap; implementation science and systemic change, including frameworks across fields and factors associated with sustained use of evidence-based interventions; and the application of Multi-Tiered Systems of Support (MTSS) across general and special education. Dr. Pierce also has a background in literacy instruction for struggling learners.

Dr. Pierce works in two capacities at AIR: to provide high-quality technical assistance to educators and to conduct meaningful research with practical application to the school setting. On the research side, Dr. Pierce serves as the implementation and coaching lead for several randomized control trials. She is also the project director for an Institute of Education Sciences (IES)–funded study examining the psychometric properties of a MTSS fidelity tool. On the technical assistance side, Dr. Pierce leads coaching and systems change projects for national technical assistance centers, including the National Center for Systemic Improvement (NCSI).

Dr. Pierce is committed to translating research into usable materials for teachers, coaches, and leaders. As a prior colead for the Global Implementation Society Standards Committee and founding member of that worldwide group, she stays attuned to the most recent findings of implementation science to improve the uptake of research in educational settings. Toward this end, she has authored peer-reviewed articles; numerous free, online tools (including coaching modules); and this book.

Dr. Pierce is originally from Seattle and earned her doctoral degree in special education from the University of Washington. She lives in New York City with her wife.

Kimberly St. Martin, Ph.D., Assistant Director, Michigan's MTSS Technical Assistance Center, Michigan Department of Education, Lansing

Dr. St. Martin is Assistant Director of Michigan's Multi-Tiered System of Support (MiMTSS) Technical Assistance Center. She regularly works with State Education Agencies, Regional Education Agencies (REAs), and districts across the country to assist them in successfully using an implementation infrastructure that can scale the components of an integrated behavior and reading Multi-Tiered Systems of Support (MTSS) model. Dr. St. Martin is a panel member for an Institute of Education Sciences (IES) Practice Guide focused on supporting adolescents in Grades 4–9 who need reading intervention supports. She collaborates with the National Implementation Research Network (NIRN) in the Bill and Melinda Gates Foundation Effective Implementation Cohort. Dr. St. Martin has also directed a federally funded adolescent literacy model demonstration grant and has been a coprincipal investigator for a Low-Cost Evaluation Trial, Integrated Tier 2 IES grant. She coauthored the Reading Tiered Fidelity Inventory (R-TFI) and implementation capacity assessments for districts and REAs to guide their supporting infrastructures for an MTSS framework. Before working with the MiMTSS Technical Assistance Center, Dr. St. Martin was a school administrator and teacher with experience in urban, urban-fringe, and rural school districts.

Introduction

BACKGROUND AND PURPOSE

In today's world, educators must develop the skills and knowledge needed to support an ever-diversifying student population. As a result, educators can no longer expect to teach in the isolation of a classroom but must instead continuously collaborate with colleagues who work at different levels of the system (e.g., across grade levels, with district leaders, with staff working at the state level) to improve outcomes among all learners (Joyce & Showers, 2002). Moreover, educators—from teachers to administrators—have a greater recognition that the overall functioning of the educational system influences the degree to which they can produce improved learner outcomes (Bryk, 2010; Fixsen et al., 2005). This complex backdrop often demands that educators have access to support mechanisms that develop their capacity, with coaches often called on to support individual teachers and teams of educators (Freeman et al., 2017; Knight et al., 2015).

Not surprisingly, then, coaching between allied educators is a critical element of effective professional learning and considered to be a cornerstone for producing improved teaching, student learning outcomes (Darling-Hammond et al., 2017; Kraft et al., 2018; Rowe et al., 2021; Yoon et al., 2007), and systems-level change in education (Fixsen et al., 2005). Although coaching is now ubiquitous across the country, with expert teachers, intervention specialists, school psychologists, administrators, counselors, and other allied professionals often serving as coaches (Denton & Hasbrouck, 2009), coaches rarely receive formal preparation or support for serving in this role (Gallucci et al., 2010). As a result, coaches often dedicate their time to a host of activities, which may lead to improved teacher practice, student outcomes, or systems-level change (Denton & Hasbrouck, 2009).

Perhaps you are one of the many coaches working with individuals or teams of educators to improve teacher, student, and systems outcomes (i.e., the day-to-day ways school systems operate, such as streamlining activities across school improvement plans) in the face of these challenges. Alternatively, your role may be to support the work of coaches (e.g., school principal, district or state specialist responsible for leading a cadre of coaches, instructor in a coaching preparation program). If so, this book aims to serve as your go-to resource in two ways. First, it contains an easily digestible synthesis of research on coaching that directly links to the work of the coach. Second, it provides practical tools, which are available in electronic format, that coaches can use to plan powerful coaching sessions, conduct efficient yet impactful sessions with teachers and teams to support their development, and reflect on sessions to ensure coaching continuously improves. Overall, use of the information, resources, and tools in this book can enhance one's capacity of a coach in the era of systems improvement.

To support your development, this book is broken into three sections. Each section is further elaborated so that you can gain a greater understanding of key content and materials. Most important, note that each of these sections provides practical information and resources for teacher coaches—coaches who seek to improve teaching and student learning—and systems coaches—coaches who support a team of educators responsible for leading implementation efforts (e.g., a Multi-Tiered

Systems of Support, or MTSS, coach). You may also apply the content of the book to coaches who work with teachers <u>and</u> teams—we call them *hybrid coaches*. We have found in our work with coaches that there is a clear need for concrete information about conducting powerful coaching cycles. We hope this book will illuminate how to productively engage in this work, whether it is with individual teachers, teams of educators leading an implementation effort, or both.

In Section I, we present foundational research about why coaching has played such a powerful role in professional learning in schools from a historical to a contemporary view. We also explicate the goals of coaching, explain typical activities completed by coaches, and bring to light common challenges coaches face. Moreover, Section I presents the defining features of a coaching framework for two types of coaching: coaching individual teachers from prekindergarten (pre-K) to high school and coaching teams of educators (e.g., principals, general and special education teachers, school psychologists) from pre-K to high school. This first section of the book concludes with an introduction to systems-level change principles and uncovers why it is so critical for coaches to apply them to their day-to-day work with teachers or teams.

Section II unpacks the coaching framework in greater detail. Readers will learn about building strong relationships or alliances with teachers and teams as well as three other core practices in coaching: observing, modeling, and providing performance feedback. This section also offers numerous tools and resources to enhance teacher and team readiness for change and coaching scenarios. Consider this section the skinny on how to plan, conduct, and reflect on conducting coaching cycles with teachers and teams.

In Section III, we focus on an often unaddressed area: considerations and strategies for implementing coaching. For example, we offer a coaching implementation checklist, resources for identifying the fiscal costs of coaching, an approach for identifying the impact of coaching, a set of coaching competencies, and a coaching fidelity measurement tool. Although Section III only contains one chapter, the information presented therein is essential for anyone who seeks to enact coaching for the long term as a mechanism for improving teacher, team, systems, and student outcomes.

We have created an extensive list of coaching resources. These include reflection exercises, activities, discussion guides, planning tools, recommendations, assessments, coaching protocols, tips, checklists, and a cost calculator. These can be found in the back matter of the print book and e-book and are also available for download on the download hub (http://downloads.brookespublishing.com). Filter or search for the book title *Coaching for Systems and Teacher Change*.

MAKING GOOD USE OF THE CONTENT

Rest assured that the three sections of this book contain multiple supportive materials, including guides to deepen thinking and discussion related to coaching, case examples to help coaches apply their thinking to their unique contexts, at-a-glance informational graphics that communicate essential information about coaching in educational systems, and tools to help coaches move beyond thinking about effective coaching to enacting powerful sessions with teachers and teams. Furthermore, each chapter contains Key Questions and Chapter Take-Aways. The former provides compelling prompts for coaches to consider whereas the latter summarizes essential ideas coaches can master.

We suggest that you read these sections as they have been organized so that you can first gain insight into the core concepts of coaching (e.g., barriers, shifting expectations of coaching), then develop a concrete understanding of the most powerful coaching moves that should be a daily part of your coaching repertoire (e.g., providing performance feedback), and finally dig into ways to offset pressing challenges that occur when coaching is not used in a structured, purposeful way in schools. We also recognize, however, that your work may dictate a different approach to using this book. The content can therefore be read in a less linear approach because each chapter and its related materials can be utilized to target specific needs related coaching (e.g., how to build alliance with teachers and teams).

A CORNERSTONE OF COACHING

Before diving into the content, take a moment to reflect on one coaching cornerstone. An underlying premise of coaching is to provide customized support to each teacher and team so that all students within an educational system can reach their fullest potential. This means that every adult and student must be valued for their unique contributions and qualities. In today's world of seemingly inconceivable circumstances (e.g., a global pandemic) and profound conditions (e.g., systemic racism) pervading our lives, coaches must conceptualize their work as a tool for counteracting such abysmal situations. Moreover, coaches' observable behaviors must fulfill the promise of helping each teacher, team, system, and student reach their fullest potential. It is therefore every coach's responsibility to take a hard look at their own biases and actively work to eradicate these negative biases. Furthermore, understand that reflecting and working on biases is an ongoing endeavor that must be attended to continually. After all, if coaching is about anything, it is about bringing out the best in everyone we support. And believing that everyone we support can be the best.

REFERENCES

Bryk, A. S. (2010). Organizing schools for improvement. *Phi Delta Kappan, 91*(7), 23–30.

Darling-Hammond, L., Hyler, M. E., & Gardner, M. (2017). *Effective teacher professional development.* Learning Policy Institute.

Denton, C. A., & Hasbrouck, J. (2009). A description of instructional coaching and its relationship to consultation. *Journal of Educational and Psychological Consultation, 19*(2), 150–175.

Fixsen, D. L., Naoom, S. F., Blase, K. A., Friedman, R. M., & Wallace, F. (2005). *Implementation research: A synthesis of the literature.* University of South Florida, Louis de la Parte Florida Mental Health Institute, The National Implementation Research Network (FMHI Publication #231).

Freeman, J., Sugai, G., Simonsen, B., & Everett, S. (2017). MTSS coaching: Bridging knowing to doing. *Theory Into Practice, 56*(1), 29–37.

Gallucci, C., Van Lare, M. D., Yoon, I. H., & Boatright, B. (2010). Instructional coaching: Building theory about the role and organizational support for professional learning. *American Educational Research Journal, 47*(4), 919–963.

Joyce, B. R., & Showers, B. (2002). *Student achievement through staff development.* Association for Supervision & Curriculum Development.

Knight, J., Elford, M., Hock, M., Dunekack, D., Bradley, B., Deshler, D. D., & Knight, D. (2015). 3 steps to great coaching. *The Learning Professional, 36*(1), 10–12, 14, 16, 18, 74.

Kraft, M. A., Blazar, D., & Hogan, D. (2018). The effect of teacher coaching on instruction and achievement: A meta-analysis of the causal evidence. *Review of Educational Research, 88*(4), 547–588.

Rowe, D. A., Collier-Meek, M. A., Kittelman, A., & Pierce, J. (2021). Ensuring effective implementation of evidence-based practices. *TEACHING Exceptional Children, 53*(6), 396–399.

Yoon, K. S., Duncan, T., Lee, S. W. Y., Scarloss, B., & Shapley, K. L. (2007). *Reviewing the evidence on how teacher professional development affects student achievement: Issues and answers* (REL 2007-No. 033). Regional Educational Laboratory Southwest (NJ1).

This book is dedicated to the educators working to improve the lives of all students, especially those children and youth who struggle the most. The work you do is tireless and often goes unrecognized; know that what you do matters.

To my best friend and wife, Cornelia:
Thank you for the joyous life we have together.
My heart is for you.
—JDP

To my parents:
No matter my age, making you proud never gets old.
I hope this book brings a smile to your face.
—KSM

I

Introduction and Core Concepts

Making the Case for Coaching

From a Historical to a Contemporary View

KEY QUESTIONS

1. Why is coaching a prominent form of professional learning in education?

2. How have educational policies and research shaped the nature of coaching in schools, particularly the evolution of the role from coaching of teachers to the role of the systems coach and hybrid coach?

3. How does knowing about the historical background of coaching help you in today's world?

CHAPTER TAKE-AWAYS

1. Teacher practice is a powerful predictor of student outcomes. In short, good teaching matters. Yet, there is wide variation in how teachers teach and a need for an effective way to support teachers' improved practice in the classroom setting. When Joyce and Shower's seminal research showed that coaching could produce improved teacher practice, coaching quickly became a dominant approach in the professional learning landscape.

2. Other coaching roles cropped up in research and policy around the new millennium, due in part to the use of schoolwide frameworks such as positive behavior interventions and supports (PBIS), response to intervention (RTI), and Multi-Tiered Systems of Support (MTSS). These new roles expanded the focus of the coach role toward improving the practice of school implementation teams, the prekindergarten (pre-K)/school system, and student outcomes.

3. The dual forces of research and policy have influenced the nature of coaching roles in schools, ultimately cementing at least two other roles—systems and hybrid coaching—as integral approaches in the professional learning landscape alongside the traditional coaching role.

CHAPTER OVERVIEW

This chapter is divided into two sections. We first provide a brief rationale for why coaching has become such a prominent form of professional learning in pre-K-12th grade schools, beginning with seminal research conducted by Joyce and Showers in the 1980s. This first section of the chapter focuses on the coaching of teachers because that is the type of coaching that originated in research, policy, and schools (Bean & Wilson, 1981). We also compile data from the National Center of Education Statistics (NCES) related to coaching to present how this role has been staffed in schools at two timepoints (2007–2008 and 2015–2016). Although these data show the overall staffing peaks and valleys of coaching, they indicate that coaching plays an integral role in professional learning within schools.

The second section of this chapter offers a historical to contemporary view of coaching, connecting information from the research and policy arenas to show how these two forces shaped the nature of coaching in schools. We also discuss the evolution of the coaching role: When coaching grew from primarily supporting individual teachers in their classroom practices to supporting teams of educators responsible for leading school implementation efforts (or supporting both teachers and teams).

Before we proceed to the main content of this chapter, we offer some important notes about terminology. We use the label *teacher coaches* when referring to those coaches who support teachers' academic instruction, use of behavioral practices, or use of socioemotional supports for students. We use this label for two reasons. Most obviously, teacher coaching indicates quickly who the coaches support. Who coaches support is important to communicate because not every coaching role is focused on teachers. Second, teacher coaching is reflective of the full scope of coaches' work, wherein those serving in the role often support teachers in an array of areas, including academic content area instruction, implementation of classroom management practices, and use of socioemotional supports. In summary, teacher coaching most accurately conveys the full nature of the role as examined in research, included in policy, and enacted in pre-K–12th-grade schools.

Systems coach is the term used when referring to those coaches who support a team of educators responsible for leading implementation efforts (McIntosh & Goodman, 2016). We also sometimes refer to systems coaching as *implementation team coaching* or even *team coaching* for shorthand. We do not, however, use the label to suggest the team is a group of teachers who are focusing on improving their classroom practices and their students' outcomes. Rather, systems coaches work with a team of educators who are charged with guiding the school's implementation of schoolwide and district priorities (e.g., MTSS, initiatives). Systems coaches aim to improve that team's practices (e.g., team's data utilization, team meeting processes), the school system or pre-K program, and even student outcomes. (We discuss these desired outcomes extensively in subsequent chapters, especially Chapter 2.)

Finally, *hybrid coaching* is used when discussing coaching that is offered to teachers and to implementation teams, indicating that the individuals providing this type of coaching work to improve teacher practice, team practices, pre-K/school systems, and, ultimately, student outcomes. The term *hybrid coaching* is not likely to be found (at this time) in research or policy, but in our experience, practitioners embrace this label because it clearly reflects the nature of work expected of those serving in the role.

We highlight the nuances of these different labels because it is important to understand from the onset who we mean when we refer to the different roles addressed in this text. In addition, we have found that the general word "coach" is commonly used in research, policy, and practice without specifying what precisely is meant by the term. Similarly, terms commonly associated with the work of the coach (e.g., professional learning, trainings, workshops) are often used differently in research and practice. Given that not all coaching roles work toward the same goals, work with the

Table 1.1. Definitions of terminology used in this text

Term	Definition and additional information
Professional learning	An umbrella term for the different types of supports coaches provide to teaches and teams. Examples of professional learning approaches include professional learning workshops, trainings, coaching, communities of practice, and professional learning communities.
Professional learning workshops	A professional learning approach that coaches typically provide to teachers or teams to build their knowledge in a certain topic (e.g., reading instruction) or educational innovation (evidence-based practices, assessment tools). Professional learning workshops may be referred to as *trainings* or simply *workshops*.
Coaching teachers	A professional learning approach provided to teachers to support their implementation of academic practices, behavioral practices, and/or socioemotional supports. The focus of coaching is on improving teacher practice and student outcomes.
Systems coaching, also referred to as *team coaching*	A professional learning approach provided to a team of educators responsible for leading a schoolwide implementation effort. The team of educators may be called the *leadership team, implementation team,* or *leadership implementation team.* The goal of systems coaching is to improve the implementation team's practice, system outcomes, and, ultimately, student outcomes.
Hybrid coaching	A professional learning approach provided to 1) teachers to support their implementation of academic practices, behavioral practices; and/or socioemotional supports and 2) a team of educators responsible for leading a schoolwide implementation effort. The goal when coaching teachers is to improve teacher practice and student outcomes. The goal when coaching a team is to improve the implementation team's practice, system outcomes, and, ultimately, student outcomes.

same coachees, or enact the same activities, it is important to clarify what we mean when we talk about coaching, as well as how coaching fits into the overall landscape of professional learning. Table 1.1 summarizes how we use these different labels throughout this text.

Whether interested in the coaching of teachers, the coaching of implementation teams, or the hybrid role, we do suggest delving into Chapter 1 before reading other chapters. Reading Chapter 1 allows you to garner a clear understanding of how coaching has been conceived and enacted in the past. Moreover, the history of coaching has shaped the nature of modern-day coaching—influencing everything from the title of the role to the expectations held about what constitutes coaching and what can be achieved from coaching. Modern-day coaches can even draw on this historical information to contemplate the future of coaching.

Similarly, we suggest reading Chapter 1 before planning, conducting, or reflecting on coaching sessions with teachers and teams. Planning, conducting, and reflecting on coaching sessions will be more productive (and more effective) when the coach holds foundational knowledge about the role and can effectively communicate this knowledge to others.

MAKING THE CASE FOR COACHING

The impact of quality teaching is unequivocal. Students show improved academic performance, from increased scores on standardized reading, math, and science tests (Hattie, 2012; RAND Corporation, 2012) to reductions in challenging classroom behavior (Reinke et al., 2014), when they are instructed by skilled teachers. The quality of teaching practices vary (Rivkin et al., 2005), however, and as a result, schools and districts often require an effective way for improving teacher practice through ongoing, classroom-based support. Enter coaching.

Why has coaching become such a prominent professional learning approach aimed at improving teacher practice? One key reason is undoubtedly linked to Joyce and Showers' (1982) seminal research findings on the difference between training and coaching. The duo found that training led to improved teacher knowledge but was insufficient for improving teachers' practice in the classroom setting. In contrast, the researchers also found that coaching—classroom-embedded, ongoing support—was the bridge between knowledge acquisition and translating that knowledge into practice in the classroom.

The alluring finding that coaching could be such a powerful force for changing teacher practice proved to be sufficient justification for it to be quickly embraced by researchers, policy makers, and educators alike. On the research side, studies on coaching exploded shortly after Joyce and Showers' original study was published (Hargreaves & Skelton, 2012). Educational policies began to attend to the notion of coaching (Denton & Hasbrouck, 2009), and schools across the country shifted into action to more widely offer coaching to teachers (Rhodes & Beneicke, 2002).

Today's coaching movement seems even stronger than it was in the 1980s. Consider the following facts:

- Hundreds of thousands of coaching studies have been conducted since Joyce and Showers' (1982) seminal examination of coaching. In 2019 alone, more than 14,000 studies were published in journals and other sources of gray literature (e.g., educational web sites, white papers).

- Every federal educational policy since 1999 has indirectly or directly called for the use of coaching to improve teaching.

- Data on coaching from the NCES (Taie & Goldring, 2017) showed that 67% of all K–12 public schools had either a coach or an instructional specialist assigned to work with teachers. A *coach* was defined as someone who (at a minimum) observed, modeled the use of teaching practices, and provided performance feedback to teachers. A *specialist* was defined as someone who coached teachers and worked directly with students.

- Of the 67% of schools previously mentioned, roughly 40% have coaches. Specialists constitute the remaining 23%. These rates are double the rates of coaches and specialists in 2000 (Domina et al., 2015).

- Nearly 60,000 K–12th-grade educators serve in the role of coach or specialist (NCES, 2017).

- Although the numbers of pre-K coaches are not available from national data sets, coaching pre-K teachers has been recommended as a necessary addition to supporting early learning (Elek & Page, 2019; Snyder et al., 2015).

Although the embrace of coaching was not a linear progression over the decades, the data offer clear signals that Joyce and Showers' (1982) case for coaching has been made. When educators require support in improving their practice, it seems safe to conclude neither researchers', educators', or policy makers' interest in coaching is unlikely to significantly wane anytime soon. Coaching is here to stay. (To learn more about the prevalence of coaching in schools, see the additional information shown in the text box.)

Coaching by the Numbers: A Deeper Look at K–12 Schools

Between 2007–2008 and 2015–2016, elementary schools with reading coaches ranged from 44% to 47%, whereas the percentage of secondary schools (i.e., combined middle and high schools) with coaches ranged from 35% to 44% (information from Taie and Goldring, 2017, & U.S. Department of Education, 2008—two reports pulled from the Schools and Staffing Survey [SASS] and the National Teacher and Principal Survey [NTPS]). Across those same years, a smaller percentage of elementary schools (from 22% in 2007–2008 to 27% in 2015–2016) than secondary schools employed math coaches (30% in the same time span). Science coaches were less common than either reading or math coaches in both elementary and secondary schools, with about 8% of elementary schools and 15%–17% of secondary schools employing this type of coach across all years (2007–2016). Table 1.2 summarizes this information.

Table 1.2. Percentage of teacher coaches by role from 2007-2008 and 2015-2016

	2007-2008		2015-2016	
Coaching Role	*Elementary*	*Secondary*	*Elementary*	*Secondary*
Reading Coach	47.3	40	44.4	35
Math Coach	22.2	30	27	30
Science Coach	8.3	17	7.5	15
Unspecified Coaching Role	Unavailable	Unavailable	34.5	43

Sources: Taie and Goldring (2017); U.S. Department of Education, National Center for Education Statistics (2008).

Looking deeper at school characteristics also offers additional insight into the nature of coaching in American schools. As shown in Table 1.3, with only one exception in 2015-2016, a greater percentage of coaches work in schools with high rates of students on free or reduced-price lunch (FRPL) than schools with low percentages of students on FRPL. In fact, with nearly every jump in FRPL rates comes a jump in the percentage of coaches working in those schools, although schools with the highest percentage of FRPL fell from roughly 70% in 2007-2008 to 67% in 2015-2016. Scanning the data related to the location of a school also highlights an interesting trend: Between 2007-2016, schools located in cities had a higher percentage of coaches than schools located in communities designated as rural, suburban, or as a township, even though township schools saw nearly a 10% jump in coaching in 2015-2016. Next, schools with 500 or more students saw coaching percentages increase, whereas smaller schools saw only slight shifts or remained the same. Looking at public and charter schools, a higher percentage of coaches worked in traditional schools than in charter schools in 2007-2008, but this trend shifted in 2015-2016. Finally, 57% of all schools had a coach in 2007-2008, but this grew to 66% by 2015-2016. Although the reasons why these trends exist are likely numerous and next to impossible to tease out, the data highlight one key point—coaching is an integral part of professional learning in schools.

Table 1.3. A contextual look at coaching in schools

School Factor	**2007-2008**	**2015-2016**
Percentage of students qualifying for FRPL 0%-34%	61.4	68.2
Percentage of students qualifying for FRPL 35%-49%	61.1	63.9
Percentage of students qualifying for FRPL 50%-74%	67.2	67
Percentage of students qualifying for FRPL 75% or more	70.2	67.6
City	72.4	73.4
Suburban	67.9	71.1
Township	58.9	59.8
Rural	54.7	55
Enrollment less than 100 students	31.2	30.5
Enrollment of students from 100-199	52.1	53.4
Enrollment of students from 200-499	69.6	69.4
Enrollment of students from 500-749	67.9	72.9
Enrollment of students from 750-999	67.2	72
Enrollment of students at or more than 1,000	60.7	63.9
Traditional public school	63.4	65.9
Charter school	61.6	69.9
Percentage of all schools with staff with coaching assignments	56.9	65.9

Sources: Taie and Goldring (2017); U.S. Department of Education, National Center for Education Statistics (2008).
Key: FRPL, free or reduced-price lunch.

COACHING ACROSS THE DECADES

Even with the significant role Joyce and Showers (1982) played in making the case for coaching, it would be too simplistic to suggest that the coaching movement rested solely on the shoulders of two individuals. Thus, this section presents a more comprehensive review of the coaching evolution that has occurred since the 1980s. It is divided into three time periods, starting from a historical perspective and building to a contemporary view. Each of the three time spans integrates information from two spheres—research and policy—to construct a phase-by-phase view to paint an overall picture of coaching, including how the role has expanded. It also allows the reader to glean a robust understanding of how coaching has been shaped by 40 years of research and educational policies to become an integral part of today's pre-K–12th grade school system.

Three notes are important to offer before moving toward the discussion of the phases of coaching. First, we begin our historical discussion of coaching in the 1980s because of the affect Joyce and Showers' work had on coaching research, educational policy, and, in turn, schools. But as Bean and Wilson (1981) noted, the deepest roots of coaching can be found in a popular role from the 1930s to the 1970s—the reading specialist. The *specialist* was defined as a teacher typically responsible for providing remediation support to struggling readers who also occasionally worked with other individual teachers outside of the classroom setting (Bean & Wilson, 1981; Ippolito et al., 2019). Second, as you will see in the following text, the role of the coach from working with teachers to working with implementation teams (or both) did not begin to shift until the second phase of coaching (roughly 2002). Information on systems and hybrid coaching roles are therefore discussed in Phases 2 and 3, whereas Phase 1 focuses on the coaching of teachers with the purpose of improving teacher practice. Third, this chapter offers a distillation of coaching research for the purposes of capturing the tenor of scholarly work and educational policy on coaching over the decades. Refer to Chapter 3 for a more comprehensive review of coaching research.

Phase 1: Laying the Groundwork for Coaching (1980s–2001)

Although Joyce and Showers were perhaps the most well-known to examine teacher coaching during the 1980s and 1990s (see Joyce & Showers, 1980, 1981; Showers, 1984; Showers & Joyce, 1996), other researchers also offered important contributions about coaching during this time span. Several of these researchers also applied a peer-to-peer coaching approach in their studies, which was the dominant coaching approach used by Joyce and Showers. For example, Kohler et al. (1995) conducted peer coaching in the pre-K setting, as did Miller (1994) and Wynn and Kromrey (1999). Others focused on peer coaching with general and special education teachers (Hasbrouck & Christen, 1997), finding it to be an effective way to support general educators' instruction for students with disabilities. Taken together, these peer coaching studies found that it was a productive approach for improving new and experienced pre-K–12th grade teachers' use of instructional and management practices across special and general education classrooms.

But as noted in one early Joyce and Showers (1980) article, successful coaching need not rely on only a peer-to-peer approach. Experts (e.g., researchers, consultants, experienced teachers) could also serve in the role. Thus, we see other researchers branching out from the peer-to-peer approach during Phase 1. Peterson Miller et al. (1991) examined the coaching of special education preservice teachers by experts, and they showed improved classroom management and instructional practices when coached. Roelof et al. (1994) and Veenman and Denessen (2001) also examined an expert-to-novice coaching model, finding it led to improved instruction and classroom management among general education teachers, although coached teachers did not outperform noncoached teachers.

Whether focused on a peer or expert coaching model, Phase 1 research offered two key takeaways. First, coaching offered teachers a unique benefit that other forms of professional learning did not offer: transferring what was learned in training to improve teacher practice in the classroom setting (Joyce & Showers, 1981). Second, but equally important, a small number of studies began to uncover that coaching could improve more than teacher practice—students may also see improved outcomes. Ross (1992) and Kohler et al. (1997) led the way to determine the impact of coaching on student outcomes. They found early evidence that coaching could lead to improvements in changing teacher practice *and* student outcomes.

As the previous research was underway, the realm of policy was slowly beginning to attend to the idea of coaching. This was influenced in part by the political desire to solidify the country's place as a global economic leader, alarmingly low student outcomes across the country on the National Assessment of Educational Progress (NAEP; Edmonson, 2005), and the release of a pivotal research synthesis on the nature of teaching reading to young children (National Research Council, 1998a). When the federal government introduced the Reading Excellence Act (REA) in 1999, a central goal of the REA was to overhaul pre-K–3 literacy instruction so that teachers used scientifically based reading (SBR) instructional practices as part of their daily work with children (https://www.govtrack.us/congress/bills/105/hr2614/text). Although not specifically cited in the act itself, coaching was viewed favorably by those in charge of awarding REA funds to states (Kraft et al., 2018), perhaps due in part to the National Research Council's strong endorsement of the 1990s version of the coaching role (the reading specialist): "Schools that lack or have abandoned the use of reading specialists should re-examine their need for them and provide the functional equivalent of these well-trained staff members" (1998b, para. 11).

With a strong push for coaching under REA and a bank of meaningful studies and scholarly articles published on the pages of some of the most widely read educational journals (e.g., *Educational Leadership, Journal of Educational Research*), Phase 1 ended with coaching of teachers as an increasingly routine part of the educational system. Even from this well-positioned place, coaching was about to capture even greater attention from the research and policy contexts.

Phase 2: The Evolution of the Coaching Role (2002–2014)

Phase 2 kicked off in the new millennium with a decisive bang as policy makers replaced REA with the No Child Left Behind (NCLB) Act of 2001 (PL 107-110) and its two funding mechanisms: Reading First and Early Reading First. Although NCLB and REA had some differences (e.g., NCLB's accountability system for schools not showing adequate student progress, requirements for teachers to be highly qualified), similarities could still be seen between the two policies (e.g., emphasis on the use of SBR, expectation that all children were proficient readers by third grade). NCLB pressed even further than REA with respect to coaching. For the first time in the history of the United States, Early Reading First and Reading First grants funded under NCLB specifically listed coaching as one recommended mechanism for improving teaching and student learning (U.S. Department of Education, 2003, 2007). Indeed, the teacher coaching role was taking the policy world by storm.

Alongside this policy push for coaching was an increase in coaching research. Studies from this phase examined Early reading First coaches, Reading First coaches, or behavioral coaches. Many of the studies from this phase focused on understanding the role of the coach, describing the critical responsibilities of literacy coaches (Deussen et al., 2007) and behavioral coaches (Bradshaw et al., 2012; Hershfeldt et al., 2012), and identifying benefits and challenges of this work (Bean et al., 2012; Shidler, 2009). Other efforts detected a positive relationship with coaching and improved teaching (Elish-Piper & L'Allier, 2011) or even causal links between coaching, improved teachers' literacy practice, and improved student literacy outcomes (Bingham & Patton-Terry, 2013; Jackson et al., 2007).

This collection of studies captured many insights about the nature and impact of coaching. For example, researchers learned that there was wide variation in how coaches allocated their time, with some coaches able to dedicate more time to directly coaching teachers while other coaches struggled to do so. Moreover, they learned that some tasks (e.g., teacher observations) were more tightly linked with improved teacher practices than other tasks (e.g., conducting student assessments) (Deussen et al., 2007).

The attempts to identify causal links between coaching and improved teaching and student outcomes were not without significant controversy. When the U.S. Department of Education's Interim Report (2006) on Reading First did not conclusively detect significant improved student outcomes in these schools, the decisively warm embrace of coaching in scholarly works was increasingly replaced by warnings to take a slow, more systematic approach to implementing coaching as the chosen professional learning approach for improving teaching and learning (Deussen et al., 2007; McKenna & Walpole, 2010). In the years after the 2006 report, NCLB increasing fell out of favor in the policy world so much that it was on a path toward demise by 2012. In this time span, coaching researchers pressed on with the message that coaching, whether literacy focused or behavioral focused, could lead to improved teaching and learning when enacted well (Kretlow & Bartholomew, 2010; Sailors & Shanklin, 2010).

Support for the coaching of teachers in schools began to waver during this messy research and policy climate. The percentage of reading, math, and science coaches and specialists working in schools in 2011–2012 remained somewhat stable compared with 2007–2008, suggesting some coaching/specialist roles were stabilizing but not growing (U.S. Department of Education, NCES, 2008, 2012). School leaders questioned if the costs (time commitments) required of coaching outweighed the benefits (Matsumura et al., 2009). Other forms of professional learning aimed at improving teaching and student learning took on increasingly prominent roles in the professional learning landscape (e.g., professional learning communities, mentoring systems, teacher inquiry, communities of practice) (Borko et al., 2010). The growth of the general instructional/not subject-specific coach, which accounted for more than one quarter of coaches working in schools, was one bright light in the area of coaching (U.S. Department of Education, NCES, 2012). This new unidentified role likely accounted for the overall increase of the percentage of coaches in schools from Phase 1 to Phase 2.

As the new millennium progressed, two variations of the traditional form of coaching began to emerge in schools and research but, interestingly, not in the policy realm: 1) coaches for teams of educators serving on implementation leadership teams, sometimes referred to as *systems coaches* (Fullan & Knight, 2011) but not always (Fixsen et al., 2005) and 2) coaches for implementation teams and individual teachers (Bradshaw et al., 2012), whom we have coined *hybrid coaches*. One reason for this evolution of coaching may be linked to the rise of RTI (Fuchs & Fuchs, 2006) and PBIS (Horner & Sugai, 2015). Some of these coaches were expected to support PBIS/RTI leadership teams in implementing multicomponent frameworks (e.g., data-based decision making) (Newton et al., 2011). Other coaches were expected to help individual teachers implement new practices while also supporting implementation leadership teams (Bradshaw et al., 2012). The prevailing thinking among researchers seemed to be that if teachers benefit from coaching, then teams of educators responsible for transforming the entire school system also likely need coaching (Barrett et al., 2008).

Second, around the time that PBIS and RTI were becoming more widely used in schools, leading implementation experts (Fixsen et al., 2005) began to promote the idea of the team coach as a necessary ingredient for the successful use, scale-up, and sustainability of educational innovations. Like key leaders of PBIS and RTI, Fixsen and colleagues maintained that implementation efforts were notoriously difficult, warranting the need for team coaches to ensure that implementation occurred. One key difference, however, was that Fixsen et al. primarily utilized the systems coaching role rather than drawing on the hybrid role, wherein the coach supports individual teachers and implementation leadership teams (Fixsen et al., 2010).

These two factors shaped the nature of the coaching role, shifting it toward new directions. The systems coach and hybrid coaching roles thus became a distinct part of the professional learning landscape alongside the teacher coach. See the text box for more background on the evolution of the coaching role.

The Systems and Hybrid Coaching Roles Evolve

Although coaching prior to 2000 focused on the coaching of teachers to improve their practice, it is important to acknowledge that those working in the role of coach prior to 2000 often did play a part in systemwide implementation efforts alongside members of school leadership teams (Hargreaves & Skelton, 2012). Yet, prior to the 2000s, coaches and specialists were typically expected to be key individuals in a school's implementation efforts by setting school assessment schedules in partnership with principals, coordinating curricular materials, and providing professional development for teachers (International Reading Association, 2010; Walpole & Blamey, 2008). If this sounds a bit like systems coaching, then you are correct. But there was a difference. Prior to the 2000s, the role of the coach was to be a part of rolling out a school reform, implementation, or improvement plan (Bean & Wilson, 1981) by *supporting individual teachers*. Post-2000, systems and hybrid coaches were increasingly expected to serve as a *primary lever* for school system improvement (Fullan & Knight, 2011; Ippolito et al., 2019; Poglinco et al., 2003) by *supporting leadership teams*.

Although the onset of the systems and hybrid coaching roles are difficult to pinpoint to a precise point in time, gone were the days when some coaches worked only with teachers. These types of coaches were expected to support leadership teams (or individual teachers *and* leadership teams) with increasing regularity. Alongside this evolved role came the additional expectation that coaches possessed the knowledge and skills necessary for improving team practice, therein transforming school systems so that student outcomes improved (McCamish et al., 2015). The bar was high for coaches working in these evolved roles.

Phase 3: Capturing the Value-Add of Coaching (2014–Present)

Phase 3 began with support for coaching, and the nature of the role was somewhat in flux. On the research side, several prominent researchers continued to issue a drumbeat of reminders that coaching teachers could not be effective if attention was not paid to how coaches worked with coachees (e.g., see Desimone & Pak, 2017). Within that same year, Darling-Hammond et al. (2017) similarly argued that coaching teachers was a cornerstone of high-quality professional learning but only when it was implemented with fidelity (i.e., adherence, appropriate dosage, quality). These messages were issued specifically in relation to the coaching of teachers, missing the opportunity to advance the idea that any coaching role (e.g., whether a systems, teacher, or hybrid role) could only be effective when implemented with fidelity.

Coaching was slowly beginning to shift toward good favor again on the policy front. In 2014, Results Driven Accountability (RDA) aimed to improve pervasively low outcomes among students with disabilities (https://www2.ed.gov/about/offices/list/osers/osep/rda/index.html). RDA required all states to identify specific strategies for dramatically improving outcomes. Although RDA did not directly reference coaching, this requirement was met by nearly half of states selecting teacher coaching, systems coaching, or hybrid coaching as a key strategy for improving teaching, systems outcomes, and student learning outcomes (Ruedel et al., 2021). Furthermore, the Every Student Succeeds Act (ESSA) of 2015 (PL 114-95) featured coaching as a way to improve teacher practice and even strongly promoted the role, emphasizing the need for coaches to support principals and other school leaders

(Rowland, 2017). It seemed that the policy world was also showing interest in evolving coaching roles.

Shortly after these policies, the effort to uncover the impact of coaching on teacher practice and student learning captured an important achievement. A team of researchers published a meta-analysis of 60 studies that clearly asserted that this type of coaching could lead to improved teaching (with an effect size of .71) and (to a lesser degree) improved student learning outcomes (with an effect size of .11) (Kraft et al., 2018). The scholarly work created a powerful buzz in the coaching world: practitioner-oriented journals disseminated the findings in a reader-friendly way (e.g., Foster, 2018), and *U.S. News and World Report* summarized the work for the lay reader (The Hechinger Report, 2018). On the heels of Kraft et al.'s work came Elek and Page's (2019) descriptive review of empirical research on coaching in early childhood contexts, highlighting that coaching could improve teaching and (again, to a lesser degree) child outcomes. Even those most critical of coaching will be hard pressed to dismiss the value of coaching teachers after reading this collection of articles.

APPENDIX A **Reflecting on My Coaching Role**

Purpose: Use this reflection sheet to think about your past, present, and future coaching role and how educational research and policy has shaped that role.

Directions:
1. Read Chapter 1.
2. Respond to the following questions about your coaching role.
3. If you can, share your reflections with a partner.

Questions	Reflections
1. What type of role did you have in the past? In what ways has educational research and policy shaped the nature of that role?	
2. How would you describe your current coaching role? Are you a coach for individual teachers, a team or systems coach, or a hybrid coach? In what ways has educational research and policy shaped the nature of that role?	
3. Think about your future coaching role. In what ways might educational research and policy shape the nature of that role?	

(page 1 of 1)

Figure 1.1. Reflecting on My Coaching Role. (*Note:* Blank versions of this form are available in Appendix A and to download.)

Alongside these scholarly works were research examinations of coaching into new arenas. Math coaching studies enjoyed a heightened interest (Bengo, 2016; Russell et al., 2019), with examinations from Phase 1 (Gersten & Kelly, 1992) and Phase 2 years (e.g., Clements & Sarama, 2008; Rudd et al., 2009) branching out to uncover the nuances of this role (Mudzimiri et al., 2014). Other Phase 3 examinations shifted toward coaching in social studies (Knowles et al., 2019) and science (Hsieh et al., 2019) classrooms. Behavior-oriented coaching research also continued to burgeon. Pas et al. (2019) studied middle school teachers' use of antibullying prevention strategies, which showed coaching was a powerful force in improving teachers' classroom management practices. Studies looking at the use of technology with coaching also began to see an uptick (Breslow, 2017), building on studies from Phase 2 (e.g., Rock et al., 2011). Many of these studies focused on uncovering findings related to virtual coaching in which a coach works remotely with teachers rather than face to face (Ippolito et al., 2021). Unfortunately, studies on systems coaching and hybrid coaching remained somewhat thin, with exceptions being Bastable, Massar, and McIntosh's (2020) examination of systems coaching activities and March and colleagues' study on systems coaching and MTSS teams' use of problem-solving procedures (March et al., 2016). Although time will cement the full implication of these studies, it seems clear there is a desire to better understand how teacher, system, and hybrid coaching roles shape teacher practice, team practice, school systems, and student outcomes across a range of contexts.

The outlook on coaching was becoming decidedly less opaque than it was during the latter years of Phase 2. In comparison to 2011–2012, the overall percentage of coaches began to slowly increase again by 2015–2016 (Taie & Goldring, 2017; U.S. Department of Education, 2012). In fact, the undefined role of the general instructional/not subject-specific coach jumped once again from about 25% to more than 36% in this same time frame (Taie & Goldring, 2017), suggesting a distinct rise in another type of coaching role not focused on supporting one content area such as reading or math—the systems or hybrid coach. The overall take-away from Phase 3 was the type of coaching roles in schools may still be in flux, but the role itself is all but cemented once again as the preferred mode of professional learning for teachers across the research, policy, and school landscape.

BRIDGING THE PAST TO THE PRESENT: IMPLICATIONS FOR TODAY'S COACH

Now that we have walked through these three timepoints in coaching research, policy, and practice, let's consider how today's coaches can use the information in their work with teachers or teams. Use the reflection sheet (see Figure 1.1; blank versions of this form are available in Appendix A and to download) to explore 1) your past, present, and future coaching role and 2) how educational research and policies have influenced your current role or may come to influence that role in the future.

SUMMARY

The appeal of coaching may wax and wane in policy, research, and practice, but where there is talk of improving teacher practice, implementation team practice, school/pre-K systems, and student outcomes, there is also talk of coaching. Although it may be a hyperbole to herald coaches as "The Heroes of the Golden Age of Educational Practice" (Petrilli, 2019), the past 4 decades have shown that coaches are indeed an integral part of the professional learning landscape for pre-K–12th grade teachers and teams.

REFERENCES

Barrett, S. B., Bradshaw, C. P., & Lewis-Palmer, T. (2008). Maryland statewide PBIS initiative: Systems, evaluation, and next steps. *Journal of Positive Behavior Interventions, 10*(2), 105–114.

Bastable, E., Massar, M. M., & McIntosh, K. (2020). A survey of team members' perceptions of coaching activities related to tier 1 SWPBIS implementation. *Journal of Positive Behavior Interventions, 22*(1), 51–61.

Bean, R. M., Draper, J. A., Hall, V., Vandermolen, J., & Zigmond, N. (2010). Coaches and coaching in Reading First schools: A reality check. *Elementary School Journal, 111*(1), 87–114.

Bean, R. M., & Wilson, R. M. (1981). *Effecting change in school reading programs: The resource role.* International Reading Association.

Bengo, P. (2016). Secondary mathematics coaching: The components of effective mathematics coaching and implications. *Teaching and Teacher Education, 60,* 88–96.

Bingham, G. E., & Patton-Terry, N. (2013). Early language and literacy achievement of early Reading First students in kindergarten and 1st grade in the United States. *Journal of Research in Childhood Education, 27*(4), 440–453.

Borko, H., Jacobs, J., & Koellner, K. (2010). Contemporary approaches to teacher professional development. *International Encyclopedia of Education, 7*(2), 548–556.

Bradshaw, C. P., Pas, E. T., Goldweber, A., Rosenberg, M. S., & Leaf, P. J. (2012). Integrating school-wide positive behavioral interventions and supports with Tier 2 coaching to student support teams: The PBIS plus model. *Advances in School Mental Health Promotion, 5*(3), 177–193.

Breslow, N. (2017). Technology takes coaching to scale. *The Learning Professional, 38*(6), 54–62.

Clements, D. H., & Sarama, J. (2008). Experimental evaluation of the effects of a research-based preschool mathematics curriculum. *American Educational Research Journal, 45*(2), 443–494.

Darling-Hammond, L., Hyler, M. E., & Gardner, M. (2017). *Effective teacher professional development.* Learning Policy Institute. https://learningpolicyinstitute.org/product/teacher-prof-dev

Denton, C. A., & Hasbrouck, J. (2009). A description of instructional coaching and its relationship to consultation. *Journal of Educational and Psychological Consultation, 19*(2), 150–175.

Desimone, L. M., & Pak, K. (2017). Instructional coaching as high-quality professional development. *Theory Into Practice, 56*(1), 3–12.

Deussen, T., Coskie, T., Robinson, L., & Autio, E. (2007). *"Coach" can mean many things: Five categories of literacy coaches in Reading First* (Issues & Answers Report, REL 2007–No. 005). U.S. Department of Education, Institute of Education Sciences, National Center for Education Evaluation and Regional Assistance, Regional Educational Laboratory Northwest. http://ies.ed.gov/ncee/edlabs

Domina, T., Lewis, R., Agarwal, P., & Hanselman, P. (2015). Professional sense-makers: Instructional specialists in contemporary schooling. *Educational Researcher, 44*(6), 359–364.

Edmondson, J. (2005). Policymaking in education: Understanding influences on the Reading Excellence Act. *Education Policy Analysis Archives/Archivos Analíticos de Políticas Educativas, 13*, 1–18.

Elek, C., & Page, J. (2019). Critical features of effective coaching for early childhood educators: A review of empirical research literature. *Professional Development in Education, 45*(4), 567–585.

Elish-Piper, L., & L'Allier, S. K. (2011). Examining the relationship between literacy coaching and student reading gains in grades K–3. *Elementary School Journal, 112*(1), 83–106.

Every Student Succeeds Act of 2015, PL 114-95, 20 U.S.C §§ 1001 *et seq.*

Fixsen, D. L., Blase, K., Metz, A., & Van Dyke, M. (2010). *Implementation teams: The active interface between interventions and effective human services.* FPG Child Development Institute, University of North Carolina.

Fixsen, D. L., Naoom, S. F., Blase, K. A., Friedman, R. M. & Wallace, F. (2005). *Implementation research: A synthesis of the literature.* The National Implementation Research Network.

Foster, E. (2018). The impact of coaching on teacher practice and student achievement. *The Learning Professional, 39*(4), 16–19.

Fuchs, D., & Fuchs, L. S. (2006). Introduction to response to intervention: What, why, and how valid is it? *Reading Research Quarterly, 41*(1), 93–99.

Fullan, M., & Knight, J. (2011). Coaches as system leaders. *Educational Leadership, 69*(2), 50–53.

Gersten, R., & Kelly, B. (1992). Coaching secondary special education teachers in implementation of an innovative videodisc mathematics curriculum. *Remedial and Special Education, 13*(4), 40–51.

Hargreaves, A., & Skelton, J. (2012). Politics and systems of coaching and mentoring. In S. J. Fletcher & C. A. Mullen (Eds.), *The SAGE handbook of mentoring and coaching in education* (pp. 122–138). Sage Publications.

Hasbrouck, J. E., & Christen, M. H. (1997). Providing peer coaching in inclusive classrooms: A tool for consulting teachers. *Intervention in School and Clinic, 32*(3), 172–177.

Hattie, J. (2012). *Visible learning for teachers: Maximizing impact on learning.* Routledge.

The Hechinger Report. (2018, March 5). *Does every teacher need a coach?* https://www.usnews.com/news/national-news/articles/2018-03-05/does-every-teacher-need-a-coach

Hershfeldt, P. A., Pell, K., Sechrest, R., Pas, E. T., & Bradshaw, C. P. (2012). Lessons learned coaching teachers in behavior management: The PBIS plus coaching model. *Journal of Educational and Psychological Consultation, 22*(4), 280–299.

Higgins, M., Weiner, J., & Young, L. (2012). Implementation teams: A new lever for organizational change. *Journal of Organizational Behavior.* https://doi.org/10.1002/job.1773

Horner, R. H., & Sugai, G. (2015). School-wide PBIS: An example of applied behavior analysis implemented at a scale of social importance. *Behavior Analysis in Practice, 8*(1), 80–85.

Hsieh, F. P., Lin, H. S., Liu, S. C., & Tsai, C. Y. (2019). Effect of peer coaching on teachers' practice and their students' scientific competencies. *Research in Science Education, 51*(6), 1569–1592.

International Reading Association. (2010). *Standards for reading professionals—Revised 2010.* Author.

Ippolito, J., Dagen, A. S., Bean, R. M., & Kern, D. (2019). *Specialists, coaches, coordinators, oh my! Looking back and looking forward on the roles and responsibilities of specialized literacy professionals.* https://digitalcommons.uri.edu/education_facpubs/30/

Ippolito, J., Swan Dagen, A., & Bean, R. M. (2021). *Elementary literacy coaching in 2021: What we know and what we wonder.* The Reading Teacher.

Jackson, R., McCoy, A., Pistorino, C., Wilkinson, A., Burghardt, J., Clark, M., Ross, C., Schochet, P., Swank, P., & Schmidt, S. R. (2007). *National evaluation of Early Reading First: Final report to Congress* (NCEE 2007-4007). National Center for Education Evaluation and Regional Assistance.

Joyce, B., & Showers, B. (1980). Improving inservice training: The messages of research. *Educational Leadership, 37*(5), 379–385.

Joyce, B. R., & Showers, B. (1981). Transfer of training: The contribution of "coaching". *Journal of Education, 163*(2), 163–172.

Joyce, B. R., & Showers, B. (1982). The coaching of teaching. *Educational Leadership, 40*, 4–10.

Knight, J. (2007). *Instructional coaching: A partnership approach to improving instruction.* Corwin Press.

Knowles, R. T., Hawkman, A. M., & Nielsen, S. R. (2019). The social studies teacher-coach: A quantitative analysis comparing coaches and non-coaches across how/what they teach. *Journal of Social Studies Research, 44*(1), 117–125.

Kohler, F. W., Crilley, K. M., Shearer, D. D., & Good, G. (1997). Effects of peer coaching on teacher and student outcomes. *Journal of Educational Research, 90*(4), 240–250.

Kohler, F. W., McCullough, K. M., & Buchan, K. A. (1995). Using peer coaching to enhance preschool teachers' development and refinement of classroom activities. *Early Education and Development, 6*(3), 215–239.

Kraft, M. A., Blazar, D., & Hogan, D. (2018). The effect of teacher coaching on instruction and achievement: A meta-analysis of the causal evidence. *Review of Educational Research, 88*(4), 547–588.

Kretlow, A. G., & Bartholomew, C. C. (2010). Using coaching to improve the fidelity of evidence-based practices: A review of studies. *Teacher Education and Special Education, 33*(4), 279–299.

Mangin, M. M. (2007). Facilitating elementary principals' support for instructional teacher leadership. *Educational Administration Quarterly, 43*(3), 319–357.

March, A. L., Castillo, J. M., Batsche, G. M., & Kincaid, D. (2016). Relationship between systems coaching and problem-solving implementation fidelity in a response-to-intervention model. *Journal of Applied School Psychology, 32*(2), 147–177.

Matsumura, L. C., Sartoris, M., Bickel, D. D., & Garnier, H. E. (2009). Leadership for literacy coaching: The principal's role in launching a new coaching program. *Educational Administration Quarterly, 45*(5), 655–693.

McCamish, C., Reynolds, H., Algozzine, B., & Cusumano, D. (2015). An investigation of characteristics, practices, and leadership styles of PBIS coaches. *Journal of Applied Educational and Policy Research, 1*(1).

McIntosh, K., & Goodman, S. (2016). *Integrated multi-tiered systems of support: Blending RTI and PBIS.* Guilford Press.

McKenna, M. C., & Walpole, S. (2010). Planning and evaluating change at scale: Lessons from Reading First. *Educational Researcher, 39*(6), 478–483.

Miller, S. P. (1994). Peer coaching within an early childhood interdisciplinary setting. *Intervention in School and Clinic, 30*(2), 109–113.

Mudzimiri, R., Burroughs, E. A., Luebeck, J., Sutton, J., & Yopp, D. (2014). A look inside mathematics coaching: Roles, content, and dynamics. *Education Policy Analysis Archives, 22*(53), n53.

National Research Council. (1998a). *Preventing reading difficulties in young children.* National Academies Press.

National Research Council. (1998b, March 18). *Reforms needed to improve children's reading skills.* http://www8.nationalacademies.org/onpinews/newsitem.aspx?RecordID=6023

Newton, J. S., Algozzine, B., Algozzine, K., Horner, R. H., & Todd, A. W. (2011). Building local capacity for training and coaching data-based problem solving with positive behavior intervention and support teams. *Journal of Applied School Psychology, 27*(3), 228–245.

No Child Left Behind Act of 2001, PL 107-110, 115 Stat. 1425, 20 U.S.C. §§ 6301 *et seq.*

Pas, E. T., Waasdorp, T. E., & Bradshaw, C. P. (2019). Coaching teachers to detect, prevent, and respond to bullying using mixed reality simulation: An efficacy study in middle schools. *International Journal of Bullying Prevention, 1*(1), 58–69.

Peterson Miller, S., Harris, C., & Watanabe, A. (1991). Professional coaching: A method for increasing effective and decreasing ineffective teacher behaviors. *Teacher Education and Special Education, 14*(3), 183–191.

Petrilli, M. J. (2019). *Toward a golden age of educational practice.* Thomas B. Fordham Institute.

Poglinco, S. M., Bach, A. J., Hovde, K., Rosenblum, S., Saunders, M., & Supovitz, J. A. (2003). *The heart of the matter: The coaching model in America's choice schools.* Consortium for Policy Research in Education.

RAND Corporation. (2012). *Teachers matter: Understanding teachers' impact on student achievement.* https://www.rand.org/pubs/corporate_pubs/CP693z1-2012-09.html

Reinke, W. M., Stormont, M., Herman, K. C., Wang, Z., Newcomer, L., & King, K. (2014). Use of coaching and behavior support planning for students with disruptive behavior within a universal classroom management program. *Journal of Emotional and Behavioral Disorders, 22*(2), 74–82.

Rhodes, C., & Beneicke, S. (2002). Coaching, mentoring and peer-networking: Challenges for the management of teacher professional development in schools. *Journal of In-Service Education, 28*(2), 297–310.

Rivkin, S. G., Hanushek, E. A., & Kain, J. F. (2005). Teachers, schools, and academic achievement. *Econometrica, 73*(2), 417–458.

Rock, M. L., Zigmond, N. P., Gregg, M., & Gable, R. A. (2011). The power of virtual coaching. *Educational Leadership, 69*(2), 42–48.

Roelof, E., Veenman, S., & Raemaekers, J. (1994). Improving instruction and classroom management behaviour in mixed-age classrooms: Results of two improvement studies. *Educational Studies, 20*(1), 105–126.

Ross, J. A. (1992). Teacher efficacy and the effects of coaching on student achievement. *Canadian Journal of Education/Revue Canadienne de l'Education, 17*(1), 51–65.

Rowland, C. (2017). *Principal professional development: New opportunities for a renewed state focus.* Education Policy Center at American Institutes for Research.

Rudd, L. C., Lambert, M. C., Satterwhite, M., & Smith, C. H. (2009). Professional development + coaching = enhanced teaching: Increasing usage of math mediated language in preschool classrooms. *Early Childhood Education Journal, 37*(1), 63–69.

Ruedel, K., Thompson, A. L., Kuchle, L., & D'Agord, C. (2021). *Highlights from five years of reviewing state systemic improvement plans.* National Center for Systemic Improvement.

Russell, J. L., Correnti, R., Stein, M. K., Bill, V., Hannan, M., Schwartz, N., Booker, L. N., Pratt, N. R., & Matthis, C. (2019). Learning from adaptation to support instructional improvement at scale: Understanding coach adaptation in the TN Mathematics Coaching Project. *American Educational Research Journal,* https://doi.org/10.3102/0002831219854050

Sailors, M., & Shanklin, N. L. (2010). Introduction: Growing evidence to support coaching in literacy and mathematics. *Elementary School Journal, 111*(1), 1–6.

Shidler, L. (2009). The impact of time spent coaching for teacher efficacy on student achievement. *Early Childhood Education Journal, 36*(5), 453–460.

Showers, B. (1984). *Peer coaching: A strategy for facilitating transfer of training.* A CEPM R&D Report. Center for Educational Policy for Management, College of Education, University of Oregon.

Showers, B., & Joyce, B. (1996). The evolution of peer coaching. *Educational Leadership, 53,* 12–16.

Snyder, P. A., Hemmeter, M. L., & Fox, L. (2015). Supporting implementation of evidence-based practices through practice-based coaching. *Topics in Early Childhood Special Education, 35*(3), 133–143.

Taie, S., & Goldring, R. (2017). *Characteristics of public elementary and secondary school teachers in the United States: Results from the 2015-16 National Teacher and Principal Survey: First look* (NCES 2017-071). National Center for Education Statistics. https://nces.ed.gov/pubs2017/2017071.pdf

U.S. Department of Education. (2003). Guidance for the Early Reading First Program. Author.

U.S. Department of Education. (2007). *State and local implementation of the No Child Left Behind Act, Volume II. Teacher quality under NCLB: Interim Report.* https://www2.ed.gov/rschstat/eval/teaching/nclb/execsum.html

U.S. Department of Education. (2016, September 27). *Non-regulatory guidance Title II, Part A of the Elementary and Secondary Education Act of 1965, as amended by the Every Student Succeeds Act of 2015.* https://www2.ed.gov /policy/elsec/leg/essa/essatitleiipartaguidance.pdf

U.S. Department of Education, National Center for Education Statistics. (2008). *Schools and Staffing Survey (SASS), 2007–08.* https://nces.ed.gov/pubs2009/2009321/tables/sass0708_2009321_s12n_06.asp

U.S. Department of Education, National Center for Education Statistics. (2012). *Schools and Staffing Survey (SASS), 2011–12.* https://nces.ed.gov/surveys/sass/tables/sass1112_2013312_s2s_005.asp

U.S. Department of Education, Office of Planning, Evaluation and Policy Development, Policy and Program Studies Service. (2006). *Reading First implementation evaluation: Interim report.* Author.

Veenman, S., & Denessen, E. (2001). The coaching of teachers: Results of five training studies. *Educational Research and Evaluation, 7*(4), 385–417.

Walpole, S., & Blamey, K. L. (2008). Elementary literacy coaches: The reality of dual roles. *The Reading Teacher, 62*(3), 222–231.

Wynn, M. J., & Kromrey, J. (1999). Paired peer placement with peer coaching in early field experiences: Results of a four-year study. *Teacher Education Quarterly, 26*(1), 21–38.

2

Coaching Goals, Activities, and Common Challenges

1. What are the goals of teacher coaches, systems coaches, and hybrid coaching?

2. What are typical coaching activities for one-to-one coaches, systems coaches, and coaches in hybrid roles? How are these activities represented in this text's coaching framework?

3. What common barriers do coaches face when working with teachers, teams, or both?

CHAPTER TAKE-AWAYS

1. Although coaching teachers may yield numerous benefits, the overall goals of coaching teachers are to improve teacher practice and student outcomes. The goals of systems coaching are to improve team practice, school/pre-K systems, and student outcomes. The goals of hybrid coaching are to improve teacher and team practice, systems, and student outcomes.

2. Although the goals of systems, teacher, and hybrid coaching are somewhat different, the work of any coach is quite similar. To achieve the goals of coaching, the core work of coaches is to conduct coaching cycles incorporating four practices: 1) using alliance strategies, 2) observing, 3) modeling, and 4) providing performance feedback. Therefore, these four practices form the basis of this book's coaching framework.

3. Coaches often face many barriers when enacting their role. Overcoming these barriers requires that coaches build their own knowledge of the role and work with other educators to offset barriers.

CHAPTER OVERVIEW

This chapter is divided into two sections. We first explicate the goals of coaching teachers and unpack key coaching activities. We then address the goals and key activities of systems and hybrid coaches. The second section of the chapter delineates common coaching barriers and briefly discusses the impact of these barriers. The chapter contains several resources to help you incorporate information into your work as a coach. We have also embedded many tools within the chapter.

We strongly suggest that coaches become familiar with the information contained within this chapter prior to planning, conducting sessions, and reflecting on coaching. Gallucci et al. (2010) noted that coaching is "inherently multifaceted and ambiguous" (p. 922). From our perspective, the multifaced nature of coaching means that 1) the goals of coaching are not always defined in precisely the same way (or even at all) in research, job descriptions, gray literature, and even existing coaching standards; 2) the educators you work with (e.g., principals, teachers, implementation teams) may have different expectations about how you will enact your role and what they will gain from coaching sessions; 3) a litany of activities are commonly associated with coaching; and 4) numerous coaching barriers can create even greater ambiguity with the role and get in the way of effective coaching. For coaching to reach its mark, you must first understand what type of coaching role you are enacting: Are you a coach for teachers or for teams responsible for leading implementation efforts? You must also immediately identify why you are conducting sessions (i.e., What will teachers or teams be able to do as a result of coaching?) Then, you can make informed, strategic decisions about how to spend your time so that you prioritize the most important coaching activities. As you make these decisions, it will be necessary to communicate a research-based rationale for recipients as to why the coaching role prioritizes some things over others. Finally, you must be ready to encounter barriers while coaching, which can derail even the savviest coach from enacting the role. Armed with the information and resources from this chapter, coaches will be better prepared to navigate the ambiguity associated with coaching. The end result is an increased likelihood that the coaching goals are achieved.

COACHING TEACHERS AND TEAMS: GOALS AND TYPICAL ACTIVITIES
Goals of Coaching Teachers

The goals of coaching are straightforward when coaching a teacher: to improve teacher practice, therein increasing the likelihood of improving student learning outcomes (see Figure 2.1; Kraft et al., 2018; Stormont et al., 2015).

The idea is that this type of coaching will build teachers' capacity one classroom at a time. The end result of this case-by-case coaching is steady progress of improved teaching and student outcomes across an entire school. Figure 2.2 outlines the logic of coaching teachers.

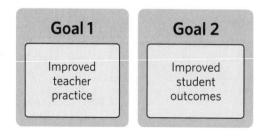

Figure 2.1. The goals of coaching teachers.

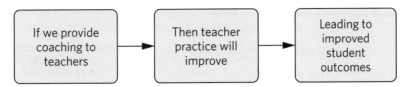

Figure 2.2.   The logic of coaching teachers.

Improvements in teaching are meant to be observable so that anyone watching the teacher could detect changes in practice. But coaching can also produce internal changes among teachers too, such as improved knowledge (Neuman & Cunningham, 2009). Other researchers have detected changes in teacher's self-efficacy (i.e., their beliefs about their ability to complete a given task) (Tschannen-Moran & McMaster, 2009). Subsequently, although the goals of coaching are to improve teaching and student learning, teachers who have benefited from coaching are likely to experience other valuable changes. These additional improvements may not be the ultimate goals of coaching but are certainly important by-products.

Common Activities for Coaching Teachers

Numerous activities are included on the coach's list of job responsibilities (Denton & Hasbrouck, 2009; Deussen et al., 2007). To be clear, not every task on the list needs to be a central part of the day-to-day work of a coach (Denton & Hasbrouck, 2009; Kraft et al., 2018). Some activities are crucial, whereas others are less critical. Topping the to-do list should be those things most strongly linked to improved teaching and student learning because these are the primary goals of coaching teachers. Other activities may be a necessary part of the coaching role but may not rise to the same level of importance.

Read the list of common coaching activities shown in Figure 2.3 (blank versions of this form are available in Appendix B and to download). Organize the items into one of two categories: those things most closely linked by experimental research to improved teaching and student outcomes (Category A) or those things that are not associated with improved teaching and learning (Category B). The things within Category B are either less likely to lead to improved teaching and student outcomes compared with what is listed in Category A or are not yet confirmed by research to be associated with improved teaching and student outcomes. After checking your answers against the key

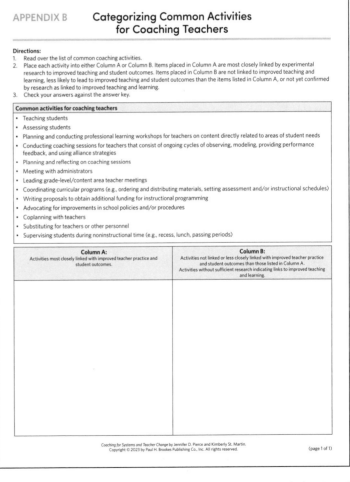

Figure 2.3.   Categorizing Common Activities for Coaching Teachers. (*Note:* Blank versions of this form are available in Appendix B and to download.)

Table 2.1. Answer key: Categorizing common activities for coaching teachers

Column A: Activities most closely linked with improved teacher practice and student outcomes.	Column B: Activities not linked or less closely linked with improved teacher practice and student outcomes than those listed in Column A. Activities without sufficient research indicating links to improved teaching and learning.
• Planning and conducting professional learning for teachers on content the coach has observed as a need and is directly related to areas of student needs • Conducting coaching sessions for teachers that consist of ongoing cycles of observing, modeling, providing performance feedback, and using alliance strategies	• Planning and reflecting on coaching sessions • Teaching students • Assessing students • Meeting with administrators • Facilitating grade-level/content-area teacher meetings • Coordinating curricular programs (e.g., ordering and distributing materials, setting assessment and/or instructional schedules) • Writing proposals to obtain additional funding for instructional programming • Advocating for improvements in school policies and/or procedures • Coplanning with teachers • Substituting for teachers

Figure 2.4. Planning for Enacting Critical Coaching Activities. (*Note:* Blank versions of this form are available in Appendix C and to download.)

(see Table 2.1), read over the summary of common coaching activities to learn more about them. Then, read the text box to better understand why some things you enact are not directly mentioned in the list of common coaching activities. Finally, use Figure 2.4 to develop a plan for how you will allocate your time (blank versions of this form are available in Appendix C and to download). This completed resource could also be used to communicate with other educators (e.g., principals, district leaders) about how you will enact your coaching role.

What About Goal Setting, Celebrating Successes, and Asking Questions?

If you are at all familiar with coaching, then chances are you have helped a teacher set goals, assisted the teacher with monitoring their progress in reaching instructional goals, celebrated success, gave specific advice, formed positive relationships, and asked powerful questions. Why aren't these activities listed as central activities in this chapter? Rest assured that all these activities are embedded within the four practices of this book's coaching framework: using alliance strategies, observing, modeling, and providing performance feedback. As you become more familiar with the coaching framework, you will see how enacting these practices is central to the work of an effective coach.

Activities Most Closely Linked With Improved Teacher Practice and Student Outcomes

When the goals of coaching are to improve teacher practice and student learning, the most critical coaching activities are firmly established by research. The most important coaching task for a teacher coach is to conduct coaching cycles (Elek & Page, 2019; Kraft et al., 2018). These cycles are the core of the role. More specifically, coaching cycles should consist of four coaching practices: 1) using alliance strategies (or relationship building strategies), 2) observing, 3) modeling, and 4) providing performance feedback. Most important, these are the core coaching practices included in this book's coaching framework. Chapter 3 outlines the research base behind these coaching practices and therefore unpacks the framework in greater detail. Chapters 5 and 6 fully elaborate on conducting coaching cycles: how, when, and why to engage in each of these coaching practices. Suffice it to say that when defining the role of the coach, these four practices must be prioritized over other things if sessions aim to produce improved teaching and student learning.

Planning and conducting professional learning workshops for teachers is a second common coaching task linked to improved teaching and student learning. These workshops are directly linked to the needs of students. After all, it does not make sense for either teachers or coaches to be a part of professional learning workshops that do not benefit students. Just as important, professional learning workshops should 1) build teacher knowledge with active learning activities, 2) embed multiple opportunities for teachers to practice and talk about what they are learning with other professional learning workshops participants, 3) be of sufficient duration and frequency to ensure teachers can adequately learn the information, and 4) connect what teachers are learning to their existing practice (Borko et al., 2010; Garet et al., 2001; Palmer & Noltemeyer 2019; Yoon et al., 2007). Professional learning workshops typically are precursors to coaching sessions. Because these workshops are often paired with coaching cycles, coaches should consider conducting professional learning workshops as a core job responsibility.

One caveat is important to offer related to professional learning workshops. It is important because it is often a key vehicle for building teacher knowledge of a given practice. But conducting a professional learning workshop is not coaching. If seeking to improve teacher practice in the classroom setting and student outcomes, then allocate more time to coaching than to providing professional learning workshops. If improved teacher knowledge, teacher practice, and student learning are your goals, then dedicate time toward both activities (i.e., professional learning workshops, coaching cycles).

Other Coaching Activities

Should other coaching activities be divorced from the day-to-day work of a coach who supports teachers? The short answer is no. Many of the activities listed in Column B can be included into the coaching role. For example, planning and reflecting on coaching cycles helps coaches get ready for conducting quality coaching sessions with teachers. Even though research has not yet linked planning and reflecting on coaching cycles with improved teaching and student learning, we do not mean to imply that coaches omit these activities from their job responsibilities. Indeed, we strongly recommend that coaches regularly plan, conduct, and reflect on coaching cycles so that sessions meet their mark. Similarly, teacher coaches should expect to occasionally coplan with teachers and regularly facilitate teacher meetings, particularly when conversations center on data analysis, which can be a difficult task for teachers (Espin et al., 2017). We encourage coaches to engage in these two activities because both offer rich opportunities for coaches and teachers to discuss and reflect on teaching and student learning. Indeed, some educational experts consider coplanning and facilitating teacher meetings to be forms of professional learning for teachers (Darling-Hammond & Richardson, 2009).

All of the remaining activities listed in Column B are valuable in some way. To illustrate, coordinating curricular programs can be a valuable thing for coaches to do because teachers need to have appropriate materials readily available for use with students. Writing proposals may be necessary to gain funding for coaching, release time for teachers, or curricular materials. But neither two activities are linked to improved teaching and student learning. We recommend that teacher coaches work with school and district leaders to consider how much of their daily responsibilities can be allocated toward these different activities that are not linked to improved teacher practice and student outcomes. Remember to refer back to Figure 2.4 so that you can meaningfully allocate your time and communicate with other educators about your role.

Goals of Systems Coaching

The goals of implementation team coaching, or systems coaching, are quite different from the goals of coaching teachers. Here, the goal is to improve how a team leads school or district-wide implementation (e.g., a school, district, or pre-K program) of a given program, practice, or intervention (e.g., a reading program, MTSS) (Horner et al., 2018). Thus, the team's processes, rather than individual teacher's practice, is what coaches aim to change first. For example, teams may improve how they build buy-in for change among staff, how they use data for decision making, or how they monitor fidelity of implementation among all school staff members (Freeman et al., 2017).

But the expected changes do not remain at the team level. The idea is that changes in the team will be a conduit for improvement to the overall system. For example, as teams become more adept at building buy-in among educators, more educators will support the implementation effort, and the overall school or pre-K program will be primed to kick off the implementation effort with high levels of educator readiness. These are improvements to the overall school system that are hypothesized to link back to the changes in team practice (Higgins et al., 2012; McIntosh & Goodman, 2016).

Of course, improving school and pre-K programs is not important in and of itself. The idea is to improve the system so that student outcomes also improve, acknowledging that systems do influence what students ultimately achieve (Fullan & Knight, 2011; Horner et al., 2018; McIntosh & Goodman, 2016). This is the logic undergirding systems coaching. Figure 2.5 explicates the goals of systems coaching, and Figure 2.6 offers for a visual representation of the logic of systems coaching.

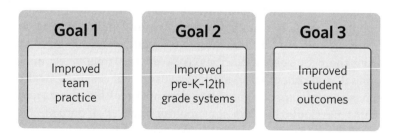

Figure 2.5.   The goals of systems coaching.

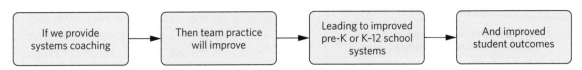

Figure 2.6. The logic of systems coaching.

Common Activities for Systems Coaching

Although the goals of systems coaching and coaching teachers are different, some systems coaching activities are quite like the work of a teacher coach. Other activities are somewhat different, given that the content of systems coaching sessions is less about educational innovations (e.g., a reading strategy) and more about the nature of change across an organization (e.g., how to conduct a Plan-Do-Study-Act cycle, sustained implementation of an innovation, how to build buy-in among staff for change) (Duda et al., 2013; Newton et al., 2011). Table 2.2 depicts the content covered by teacher coaches and systems coaches. The list is not exhaustive but rather serves as an illustration of how the content of coaching sessions varies based on the coaching role. The text box also highlights how systems coaches typically use assessments to guide their work with implementation teams.

Table 2.2.   Content covered in coaching sessions based on coaching role

Sample of content covered in coaching sessions with teachers	Sample of content covered in systems coaching sessions
• Use of classroom management and positive behavioral practices • Guidance in academic content area • Use of instructional teaching practices • Use of student data for improving teaching	• Conducting effective team meetings • Collecting, entering, analyzing, and using data efficiently and accurately • Setting a vision and goal for student improvement in the school • Building buy-in for school implementation effort • Creating communication protocols and feedback loops between the implementation team and other groups at the school • Developing a high-quality professional learning plan • Writing and enacting a school implementation plan • Conducting Plan-Do-Study-Act cycles to continuously improve the implementation effort • Conducting fidelity measurement of teacher practice • Using fidelity data to improve school implementation effort • Understanding phases of implementation (exploring, planning, initial implementation, implementation, sustaining, and scaling up)

Fidelity Assessment Data and Coaching

Systems coaches often use data from school-level fidelity assessments (e.g., Reading Tiered Fidelity Inventory) as a road map for their work with teams. Why is this the case? These fidelity measures yield data about the school or pre-K program's use of systemwide innovations such as MTSS or PBIS: What is working well and what is not? Coaches and teams analyze the data and then identify what they need to focus on to continuously improve their implementation effort. Similarly, teacher coaches may find it useful to use fidelity assessment data to guide their work with teachers. The measures used, however, must yield data on teacher practice. Unfortunately, many instructional programs used by teachers do not have such fidelity assessments. If such assessments are available, then we recommend teacher coaches also use the tools to guide their work with teachers.

Next, you will find a list of common systems coaching activities. As with the prior section, use the template to organize this list of items into one of two categories (see Figure 2.7; blank versions of this form are available in Appendix D and to download). Recall the items placed in Column A are hypothesized to be associated with improved team practice and system outcomes. The items placed in Column B are hypothesized to not be associated with improved team and systems or are less likely to lead to these improvements than the items listed in Column A. Note we use "hypothesized" because research on systems coaching (and hybrid coaching for that matter) is not yet as robust as research

---

APPENDIX D   **Blank Template for Categorizing Systems Coaching Activities**

Directions:
1. Read over the list of common systems coaching activities.
2. Place each task into either Column A or Column B. Items placed in Column A are hypothesized to lead to improved team practice, systems, and student outcomes. Items placed in Column B are not linked to these improvements, less likely to lead to these improvements than the activities listed in Column A, or not yet confirmed by research as linked to improved teaching and learning.
3. Check your answers against the answer key.

Common Systems Coaching Activities:
- Planning and conducting professional learning workshops for teachers and/or the leadership team
- Conducting coaching sessions for the leadership team that consist of ongoing cycles of observing, modeling, providing performance feedback, and using alliance strategies
- Planning and reflecting on coaching sessions
- Meeting with administrators outside of the leadership team meeting
- Facilitating leadership team meetings
- Coordinating materials (e.g., ordering and distributing materials, setting assessment and/or instructional schedules)
- Writing proposals to obtain additional funding for the ongoing implementation of the selected innovation
- Advocating for improvements in school policies and/or procedures related to the innovation

Column A: Activities hypothesized to be linked to improved team practice and systems (e.g., use of Plan-Do-Study-Act cycles, staff buy-in for implementation effort, improved student outcomes).	**Column B:** Activities hypothesized as unlinked or less closely linked with improved team practice and systems than those listed in Column A. Activities with insufficient research indicating links to improved team practice and systems.

Figure 2.7. Blank Template for Categorizing Systems Coaching Activities. (*Note:* Blank versions of this form are available in Appendix D and to download.)

Table 2.3. Answer key: Categorizing common systems coaching activities

Column A: Activities hypothesized to be linked to improved team practice and systems (e.g., use of Plan-Do-Study-Act cycles, staff buy-in for implementation effort, improved student outcomes).	**Column B:** Activities hypothesized as unlinked or less closely linked with improved team and systems than those listed in Column A. Activities with insufficient research indicating links to improved team and systems.
• Planning and conducting professional learning workshops for the leadership team and/or the entire staff within the system on the implementation effort • Conducting coaching sessions with the implementation/leadership team that consist of ongoing cycles of observing, modeling, providing performance feedback, and using alliance strategies	• Conducting fidelity assessments at the teacher level • Evaluating the system's implementation effort • Meeting with administrators outside of the leadership team meeting • Planning and reflecting on coaching sessions • Facilitating team meetings • Coordinating materials related to the implementation effort for the team (e.g., compiling implementation or evaluation data for the team, purchasing materials) • Writing system-level improvement plans related to the implementation effort • Writing proposals to obtain additional funding for the implementation effort • Advocating for improvements in school policies and/or procedures related to the implementation effort

on coaching teachers. Therefore, much of the thinking included here is theorized rather than firmly established from research findings, as discussed briefly in the text box. After checking your answers against the key (see Table 2.3), read over the summary of common systems coaching activities to learn more about what coaches are commonly expected to do as a part of their job responsibilities.

Systems and Hybrid Coaching Caveat

Systems and hybrid coaching are hypothesized as effective approaches for improving team practice, systems, and student outcomes. Research on these newer coaching roles is not as robust as research on coaching teachers. Therefore, it is possible that future research will require a change to this hypothesis. We suggest you keep in mind this coaching caveat until additional research is conducted on systems and hybrid coaching roles.

Activities Most Closely Linked With Improved Team Practice, Systems, and Student Outcomes

As noted in Table 2.3, systems coaches can allocate their time toward two central activities: 1) facilitating professional learning workshops for teams or an entire school staff and 2) conducting coaching sessions with the implementation team that consist of ongoing cycles of using alliance strategies, observing, modeling, and providing performance feedback (Duda et al., 2013; Fullan & Knight, 2011). Professional learning workshops should be aligned to definitions of high quality (Garet et al., 2001; Yoon et al., 2007). Subsequently, the structure of these workshops should mirror sessions offered to teachers. The content is one key difference with professional learning workshops conducted by systems coaches. Systems coaches deliver information that focuses on systems change concepts, including how to use assessments to improve the school implementation effort. For example, the systems coach may offer professional learning workshops on how to conduct a Plan-Do-Study-Act (Deming & Edwards, 1982) cycle because these cycles are central to the work of the leadership team but are quite difficult to enact (Tichnor-Wagner et al., 2017). They may commonly train on how to conduct and analyze student assessments (e.g., Reading Tiered Fidelity Inventory; St. Martin et al., 2015) and fidelity measures (e.g. TFI; Algozzine et al., 2014) that are used across the entire school or pre-K program. Many systems coaches are also expected to provide workshops on the innovation being implemented schoolwide, like PBIS or MTSS.

Related to the second task, systems coaches conduct coaching sessions with teams responsible for leading the implementation effort. As with coaches who work solely with teachers, these sessions should consist of the most effective coaching practices: 1) using alliance strategies (or relationship strategies), 2) observing, 3) modeling, and 4) providing performance feedback. The nature of systems coaching sessions will be different from a coaching session that occurs with teachers. Those serving in the systems coaching role can expect to focus on strategies for developing ongoing buy-in for the implementation effort, helping the team conduct teacher and systems fidelity assessments and use the data for improving implementation, and evaluating the overall implementation effort (March et al., 2016). See Chapter 4 for more information about common topics covered in systems coaching sessions.

As with those serving in the teacher coaching role, systems coaches will need to critically reflect on how to allocate time. Thus, the same caveat offered to teacher coaches related to professional learning workshops will also be offered here—conducting these workshops is not coaching. When the goal is to improve team practice and the overall system, allocate more time to coaching than to delivering professional learning workshops. If improved team knowledge, team practice, and systems are your goals, then dedicate time toward both professional learning workshops and coaching.

Other Team Coaching Activities   Like coaches who work with teachers, systems coaches should be prepared to engage in other activities beyond the two listed in Column A. In fact, systems coaches need to be open to allocating time toward activities across both columns because research has not yet clearly delineated which are more critical than others. It is possible that some of the activities in Column B (e.g., planning and reflecting on coaching sessions) will shift toward Column A, making it imperative that the systems coach allocate time toward these newly identified critical activities. Until this research has been conducted, we suggest that systems coaches include Column B activities into their job scope but with less time allocated toward them than conducting professional learning workshops and coaching cycles.

To make this feasible, remember that the system coach's role is to build team and system capacity, not to take responsibility for the overall implementation effort. Building team capacity happens best when team members become responsible for completing activities rather than expecting the coach to be solely responsible for enactment. Thus, instead of conducting fidelity assessments or evaluations of the overall implementation effort, build the teams' capacity in these activities rather than completing these activities yourself. After all, as a systems coach you likely already possess the capacity to complete these activities. Focus on building the capacity of the team so that they improve their knowledge and skills, therein improving the overall system and educator's capacity to sustain the system.

COACHING INDIVIDUAL TEACHERS AND TEAMS OF EDUCATORS: THE HYBRID ROLE

Let's unpack the third coaching role described in this text—the hybrid coach. It is likely that you can surmise the goals and logic of hybrid coaching given the previous information on coaching teachers and coaching implementation teams (see Figures 2.8 and 2.9).

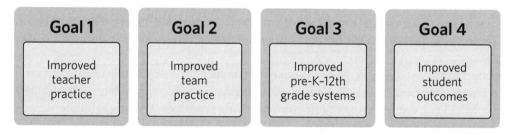

Figure 2.8.   The goals of hybrid coaching.

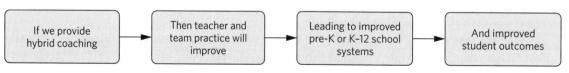

Figure 2.9.   The logic of hybrid coaching.

Dear Administrator:

I'd like to work with you on the allocation of my time as a coach. My understanding is that I am expected to support two different coaching recipients: individual teachers and the team responsible for leading the implementation effort at our school. The goal of coaching sessions when working with teachers is to improve teaching and student learning. The goal of coaching sessions when working with teams of educators is to improve team practices and systems (e.g., increased collaboration across grade levels) and student outcomes. I've developed some initial plans about how to structure my time, and I'd like to share my thinking with you. We can adjust this plan based on your feedback. I look forward to hearing your thoughts and developing a coherent schedule so that the goals of coaching can be achieved.

Thank you!

Coach Name

Figure 2.10.   Template for talking with administrators: hybrid coaching.

You are also likely able to identify the two most critical activities for the hybrid coach: conducting professional learning workshops and coaching cycles. These two activities are most closely linked to improved teaching, student outcomes, team practices, and systems improvements (Kraft et al., 2018), so it is important that the hybrid coach focus on these things. Then, allocate remaining time toward other coaching activities, knowing that the hybrid role will require you to balance time between working with individual teachers and working with teams of educators. Figure 2.10

Table 2.4.   Summary of coaching roles, recipients, goals, and critical coaching activities

	Coach	Recipient of coaching	Goals	Critical coaching activities
Coaching teachers	• School, district personnel, or external agent (e.g., researcher, consultant) • Peer (e.g., another teacher)	Individual teachers	• Improved teacher practice • Improved student outcomes	• Planning and conducting professional learning workshops • Conducting coaching sessions that consist of ongoing cycles of observing, modeling, providing performance feedback, and using alliance strategies
Systems coach	• School, district personnel, or external agent (e.g., researcher, consultant) • Peer (e.g., another teacher)	Implementation/ leadership team	• Improved team practices • Improved systems (e.g., scale-up and sustained implementation of an innovation) • Improved student outcomes	
Hybrid model	• School, district personnel, or external agent (e.g., researcher, consultant) • Peer (e.g., another teacher)	Individual teachers and an implementation/ leadership team	• Improved teacher practice • Improved team practice • Improved systems (e.g., sustained implementation of an innovation) • Improved student outcomes	

may be a particularly helpful tool for those in the hybrid coaching role because it provides a template for talking with district and school program administrators about how time will be balanced between supporting teachers and supporting teams. Yet, any coach may use this template with minor adjustments to facilitate a conversation with supervisors. Similarly, Table 2.4 provides an at-a-glance summary of coaching roles, coaching recipients, critical coaching activities, and goals. This tool may be used to communicate the differences and key ideas of the various coaching roles with other educators.

GETTING READY FOR COACHING CHALLENGES

As can be seen in the prior section, the role of any coach can include many activities, some more critical than others. Unfortunately, several obstacles can get in the way of focusing on the most critical coaching activities, therein affecting the degree to which coaching goals can be attained. The next section summarizes these key barriers, all of which can impede even the most skilled coach from staying focused on their most impactful work. To avoid a situation of "problem admiring," we first describe each barrier and indicate specific chapters in the book that present strategies for offsetting barriers. These barriers are summarized in Figure 2.11 and discussed in the next section.

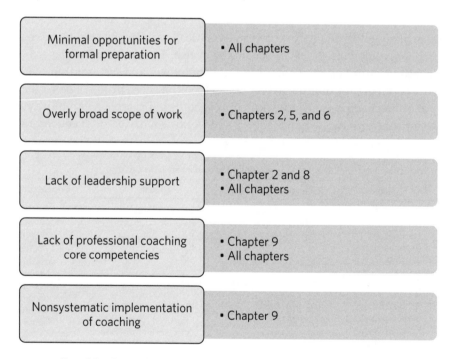

Minimal opportunities for formal preparation	• All chapters
Overly broad scope of work	• Chapters 2, 5, and 6
Lack of leadership support	• Chapter 2 and 8 • All chapters
Lack of professional coaching core competencies	• Chapter 9 • All chapters
Nonsystematic implementation of coaching	• Chapter 9

Figure 2.11.   Common coaching barriers and location of strategies for addressing barriers.

Minimal Opportunities for Formal Preparation

Whether working as a coach for teachers, a system coach, or a hybrid coach, there are minimal opportunities for formal preparation for those serving in the roles (Denton & Hasbrouck, 2009). Therefore, coaches are left on their own to figure out how to enact their role. Imagine being hired for the role of coach and having to answer the following questions:

• How do I identify which teachers to coach?

- What are the best practices for developing relationships with teachers before I begin critical coaching activities?

- Is every teacher or team coached in the same way, or are there adjustments I can make to supports based on the coaching recipients? What types of adjustments are ideal, acceptable, unacceptable, or potentially harmful to achieving outcomes?

- Where do I begin when coaching an implementation team?

- Do some implementation teams and teachers need more coaching than others?

- How do I know how much coaching is enough and when to begin to fade my coaching supports?

Although some coaches thrive in knowing the answers to these questions despite a lack of advance preparation, others inevitably struggle to determine how to coach others.

Are you looking to answer these questions? This text offers content and resources that enhance coach knowledge and skills. Rest assured that by the end of this book, you will be able to answer all these questions—plus more. In addition, you will want to gain access to the case studies in Chapter 8, which illustrate how one coach with just 1 year of prior experience enacts his role.

Overly Broad Scope of Work

Far too often the scope of the coach's job is too broad, requiring that the coach engage in too many surface-level activities. Related to this, the job responsibilities may be directed toward things that do not match the desired goals of coaching. When the list of expected job responsibilities is overwhelming and nearly impossible to manage, there is little time for the most critical aspect of the coaching role: conducting coaching cycles that include observing, modeling, providing performance feedback, and using alliance strategies.

In addition, some proponents of coaching maintain that the coach's job should not be structured around a set of specific practices (Wolpert-Gawron, 2016). Although we do not suggest that coaches need to follow a minute-by-minute schedule of nonstop coaching cycles, coaches are advised to narrow the scope of the job around critical activities.

Use the information from this chapter to focus the work of coaches around the most impactful activities. You will also find helpful information and tools in Chapters 3, 5, and 6 on the coaching framework, which centers on the use of coaching cycles. Then, work through Chapter 8's case studies to identify how the scope of the coaching role can focus on central coaching activities.

Lack of Leadership Support

Leaders (e.g., principals, pre-K directors) play a central role in shaping what coaching looks like and how recipients of coaching react to it as a vehicle for reaching their goals (Mangin, 2007). Unfortunately, principals often do not communicate the vision and purpose of coaching, clarify whether coaching is optional or mandatory, or even tell recipients what to expect from coaching sessions. Most concerning is when principals do not explicitly dispel the myth that the coach is in a position to evaluate teachers. When principals do not clearly communicate what coaching is (and is not), it is met with mixed reactions at best and clear hostility at worst. Therefore, explicitly communicating the purpose and type of coaching is the most pressing issue for principals. The purpose of coaching is to develop capacity so educators can enact high-quality practices; thus, it is something leaders can promote as helpful for all educators.

All the chapters contain information you can use to productively communicate with principals about coaching. For specific tools, refer to Chapter 8 as well as Figure 2.4 to help your efforts.

Lack of Professional Coaching Core Competencies

Guidance regarding core competencies is a fourth reason why coaching misses the mark. Core competencies serve to clarify how coaches conduct their work and offer concrete guidance about conducting coaching sessions. Although some noneducational coaching core competencies do exist (e.g., International Coaching Federation's Core Competencies, n.d.), most teacher and team coaches do not have a set of widely accepted core competencies (one exception being the International Reading Association's 2010 set of standards for literacy coaches). Moreover, coaches must independently translate this information into their daily practice. Thus, not only are coaches unlikely to have any formal preparatory experiences as they enter their roles, but they also cannot reference an agreed-on set of standards to guide their work. It is little wonder why coaching can be difficult for those serving in the role and why coaching sessions might miss their mark.

Refer to Chapter 9 for a set of coaching core competencies that can be used to shape the day-to-day work of coaches. These competencies directly build from the information presented in Chapters 1–8. In addition, all of the case studies found in Chapter 8 illustrate how competencies influence coaching practice.

Figure 2.12. Discussion Guide: Preparing for Coaching Barriers. (*Note:* Blank versions of this form are available in Appendix E and to download.)

Nonsystematic Implementation of Coaching

A final common coaching barrier is that coaching is typically implemented in a less than systematic way. Educators often gloss over important steps that need to be taken when coaching in schools, assuming it is a quick fix that will easily lead to improving teaching, team practice, systems, and student outcomes. Like the implementation of any other innovation used in schools, we must be methodical in our use of coaching if we want it to lead to these desired goals (Pierce, 2019).

The good news is that taking a methodical approach to enacting coaching is not impossible to do. More researchers are

APPENDIX F	Action Planning Tool

Purpose: Use this tool to identify what you will do to overcome coaching barriers. You may update this form as you read other chapters of this book.

Directions:
1. List the coaching barriers you currently face or may face.
2. In the next column, identify what action steps you may need to take to offset barriers. List who you need to communicate with to offset the challenge (e.g., principal, pre-K director).
3. In the third column, identify what happened when you took the actions steps.
4. List ideas for what you need to do next.
5. Use the final column to record any other information or comments.

Barrier	What do I need to do (action steps to take to offset barriers)? With whom do I need to communicate?	What happened?	What is next?	Other comments

Figure 2.13. Action Planning Tool. (*Note:* Blank versions of this form are available in Appendix F and to download.)

promoting the idea that how coaching is enacted matters (Darling-Hammond et al., 2017; Pierce et al., 2019).

Chapter 9 offers content and tools you can use to take a strategic approach to implementing coaching. You may also want to refer to coaching case examples in Chapter 8, which include situations when coaching is enacted without a strategic approach.

The Impact of Barriers: Unachieved Goals

Sadly, the barriers previously cited are not new—they have been noted in research and practice for decades (Rhodes & Beneicke, 2002). Just as concerning are the consequences of these barriers. First, resources are not being maximized when coaches are hired but are unable to dedicate their time to critical coaching activities. Second, coaching recipients may become unsatisfied with participating in sessions when coaches seem unprepared to conduct critical coaching activities. Recipients may resist participating in coaching sessions when principals expect coaching to be evaluative or when principals do not explicitly set the vision of coaching on capacity building. No less important, coaches may face frustration with the role, making them less likely to remain in their chosen profession. Perhaps most alarming is that when these barriers are occurring, coaching is unlikely to live up to the promise of improved teacher practice, team practice, systems, and student outcomes.

Complete the reflection tool (Figure 2.12; blank versions of this form are available in Appendix E and to download) now that you have read over the most critical coaching activities and have a better sense of some of the pressing barriers that exist in coaching. This tool is designed to help you think about your coaching role, the goals of that role, and the potential challenges you may face when enacting that role. Complete the action plan (Figure 2.13; blank versions of this form are available in Appendix F and to download) so that you can develop some ways to offset these challenges. If you find that you are not ready yet to complete the action plan, then revisit the form as you read additional chapters from this book.

SUMMARY

Working as a teacher coach, systems coach, or hybrid coach is clearly a large role that holds the potential to be a powerful way to lead to improved teacher practice, team practice, systems, and student outcomes. Help coaching live up to its promise. Use the information within this chapter to make strategic decisions about how to allocate your time toward the most critical coaching activities. You may run into some coaching barriers along the way, but with a focus on the most critical coaching activities, there is increased confidence you will be able to enact your coaching role with success.

REFERENCES

Algozzine, B., Barrett, S., Eber, L., George, H., Horner, R., Lewis, T., Putnam, B., Swain-Bradway, J., McIntosh, K., & Sugai, G. (2014). *School-wide PBIS tiered fidelity inventory.* OSEP Technical Assistance Center on Positive Behavioral Interventions and Supports. www.pbis.org

Barrett, S. B., Bradshaw, C. P., & Lewis-Palmer, T. (2008). Maryland statewide PBIS initiative: Systems, evaluation, and next steps. *Journal of Positive Behavior Interventions, 10*(2), 105–114.

Bean, R. M., & Wilson, R. M. (1981). *Effecting change in school reading programs: The resource role.* International Reading Association.

Borko, H., Jacobs, J., & Koellner, K. (2010). Contemporary approaches to teacher professional development. *International Encyclopedia of Education, 7*(2), 548–556.

The Consolidated Framework for Implementation Research. (2019). *Research team-center for clinical management research.* https://cfirguide.org

Darling-Hammond, L., Hyler, M. E., & Gardner, M. (2017). *Effective teacher professional development.* Learning Policy Institute.

Darling-Hammond, L., & Richardson, N. (2009). Research review/teacher learning: What matters. *Educational Leadership, 66*(5), 46–53.

Deming, W. E., & Edwards, D. W. (1982). *Quality, productivity, and competitive position* (Vol. 183). Massachusetts Institute of Technology, Center for Advanced Engineering Study.

Denton, C. A., & Hasbrouck, J. (2009). A description of instructional coaching and its relationship to consultation. *Journal of Educational and Psychological Consultation, 19*(2), 150–175.

Desimone, L. M., & Pak, K. (2017). Instructional coaching as high-quality professional development. *Theory Into Practice, 56*(1), 3–12.

Deussen, T., Coskie, T., Robinson, L., & Autio, E. (2007). *"Coach" can mean many things: Five categories of literacy coaches in Reading First* (Issues & Answers Report, REL 2007–No. 005). U.S. Department of Education, Institute of Education Sciences, National Center for Education Evaluation and Regional Assistance, Regional Educational Laboratory Northwest. http://ies.ed.gov/ncee/edlabs

Domina, T., Lewis, R., Agarwal, P., & Hanselman, P. (2015). Professional sense-makers: Instructional specialists in contemporary schooling. *Educational Researcher, 44*(6), 359–364.

Duda, M. A., Fixsen, D. L., & Blase, K. A. (2013). Setting the stage for sustainability: Building the infrastructure for implementation capacity. In V. Buysse & E. S. Peisner-Feinberg (Eds.), *Handbook of response to intervention in early childhood* (pp. 397–416). Paul H Brookes Publishing Co.

Elek, C., & Page, J. (2019). Critical features of effective coaching for early childhood educators: A review of empirical research literature. *Professional Development in Education, 45*(4), 567–585.

Espin, C. A., Wayman, M. M., Deno, S. L., McMaster, K. L, & de Rooij, M. (2017). Data-based decision-making: Developing a method for capturing teachers' understanding of CBM graphs. *Learning Disabilities Research and Practice, 32*(1), 2–21.

Fixsen, D., Blase, K., Metz, A., & Van Dyke, M. (2013). Statewide implementation of evidence-based programs. *Exceptional Children, 79*(2), 213–230.

Fixsen, D. L., Naoom, S. F., Blase, K. A., Friedman, R. M. & Wallace, F. (2005). *Implementation research: A synthesis of the literature* (FMHI Publication #231). University of South Florida, Louis de la Parte Florida Mental Health Institute, National Implementation Research Network.

Freeman, J., Sugai, G., Simonsen, B., & Everett, S. (2017). MTSS coaching: Bridging knowing to doing. *Theory Into Practice, 56*(1), 29–37.

Fuchs, D., & Fuchs, L. S. (2006). Introduction to response to intervention: What, why, and how valid is it? *Reading Research Quarterly, 41*(1), 93–99.

Fullan, M. (2005). *Leadership and sustainability: System thinkers in action.* Corwin Press.

Fullan, M., & Knight, J. (2011). Coaches as system leaders. *Educational leadership, 69*(2), 50–53.

Gallucci, C., Van Lare, M. D., Yoon, I. H., & Boatright, B. (2010). Instructional coaching: Building theory about the role and organizational support for professional learning. *American Educational Research Journal, 47*(4), 919–963.

Garet, M. S., Porter, A. C., Desimone, L., Birman, B. F., & Yoon, K. S. (2001). What makes professional development effective? Results from a national sample of teachers. *American Educational Research Journal, 38*(4), 915–945.

Hargreaves, A., & Skelton, J. (2012). Politics and systems of coaching and mentoring. In S. Fletcher & C. A. Mullen (Eds.), *The Sage handbook of mentoring and coaching in education* (pp. 122–138). Sage Publications.

Hasbrouck, J. E., & Christen, M. H. (1997). Providing peer coaching in inclusive classrooms: A tool for consulting teachers. *Intervention in School and Clinic, 32*(3), 172–177.

Hershfeldt, P. A., Pell, K., Sechrest, R., Pas, E. T., & Bradshaw, C. P. (2012). Lessons learned coaching teachers in behavior management: The PBIS plus coaching model. *Journal of Educational and Psychological Consultation, 22*(4), 280–299.

Higgins, M. C., Weiner, J., & Young, L. (2012). Implementation teams: A new lever for organizational change. *Journal of Organizational Behavior, 33*(3), 366–388.

Horner, R. H., Newton, J. S., Todd, A. W., Algozzine, B., Algozzine, K., Cusumano, D., & Preston, A. (2018). A randomized waitlist controlled analysis of team-initiated problem solving professional development and use. *Behavioral Disorders, 43*(4), 444–456.

Horner, R. H., & Sugai, G. (2015). School-wide PBIS: An example of applied behavior analysis implemented at a scale of social importance. *Behavior Analysis in Practice, 8*(1), 80–85.

International Coaching Federation. (n.d.). *ICF core competencies.* https://coachingfederation.org/core-competencies

International Reading Association. (2010). *Standards for reading professionals—Revised 2010.* Author.

Ippolito, J., Bean, R. M., Kern, D., & Dagen, A. S. (2019). *Specialists, coaches, coordinators, oh my! Looking back and looking forward on the roles and responsibilities of specialized literacy professionals.*

Kraft, M. A., Blazar, D., & Hogan, D. (2018). The effect of teacher coaching on instruction and achievement: A meta-analysis of the causal evidence. *Review of Educational Research, 88*(4), 547–588.

Lewis, C. (2015). What is improvement science? Do we need it in education? *Educational Researcher, 44*(1), 54–61.

Mangin, M. M. (2007). Facilitating elementary principals' support for instructional teacher leadership. *Educational Administration Quarterly, 43*(3), 319–357.

March, A.L., Castillo, J.M., Batsche, G.M., & Kincaid, D. (2016). Relationship between systems coaching and problem-solving implementation fidelity in a Response to Intervention model. *Journal of Applied School Psychology, 32*(2), 147–177.

McCamish, C., Reynolds, H., Algozzine, B., & Cusumano, D. (2015). An investigation of characteristics, practices, and leadership styles of PBIS coaches. *Journal of Applied Educational and Policy Research, 1*(1), 15–34.

McIntosh, K., & Goodman, S. (2016). *Integrated multi-tiered systems of support: Blending RTI and PBIS.* Guilford Publications.

McKenna, M. C., & Walpole, S. (2010). Planning and evaluating change at scale: Lessons from Reading First. *Educational Researcher, 39*(6), 478–483.

Mellard, D. (2010). *Fidelity of implementation within a response to intervention (RtI) framework.* https://webnew.ped.state.nm.us/wp-content/uploads/2018/03/Fidelity-of-Implementation-guidev5-1.pdf

Neuman, S. B., & Cunningham, L. (2009). The impact of professional development and coaching on early language and literacy instructional practices. *American Educational Research Journal, 46*(2), 532–566.

Newton, J. S., Algozzine, B., Algozzine, K., Horner, R. H., & Todd, A. W. (2011). Building local capacity for training and coaching data-based problem solving with positive behavior intervention and support teams. *Journal of Applied School Psychology, 27*(3), 228–245.

Palmer, K., & Noltemeyer, A. (2019). Professional development in schools: Predictors of effectiveness and implications for statewide PBIS trainings. *Teacher Development, 23*(5), 511–528.

Pierce, J. D. (2019). How good coaches build alliance with teachers. *Educational Leadership, 77*(3), 78–82.

Poglinco, S. M., Bach, A. J., Hovde, K., Rosenblum, S., Saunders, M., & Supovitz, J. A. (2003). *The heart of the matter: The coaching model in America's choice schools.* Consortium for Policy Research in Education.

Rhodes, C., & Beneicke, S. (2002). Coaching, mentoring and peer-networking: Challenges for the management of teacher professional development in schools. *Journal of In-service Education, 28*(2), 297–310.

St. Martin, K., Nantais, M., & Harms, A. (2015). *Reading Tiered Fidelity Inventory (Elementary-Level Edition).* Michigan Department of Education, Michigan's Integrated Behavior and Learning Support Initiative.

Stormont, M., Reinke, W. M., Newcomer, L., Marchese, D., & Lewis, C. (2015). Coaching teachers' use of social behavior interventions to improve children's outcomes: A review of the literature. *Journal of Positive Behavior Interventions, 17*(2), 69–82.

Tichnor-Wagner, A., Wachen, J., Cannata, M., & Cohen-Vogel, L. (2017). Continuous improvement in the public school context: Understanding how educators respond to plan–do–study–act cycles. *Journal of Educational Change, 18*(4), 465–494.

Tschannen-Moran, M., & McMaster, P. (2009). Sources of self-efficacy: Four professional development formats and their relationship to self-efficacy and implementation of a new teaching strategy. *Elementary School Journal, 110*(2), 228–245.

Walpole, S., & Blamey, K. L. (2008). Elementary literacy coaches: The reality of dual roles. *The Reading Teacher, 62*(3), 222–231.

Wolpert-Gawron, H. (2016). The many roles of an instructional coach. *Educational Leadership, 73*(9), 56–60.

Yoon, K. S., Duncan, T., Lee, S. W. Y., Scarloss, B., & Shapley, K. L. (2007). *Reviewing the evidence on how teacher professional development affects student achievement.* Regional Educational Laboratory Southwest.

Effective Coaching Practices

A Synthesis of Research

KEY QUESTIONS

1. What are the most effective practices coaches use when supporting teachers?

2. What are the most effective practices coaches use when supporting implementation teams?

3. How do coaches apply these practices in a three-phase recursive cycle?

CHAPTER TAKE-AWAYS

1. Different types of coaching have been examined in research, including expert-to-expert peer coaching and expert-to-novice coaching. Findings from this research indicate that the type of coaching is not as important as *what* the coach does when working with teachers or teams.

2. Although some debate continues about what constitutes effective coaching of teachers, experimental and qualitative research indicates that four specific coaching practices are linked to improved teaching and student outcomes: 1) using alliance strategies, 2) observing, 3) modeling, and 4) providing performance feedback.

3. A less robust body of research exists on the impact of coaching teams of educators (e.g., implementation teams, school leadership teams) than the research on coaching teachers. Findings suggest, however, that the same four effective practices used with coaching teachers can be used with teams of educators to improve team practice, systems, and student outcomes.

4. Coaches apply the four practices in a three-phase recursive cycle. In the first phase, coaches conduct a premeeting with the coachee(s). In the second phase, coaches work directly in the classroom with the teacher or attend the team meeting. In the third phase, coaches conduct a postmeeting with the teacher or team to provide performance feedback (e.g., sharing notes from observations, product reviews, checklist data, or charts).

CHAPTER OVERVIEW

This chapter is divided into three sections. We first provide a synthesis of coaching research, focusing initially on coaching that occurs between a teacher and a coach. We shift toward research related to the coaching of teams of educators who are responsible for leading implementation efforts across an entire school or pre-K program, or systems coaches (Adelman & Taylor, 2007; Fullan & Knight, 2011). In the second section of this chapter, we present the four effective practices that comprise this text's coaching framework: 1) using alliance strategies, 2) observing, 3) modeling, and 4) providing performance feedback. We also briefly clarify when coaches enact each of the four practices: first in a premeeting with a teacher or team, next when working with the teacher (in the classroom) or with the implementation team in the team meeting setting, and finally in a postmeeting with the teacher or team. The final section of the chapter contains a reflection and discussion tool you can use to integrate the chapter's information into your coaching role.

Ideally, we suggest that coaches become familiar with this content prior to planning coaching sessions. Planning for coaching sessions, conducting sessions with one or more teachers, and reflecting on coaching requires a nuanced knowledge of each coaching practice: when to integrate each practice into a session, why some practices are used in every session and others are not, and how to adjust the use of each practice to best suit the needs of the coaching situation. Coaches who understand such nuances before beginning to coach will be well prepared to plan, conduct, and reflect on sessions to improve teacher practice, team practice, systems, or student outcomes.

RESEARCH ON COACHING

Coaching Teachers

An extensive body of experimental and qualitative research exists on the impact of coaching on teaching and student learning. Some of this research focuses on educators working in early childhood classrooms (e.g., Fox et al., 2011; Neuman & Cunningham, 2009), whereas other studies examine teacher coaching in K–12 settings (Biancarosa et al., 2010; Gregory et al., 2014; Kraft, & Blazar, 2017). Several variations of coaching are seen across these studies. For example, Joyce and Showers (1982) examined the use of peer coaching in their seminal research, wherein experienced teachers were partnered with other experienced teachers to support each others' implementation of newly learned practices. Teachers working within these dyads observed each other, modeled if their partner did not know how to implement a new practice, and provided their partners with performance feedback, which resulted in improved teaching.

In the nearly 4 decades since this research, peer coaching continues to be examined, with studies expanding to focus on dyads of teachers as they coach each other in pre-K settings and K–12 settings (see Britton & Anderson, 2010; Lu, 2010). Across these studies, results affirm that peer coaching, particularly experienced teacher to experienced teacher dyads, can be a productive way of improving teachers' overall instructional practices (e.g., Ackland, 1991; Kohler et al., 1997). Experienced teacher to experienced teacher peer coaching can also lead to improvements in specific aspects of teaching, such as math instruction (Murray et al., 2009), literacy instruction (Fisher et al., 2011), use of positive classroom management strategies (Duchaine et al., 2011), and implementation of social-emotional supports (Stormont et al., 2015).

Peer coaching is not the only type of dyad examined in research. Expert-to-novice coaching dyads are also prevalent in research (e.g., Kraft et al., 2018; Neuman & Wright, 2010; Stormont et al., 2015). In these studies, a more expert teacher (e.g., Biancarosa et al., 2010), researcher, or doctoral student (e.g., Hemmeter et al., 2015; Stitcher et al., 2006) serves as the coach for a teacher with less expertise. Recipients of coaching include preservice teachers (i.e., those enrolled in a preparatory program) (see Stahl et al., 2018) or teachers in their first few years of teaching (Veenman & Denessen, 2001). Expert-to-novice coaching studies from early childhood settings suggest that teachers can improve their use of promising or evidence-based literacy and classroom management practices (Artman-Meeker et al., 2014; Pianta et al., 2017; Snyder et al., 2015) and even programs designed for use with children with specific disabilities such as autism (Ruble et al., 2013). Similarly, expert-to-novice coaching research in K–12 can lead to teachers' improved use of behavioral interventions (e.g., Hershfeldt et al., 2012; Reinke et al., 2008; Stormont et al., 2015), overall instructional practices (Gilmour et al., 2017; Jager et al., 2002; Kretlow et al., 2012), use of social-emotional supports (Stormont et al., 2015), math instruction (Kretlow et al., 2012), and literacy instruction (Maheady et al., 2004; Matsumura et al., 2012).

Whether the coaching occurs between two experienced teachers or from an expert to a novice teacher, and regardless of the grade level in which the teachers work, the prominent form of coaching in many of these studies is a face-to-face approach. Technological advances, however, have resulted in the use of various platforms (e.g., e-mail, video) (Artman-Meeker et al., 2014; Barton et al., 2013; Krick Oborn & Johnson, 2015; Ruble et al., 2013) or other tools (e.g., bug-in-ear devices) (Owens et al., 2020; Rock et al., 2014; Scheeler et al., 2010) to conduct coaching sessions virtually. Some studies have even examined fusion models of coaching in which sessions occur in a face-to-face and virtual format (Hemmeter et al., 2015; Powell et al., 2010; Ruble et al., 2013). The use of virtually mediated coaching can result in pre-K teachers' improved use of general instructional and interaction skills (Pianta et al., 2008) and literacy and social-emotional practices (Artman-Meeker & Hemmeter, 2013; Powell et al., 2010). Virtual approaches to coaching in K–12 settings have shown improved math instruction (Campbell & Malkus, 2011), science instruction (Cotabish et al., 2013), overall instruction (Rimm-Kauffman et al., 2014), and classroom management strategies (Gregory et al., 2014). Thus, findings on virtual and face-to-face coaching show both approaches can be beneficial for teachers. Such research provided reassurance that coaching could continue even during the height of the COVID pandemic, when teachers and coaches could not work together in a face-to-face format.

Important conclusions can be drawn from the research described above—coaching can result in improved teacher practice, with some research also showing improved learner outcomes (Garbacz et al., 2015; Kraft et al., 2018; Kretlow & Bartholomew, 2010; Mashburn et al., 2010; Sailors & Price, 2010; Walpole et al., 2010). A critical caveat is necessary at this juncture, however: Not all behaviors enacted by the coach (i.e., coaching practices) produce such results (Kraft et al., 2018; Piasta et al., 2017). Coaching that specifically includes reoccurring cycles of observing, modeling, and providing performance feedback can lead to improved teaching and student learning (Wood et al., 2016). Furthermore, the alliance formed (including how the coach collaborates with the coachees and the coach's expertise) between coaches and teachers seems to influence the degree to which coaching results in improved teaching and student learning (Johnson et al., 2016; Pierce, 2019). When relationships are not positive, the coach may struggle to help the teacher make improvements to teaching (Wehby et al., 2012). Thus, alliance also plays an effective role in coaching, and coaches can use strategies to support a positive teacher–coach alliance.

Systems Coaching

Although experimental research on coaching implementation teams is not yet as prolific as coaching teachers, non–research-oriented literature is available. Much of this literature clarifies the nature of the job in comparison to a teacher coach (Duda & Barrett, 2013; Fullan & Knight, 2011) and presents the reasons why team coaching is a necessary support mechanism for these teams (e.g., Adelman & Taylor, 2007; Bradshaw et al., 2012; Freeman et al., 2015; Horner et al., 2014).

Turning to the experimental research, studies on coaching teams of educators has occurred primarily in K–12 settings (e.g., Horner et al., 2014). The focal point of this research has been on coaching to support a team of educators responsible for leading an implementation effort across a school or districtwide. Subsequently, the emphasis with team coaching is on team practice—therein improving the system (e.g., initial and sustained implementation of an innovation with fidelity at a school; teaming procedures used by the implementation leadership team [Pas et al., 2020]; use of data for decision making [McIntosh et al., 2018])—rather than on coaching to improve the practice of teachers. Given this focal point, team coaching is also referred to as *systems coaching* (Freeman et al., 2017).

Moreover, some conclusions can be drawn from experimental examinations of this coaching role. Systems coaching is cited as an essential support during initial and sustained school-level implementation of PBIS (McIntosh et al., 2018) and RTI (March et al., 2016). Although research on coaching teams in the context of implementing MTSS seems relatively new to the field (see Bastable et al., 2020), much can be learned about systems coaching from research on PBIS. Several have argued that team coaching is essential for initial and sustained implementation of the framework (Eagle et al., 2015; Freeman et al., 2017). Like teacher coaches, systems coaches seem to be most impactful when they observe, model, build alliance, and provide performance feedback to implementation teams they support (Horner et al., 2014; McIntosh et al., 2018). When coaches applied such practices, teams were better equipped to lead implementation efforts, which in turn facilitated the school's or district's ability to initiate and sustain the implementation of three-tiered frameworks (Horner et al., 2014; McIntosh et al., 2018). Interestingly, the continuity of coaching (i.e., whether the coach supported a school for at least 3 consecutive years) may be a particularly salient factor in a team's use of problem-solving procedures within an MTSS or RTI framework (March et al., 2016).

Other commonalities exist between coaching teachers and coaching implementation teams in research. Systems coaches often have expertise in the area in the innovation being implemented (e.g., PBIS). These coaches also hold a variety of professional backgrounds, such as school psychologists, reading specialists, special educators, or university-based researchers (March et al., 2016). One distinction with teacher coaching and systems coaching research, however, is that all studies rely on face-to-face coaching rather than a virtually mediated approach.

THE FRAMEWORK FOR EFFECTIVE COACHING

Four Effective Coaching Practices

Given the findings on coaching teachers and coaching teams, coaching is most beneficial when it includes four effective practices: 1) using alliance strategies, 2) observing, 3) modeling, and 4) providing performance feedback (see Figure 3.1; see also Dunst et al., 2015; Garbacz et al., 2015; Kraft et al., 2018; Kretlow & Bartholomew, 2010; and Polly et al., 2013).

Using alliance strategies

Observing

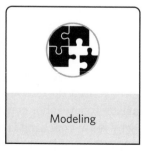
Modeling

Providing performance feedback

Figure 3.1.   Effective coaching practices. (*Source:* Pierce, 2015.)

Applying the Practices in a Three-Phase Cycle

Coaches apply the four effective coaching practices with teachers and implementation teams in a three-phase recursive cycle (Cornett & Knight, 2009; Freeman et al., 2017; Kretlow & Bartholomew, 2010). In the first phase of the cycle, coaches conduct a premeeting with the teacher or team, using alliance strategies to set a positive foundation for the upcoming work between the coach and the recipient(s) of coaching. Next, the coach observes the teacher or team, models if the teacher or team struggles to engage in a specific task (use of a reading strategy), and continues to use alliance strategies. In the third phase of the cycle, the coach conducts a postmeeting with the teacher or team, again applying alliance strategies and providing performance feedback. This three-phase cycle of coaching continues in recursive fashion so that teachers or teams continually receive support from the coach. Figure 3.2 and the next section of this chapter briefly defines each of the four coaching practices. We also provide additional information about how coaches enact these practices during each phase of the coaching cycle. Chapters 5 and 6 fully define each coaching practice and further clarify how practices are used in the three-phase coaching cycle.

Using Alliance Strategies   The first aspect of the coach's work is to create (and maintain) a positive alliance (i.e., relationship) with the team being coached (Atteberry & Bryk, 2011; Lowenhaupt et al., 2014; Neuman & Cunningham, 2009). Although alliance may seem like an

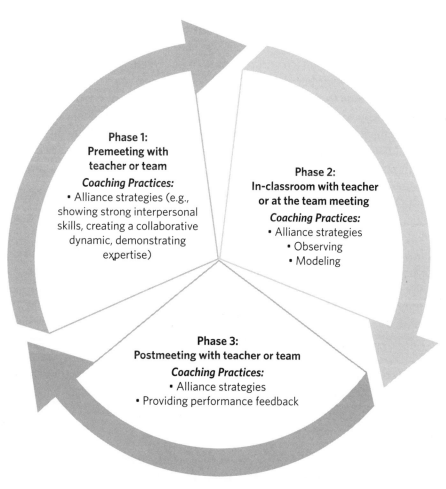

Figure 3.2.   Effective coaching practices in a three-phase recursive cycle. (*Source:* Pierce, 2015.)

abstract concept, it is shaped by at least three factors (Horvath, 2001): 1) the interpersonal skills of the coach, including the coach's communication skills and the capacity of the coach to build trust with the recipient of coaching (i.e., the coachee); 2) the degree to which the coach and coachee collaborate, particularly when setting goals for improved teaching or team practice, approaching their work together as partners, coming to consensus about how to work together, and prioritizing the needs of the teacher or team; and 3) the depth of the coach's expertise in the content area in which the coaching occurs and the context (e.g., teaching elementary students with disabilities, implementing pre-K PBIS, instructing secondary students in math and science).

To illustrate, coaches can build and maintain positive alliance with teachers or teams by asking open-ended questions, actively listening, summarizing ideas shared, and clearly articulating next steps. Coaches also champion the incremental improvements of teachers and teams and partner with the teacher or team to develop a coherent plan to move teacher or implementation forward (Garbacz et al., 2015; Pierce, 2015). In fact, building and maintaining positive alliance is a foundational task for coaching teachers and implementation (Johnson, 2017).

Moreover, using alliance strategies occurs throughout every phase of the coaching cycle. For example, when kicking off the cycle (i.e., during the premeeting), coaches may find it helpful to ascertain the teacher's or team's goal for the coaching session by asking open-ended questions such as, "How do you envision us working together as partners?" or "Do you have a particular goal you'd like me to help you progress toward?" As the teacher or team talks, the coach can closely listen, summarizing what is stated, showing interest in the ideas of the teacher or team, and clearly articulating next steps. In the second phase of the cycle (i.e., working directly in the classroom, at the team meeting), the coach can focus their attention on the area identified by the teacher or team to indicate to coachee(s)' needs are a priority to the coach as well. During the third phase of the cycle (i.e., postmeeting), the coach can continue to ask open-ended questions (e.g., "How did the lesson/meeting go from your perspective?" "What surprised you about the lesson and student engagement?") to encourage the coachees to share insights. The coach will infuse their observations and perspectives by building on the team's insights. The coach will work with the teacher or team to pinpoint some next steps. By using alliance strategies during each phase of the coaching cycle, the coachee(s) gain a deepening understanding that the coach is a trustworthy ally on the journey toward improvement.

Observing   Observing teachers and teams may seem like it is the simplest of the four coaching practices but, in reality, it is just as nuanced as other coaching practices. In the case of coaching teachers, the coach watches the teacher work with students to gather information about what transpires in the classroom. As a part of the information-gathering aspect of the observation, the coach may also take notes or collect data on teacher practice. When observing teams, the coach typically attends the team meeting that is focused on the educational innovation being implemented (e.g., meeting focused on the PBIS components of MTSS, literacy components of MTSS). As with coaching teachers, the observation occurs so that the coach can gain insight into how the team currently operates. Although watching a teacher or a team seems like an obvious component of any coaching session, it is an important part of the second phase of the coaching cycle. The coach must have a clear understanding of how the teacher works with students or how the team is managing the implementation effort before using at least two other coaching practices—modeling or providing performance feedback (Dunst et al., 2015; Garbacz et al., 2015; Kraft et al., 2018; Kretlow & Bartholomew, 2010; Polly et al., 2013).

Modeling   Modeling is a third practice that can be a regular part of a coaching session (Akhavan, 2015; Dunst et al., 2015; Garbacz et al., 2015; Kraft et al., 2018; Kretlow & Bartholomew, 2010;

Polly et al., 2013). Modeling is akin to providing scaffolded instruction to students. In the case of coaching teachers, the coach shows the teacher how to implement a practice, implements the practice in tandem with them, and offers the teacher opportunities to independently use the practice. Modeling should only be used when teachers or teams are unsuccessful at implementing a practice (Kretlow & Bartholomew, 2010; State et al., 2019) and when the coach has already established with the teacher that modeling may be a part of a coaching session. If a teacher implements a given practice and the students are benefiting from that instruction, then modeling may be omitted from the coaching session (Dunst et al., 2015; Garbacz et al., 2015). Yet, if modeling does not occur but is needed, then the teacher may continue to implement a practice incorrectly. In turn, students may not receive the instruction that they need. If modeling is needed, then this coaching practice occurs in the second phase of the coaching cycle because the coach has gathered information about teaching from the observation phase.

Modeling for a team of educators is essentially the same as the process previously described. For example, implementation teams seem to benefit from demonstrations of how to engage in data-based decision-making procedures (March et al., 2016). As in the case of coaching teachers, modeling is not always needed when coaching a team of educators. Imagine that a coach has observed an implementation team as they analyze student reading scores. The team members clearly understand how to engage in this task, doing so without any errors. The coach would not need to model how to analyze the scores in this case. In contrast, if the team members did not know how to examine the data and drew inaccurate conclusions, then the coach could model for the team members as long as the team and coach have already come to agreement that modeling may be a part of coaching sessions. Modeling would continue until the team members were accurate in the skill. Like modeling for one teacher, this coaching practice most commonly occurs in the second phase of the coaching cycle because the coach must first observe to gather information about what the team is doing before modeling.

Providing Performance Feedback   Providing performance feedback to teachers and implementation teams is the fourth effective coaching practice (Cavanaugh, 2013; Dunst et al., 2015; Garbacz et al., 2015; Kraft et al., 2018; Kretlow & Bartholomew, 2010; Polly et al., 2013). In fact, performance feedback has been cited as an evidence-based practice for coaching teachers because it can serve as a powerful catalyst for changing human behavior (Solomon et al., 2012). Yet, not all performance feedback offers this effect. High-quality performance feedback is more positive than corrective. In the case of coaching teachers, feedback is a precise description of what the teacher did and what the students did in response to the teacher. In the case of coaching an implementation team, feedback is just as precise, but the description should be of what the team members did to advance their implementation effort (e.g., correctly analyzed and used students' reading progress monitoring data to inform an implementation decision). Timeliness is another aspect of high-quality performance feedback so the teacher or team receives the feedback shortly after working with students or after conducting their team meeting (Cavanaugh, 2013; March et al., 2016; Scheeler et al., 2004).

Perhaps not surprisingly, performance feedback is typically provided in a postmeeting. Feedback is often summarized in written form or compiled within checklists that document what transpired in the classroom or team meeting. (See Figure 6.2, which can help you determine how you might collect data.) By the time of the postmeeting, coaches have 1) used alliance strategies to form a positive foundation of trust, common commitment, and clarify how the partnership will proceed between the coach and coachees; 2) observed to gain information about the work of the teacher or team; and 3) modeled if the teacher or team needed that support. Therefore, the coach should have adequate information to share with the teacher or team and maintain the positive rapport so that feedback can be well received.

SUMMARY

If you have ever searched research and gray literature on coaching, then chances are it was difficult to glean the most important conclusions about what coaches can do to productively support teachers and teams. Let us remind you of the good news: Four effective practices are most closely connected to the goals of coaching, whether you are coaching teachers or teams. By now you have at least a general understanding of what those practices are and a better sense of when those practices are used throughout a three-phase coaching cycle. If you are ready to fully unpack each of these practices and how they are used in the coaching cycle, then shift your attention to Chapters 5 and 6. Shift your attention to Chapter 4 if you would like to learn more about another core coaching concept—coaching for systems improvement with teachers and teams.

RESOURCES

Read over the tool shown in Figure 3.3 (blank versions of this form are available in Appendix G and to download). This tool can be used to link what you learned from this chapter to your role as a coach. You may find it helpful to share and discuss your responses with a partner.

APPENDIX G

Connecting the Dots: Research, the Coaching Framework, and Your Coaching Role

Purpose: Use this tool to reflect on what you learned about the four effective coaching practices used during the three-phase coaching cycle.

Directions:
1. Complete each section of this tool so that you can integrate what you learned from the chapter into your coaching practice.
2. You may find it helpful to discuss your responses with a partner and record any notes in the space provided.

	Questions
Phase 1: The premeeting	1. What did you learn about using coaching practices that could be applied to Phase 1 of the coaching cycle? 2. What questions remain for you? 3. What are you most excited to apply to your coaching practice? What do you think will be tricky? Why?
Phase 2: In the classroom or at the team meeting	1. What did you learn about using coaching practices that could be applied to Phase 2 of the coaching cycle? 2. What questions remain for you? 3. What are you most excited to apply to your coaching practice? What do you think will be tricky? Why?
Phase 3: The postmeeting	1. What did you learn about using coaching practices that could be applied to Phase 3 of the coaching cycle? 2. What questions remain for you? 3. What are you most excited to apply to your coaching practice? What do you think will be tricky? Why?

Figure 3.3. Connecting the Dots: Research, the Coaching Framework, and Your Coaching Role. (*Note:* Blank versions of this form are available in Appendix G and to download.)

REFERENCES

Ackland, R. (1991). A review of the peer coaching literature. *Journal of Staff Development, 12*(1), 22–27.

Adelman, H. S., & Taylor, L. (2007). Systemic change for school improvement. *Journal of Educational and Psychological Consultation, 17*(1), 55–77.

Akhavan, N. (2015). Coaching side by side: One-on-one collaboration creates caring, connected teachers. *Journal of Staff Development, 36,* 34–37.

Artman-Meeker, K. M., & Hemmeter, M. L. (2013). Effects of training and feedback on teachers' use of classroom preventive practices. *Topics in Early Childhood Special Education, 33,* 112–123.

Artman-Meeker, K., Hemmeter, M. L., & Snyder, P. (2014). Effects of distance coaching on teachers' use of pyramid model practices: A pilot study. *Infants & Young Children, 27*(4), 325–344.

Atteberry, A., & Bryk, A. S. (2011). Analyzing teacher participation in literacy coaching activities. *Elementary School Journal, 112*(2), 356–382.

Barton, E. E., Pribble, L., & Chen, C. I. (2013). The use of e-mail to deliver performance-based feedback to early childhood practitioners. *Journal of Early Intervention, 35*(3), 270–297.

Bastable, E., Massar, M. M., & McIntosh, K. (2020). A survey of team members' perceptions of coaching activities related to tier 1 SWPBIS implementation. *Journal of Positive Behavior Interventions, 22*(1), 51–61.

Biancarosa, G., Bryk, A. S., & Dexter, E. R. (2010). Assessing the value-added effects of literacy collaborative professional development on student learning. *Elementary School Journal, 111*(1), 7–34.

Bradshaw, C. P., Pas, E. T., Goldweber, A., Rosenberg, M. S., & Leaf, P. J. (2012). Integrating school-wide positive behavioral interventions and supports with tier 2 coaching to student support teams: The PBIS plus model. *Advances in School Mental Health Promotion, 5*(3), 177–193.

Britton, L. R., & Anderson, K. A. (2010). Peer coaching and pre-service teachers: Examining an underutilised concept. *Teaching and Teacher Education, 26*(2), 306–314.

Campbell, P. F., & Malkus, N. N. (2011). The impact of elementary mathematics coaches on student achievement. *Elementary School Journal, 111*(3), 430–454. https://doi.org/10.1086/657654

Cavanaugh, B. (2013). Performance feedback and teachers' use of praise and opportunities to respond: A review of the literature. *Education and Treatment of Children, 36*(1), 111–136.

Cornett, J., & Knight, J. (2009). Research on coaching. In J. Knight (Ed.), *Coaching: Approaches and perspectives* (pp. 192–216). Corwin Press.

Cotabish, A., Dailey, D., Robinson, A., & Hughes, G. (2013). The effects of a STEM intervention on elementary students' science knowledge and skills. *School Science and Mathematics, 113*(5), 215–226.

Duchaine, E. L., Jolivette, K., & Fredrick, L. D. (2011). The effect of teacher coaching with performance feedback on behavior-specific praise in inclusion classrooms. *Education and Treatment of Children, 34*(2), 209–227.

Duda, M. A., & Barrett, S. (2013). *Systems coaching: Coaching for competence and impact—Brief #1: Defining coaching.* https://www.pbis.org/resource/coaching-for-competence-and-impact-brief-1-defining-coaching

Dunst, C. J., Bruder, M. B., & Hamby, D. W. (2015). Metasynthesis of in-service professional development research: Features associated with positive educator and student outcomes. *Educational Research and Reviews, 10*(12), 1731–1744

Eagle, J. W., Dowd-Eagle, S. E., Snyder, A., & Holtzman, E. G. (2015). Implementing a multi-tiered system of support (MTSS): Collaboration between school psychologists and administrators to promote systems-level change. *Journal of Educational and Psychological Consultation, 25*(2-3), 160–177.

Fisher, D., Frey, N., & Lapp, D. (2011). Coaching middle-level teachers to think aloud improves comprehension instruction and student reading achievement. *The Teacher Educator, 46*(3), 231-243.

Fox, L., Hemmeter, M. L., Snyder, P., Binder, D. P., & Clarke, S. (2011). Coaching early childhood special educators to implement a comprehensive model for promoting young children's social competence. *Topics in Early Childhood Special Education, 31*(3), 178–192.

Freeman, J., Sugai, G., Simonsen, B., & Everett, S. (2017). MTSS coaching: Bridging knowing to doing. *Theory Into Practice, 56*(1), 29–37.

Freeman, R., Miller, D., & Newcomer, L. (2015). Integration of academic and behavioral MTSS at the district level using implementation science. *Learning Disabilities: A Contemporary Journal, 13*(1), 59–72.

Fullan, M., & Knight, J. (2011). Coaches as system leaders. *Educational Leadership, 69*(2), 50–53.

Garbacz, S. A., Lannie, A. L., Jeffery-Pearsall, J. L., & Truckenmiller, A. J. (2015). Strategies for effective classroom coaching. *Preventing School Failure, 59*(4), 263–273.

Gilmour, A. F., Wehby, J. H., & McGuire, T. M. (2017). A preliminary investigation of using school-based coaches to support intervention fidelity of a classwide behavior management program. *Preventing School Failure: Alternative Education for Children and Youth, 61*(2), 126–135.

Gregory, A., Allen, J. P., Mikami, A. Y., Hafen, C. A., & Pianta, R. C. (2014). Effects of a professional development program on behavioral engagement of students in middle and high school. *Psychology in the Schools, 51*(2), 143–163.

Hemmeter, M. L., Hardy, J. K., Schnitz, A. G., Adams, J. M., & Kinder, K. A. (2015). Effects of training and coaching with performance feedback on teachers' use of Pyramid Model practices. *Topics in Early Childhood Special Education, 35*(3), 144–156.

Hershfeldt, P. A., Pell, K., Sechrest, R., Pas, E. T., & Bradshaw, C. P. (2012). Lessons learned coaching teachers in behavior management: The PBIS plus coaching model. *Journal of Educational and Psychological Consultation, 22*(4), 280–299.

Horner, R. H., Kincaid, D., Sugai, G., Lewis, T., Eber, L., Barrett, S., Dickey, C. R., Richter, M., Sullivan, E., Boezio, C., & Algozzine, B. (2014). Scaling up school-wide positive behavioral interventions and supports: Experiences of seven states with documented success. *Journal of Positive Behavior Interventions, 16*(4), 197–208.

Horvath, A. O. (2001). The alliance. *Psychotherapy: Theory, Research, Practice, Training, 38*(4), 365–372.

Jager, B., Reezigt, G. J., & Creemers, B. P. (2002). The effects of teacher training on new instructional behaviour in reading comprehension. *Teaching and Teacher Education, 18*(7), 831–842.

Johnson, L. D. (2017). Scaling the Pyramid Model across complex systems providing early care for preschoolers: Exploring how models for decision making may enhance implementation science. *Early Education and Development, 28*(7), 822–838.

Johnson, S. R., Pas, E. T., & Bradshaw, C. P. (2016). Understanding and measuring coach–teacher alliance: A glimpse inside the 'black box'. *Prevention Science, 17*(4), 439–449.

Joyce, B., & Showers, B. (1982). The coaching of teaching. *Educational Leadership, 40*(1), 4–8.

Kohler, F. W., Crilley, K. M., Shearer, D. D., & Good, G. (1997). Effects of peer coaching on teacher and student outcomes. *Journal of Educational Research, 90*(4), 240–250.

Kraft, M. A., & Blazar, D. (2017). Individualized coaching to improve teacher practice across grades and subjects: New experimental evidence. *Educational Policy, 31*(7), 1033–1068.

Kraft, M. A., Blazar, D., & Hogan, D. (2018). The effect of teacher coaching on instruction and achievement: A meta-analysis of the causal evidence. *Review of Educational Research, 88*(4), 547–588.

Kretlow, A. G., & Bartholomew, C. C. (2010). Using coaching to improve the fidelity of evidence-based practices: A review of studies. *Teacher Education and Special Education, 33*, 279–299.

Kretlow, A. G., Cooke, N. L., & Wood, C. L. (2012). Using in-service and coaching to increase teachers' accurate use of research-based strategies. *Remedial and Special Education, 33*, 348–361.

Kretlow, A. G., Wood, C. L., & Cooke, N. L. (2012). Using in-service and coaching to increase kindergarten teachers' accurate delivery of group instructional units. *Journal of Special Education, 44*, 234–246.

Krick Oborn, K. M., & Johnson, L. D. (2015). Coaching via electronic performance feedback to support home visitors' use of caregiver coaching strategies. *Topics in Early Childhood Special Education, 35*(3), 157–169.

Lowenhaupt, R., McKinney, S., & Reeves, T. (2014). Coaching in context: The role of relationships in the work of three literacy coaches. *Professional Development in Education, 40*(5), 740–757.

Lu, H. L. (2010). Research on peer coaching in preservice teacher education: A review of literature. *Teaching and Teacher Education, 26*(4), 748–753.

Maheady, L., Harper, G. F., Mallette, B., & Karnes, M. (2004). Preparing preservice teachers to implement class wide peer tutoring. *Teacher Education and Special Education, 27*(4), 408–418.

March, A. L., Castillo, J. M., Batsche, G. M., & Kincaid, D. (2016). Relationship between systems coaching and problem-solving implementation fidelity in a response-to-intervention model. *Journal of Applied School Psychology, 32*(2), 147–177.

Mashburn, A. J., Downer, J. T., Hamre, B. K., Justice, L. M., & Pianta, R. C. (2010). Consultation for teachers and children's language and literacy development during pre-kindergarten. *Applied Developmental Science, 14*(4), 179–196.

Matsumura, L. C., Garnier, H. E., & Spybrook, J. (2012). The effect of content-focused coaching on the quality of classroom text discussions. *Journal of Teacher Education, 63*, 214–228.

McIntosh, K., Mercer, S. H., Nese, R. N., Strickland-Cohen, M. K., Kittelman, A., Hoselton, R., & Horner, R. H. (2018). Factors predicting sustained implementation of a universal behavior support framework. *Educational Researcher, 47*(5), 307–316. https://doi.org/10.3102/0013189X18776975

Murray, S., Ma, X., & Mazur, J. (2009). Effects of peer coaching on teachers' collaborative interactions and students' mathematics achievement. *Journal of Educational Research, 102*(3), 203–212.

Neuman, S. B., & Cunningham, L. (2009). The impact of professional development and coaching on early language and literacy instructional practices. *American Educational Research Journal, 46*(2), 532–566.

Neuman, S. B., & Wright, T. S. (2010). Promoting language and literacy development for early childhood educators: A mixed-methods study of coursework and coaching. *Elementary School Journal, 111*(1), 63–86.

Owens, T. L., Lo, Y. Y., & Collins, B. C. (2020). Using tiered coaching and bug-in-ear technology to promote teacher implementation fidelity. *The Journal of Special Education, 54*(2), 67–79.

Pas, E. T., Lindstrom Johnson, S., Alfonso, Y. N., & Bradshaw, C. P. (2020). Tracking time and resources associated with systems change and the adoption of evidence-based programs: The "hidden costs" of school-based coaching. *Administration and Policy in Mental Health and Mental Health Services Research, 47*, 720–734.

Pianta, R., Hamre, B., Downer, J., Burchinal, M., Williford, A., LoCasale-Crouch, J., Howes, C., La Paro, K., & Scott-Little, C. (2017). Early childhood professional development: Coaching and coursework effects on indicators of children's school readiness. *Early Education and Development, 28*(8), 956–975.

Pianta, R. C., Mashburn, A. J., Downer, J. T., Hamre, B. K., & Justice, L. (2008). Effects of web-mediated professional development resources on teacher–child interactions in pre-kindergarten classrooms. *Early Childhood Research Quarterly, 23*(4), 431–451.

Piasta, S. B., Justice, L. M., O'Connell, A. A., Mauck, S. A., Weber-Mayrer, M., Schachter, R. E., Farley, K. S., & Spear, C. F. (2017). Effectiveness of large-scale, state-sponsored language and literacy professional development on early childhood educator outcomes. *Journal of Research on Educational Effectiveness, 10*(2), 354–378.

Pierce, J. D. (2015). *Teacher–coach alliance as a critical component of coaching: Effects of feedback and analysis on teacher practice.* http://hdl.handle.net/1773/33786

Pierce, J. D. (2019). How good coaches build alliance with teachers. *Educational Leadership, 77*(3), 78–82.

Polly, D., Mraz, M., & Algozzine, R. (2013). Implications for developing and researching elementary school mathematics coaches. *School Science and Mathematics, 113,* 297–307. https://doi.org/10.1111/ssm.12029

Powell, D. R., Diamond, K. E., Burchinal, M. R., & Koehler, M. J. (2010). Effects of an early literacy professional development intervention on head start teachers and children. *Journal of Educational Psychology, 102*(2), 299–312.

Reinke, W. M., Lewis-Palmer, T., & Merrell, K. (2008). The classroom check-up: A classwide teacher consultation model for increasing praise and decreasing disruptive behavior. *School Psychology Review, 37*(3), 315–332.

Rimm-Kaufman, S. E., Larsen, R. A. A., Baroody, A. E., Curby, T. W., Ko, M., Thomas, J. B., Merritt, E. G., Abry, T., & DeCoster, J. (2014). Efficacy of the responsive classroom approach: Results from a 3-year, longitudinal randomized controlled trial. *American Educational Research Journal, 51*(3), 567-603.

Rock, M. L., Schumacker, R. E., Gregg, M., Howard, P. W., Gable, R. A., & Zigmond, N. (2014). How are they now? Longer term effects of e-coaching through online bug-in-ear technology. *Teacher Education and Special Education, 37*(2), 161–181.

Ruble, L. A., McGrew, J. H., Toland, M. D., Dalrymple, N. J., & Jung, L. (2013). A randomized controlled trial of COMPASS web-based and face-to-face teacher coaching in autism. *Journal of Consulting and Clinical Psychology, 81,* 566–572.

Sailors, M., & Price, L. R. (2010). Professional development that supports the teaching of cognitive reading strategy instruction. *Elementary School Journal, 110*(3), 301–322.

Scheeler, M. C., Congdon, M., & Stansbery, S. (2010). Providing immediate feedback to co-teachers through bug-in-ear technology: An effective method of peer coaching in inclusion classrooms. *Teacher Education and Special Education, 33*(1), 83–96.

Scheeler, M. C., Ruhl, K. L., & McAfee, J. K. (2004). Providing performance feedback to teachers: A review. *Teacher Education and Special Education, 27*(4), 396–407.

Snyder, P. A., Hemmeter, M. L., & Fox, L. (2015). Supporting implementation of evidence-based practices through practice-based coaching. *Topics in Early Childhood Special Education, 35*(3), 133–143.

Solomon, B. G., Klein, S. A., & Politylo, B. C. (2012). The effect of performance feedback on teachers' treatment integrity: A meta-analysis of the single-case literature. *School Psychology Review, 41*(2). 160–175.

Stahl, G., Sharplin, E., & Kehrwald, B. (2018). A review of the literature on coaching in pre-service teacher education. In G. Stahl, E. Sharplin, & B. Kehrwald *Real-time coaching and pre-service teacher education* (pp. 13–30). Springer.

State, T. M., Simonsen, B., Hirn, R. G., & Wills, H. (2019). Bridging the research-to-practice gap through effective professional development for teachers working with students with emotional and behavioral disorders. *Behavioral Disorders, 44*(2), 107–116.

Stichter, J. P., Lewis, T. J., Richter, M., Johnson, N. W., & Bradley, L. (2006). Assessing antecedent variables: The effects of instructional variables on student outcomes through in-service and peer coaching professional development models. *Education and Treatment of Children, 29*(4) 665–692.

Stormont, M., Reinke, W. M., Newcomer, L., Marchese, D., & Lewis, C. (2015). Coaching teachers' use of social behavior interventions to improve children's outcomes: A review of the literature. *Journal of Positive Behavior Interventions, 17*(2), 69–82.

Veenman, S., & Denessen, E. (2001). The coaching of teachers: Results of five training studies. *Educational Research and Evaluation, 7*(4), 385–417.

Walpole, S., McKenna, M. C., Uribe-Zarain, X., & Lamitina, D. (2010). The relationships between coaching and instruction in the primary grades: Evidence from high-poverty schools. *Elementary School Journal, 111*(1), 115–140.

Wehby, J. H., Maggin, D. M., Partin, T. C. M., & Robertson, R. (2012). The impact of working alliance, social validity, and teacher burnout on implementation fidelity of the good behavior game. *School Mental Health, 4*(1), 22–33.

Wood, C. L., Goodnight, C. I., Bethune, K. S., Preston, A. I., & Cleaver, S. L. (2016). Role of professional development and multi-level coaching in promoting evidence-based practice in education. *Learning Disabilities: A Contemporary Journal, 14,* 159–170.

Applying Systems-Level Change Principles to the Coaching Process

4

KEY QUESTIONS

1. What is a system, and why do systems matter to teachers, teams, and coaches?

2. How can a coach help teachers or teams change aspects of their education systems that get in the way of improved student outcomes?

CHAPTER TAKE-AWAYS

1. Coaching teams or teachers occurs within a larger context of a system, such as a classroom, school, or district. These systems are comprised of five components: 1) human resources, 2) material resources, 3) fiscal resources, 4) processes and procedures, and 5) policies and regulations.

2. The five components interact with each other to produce the system's outcomes, including student outcomes.

3. Understand the strengths and weaknesses of the five system components to know why or why not a system is reaching improved student outcomes.

4. Apply three key systems-level change principles to help teachers or teams improve their systems: 1) understand the strengths and weaknesses of the system, 2) intentionally and continuously address system barriers with Plan-Do-Study-Act cycles, and 3) support teachers and teams with the nontechnical or adaptive aspects of change.

CHAPTER OVERVIEW

Chapter 4 may be that one chapter a coach is tempted to skip, assuming systems and systems-level change principles may not directly apply to working with teachers or teams. If this is the case for you, then reconsider. All coaches work within systems whether it is a classroom, school, pre-K program, or district. Moreover, systems shape student outcomes, for better or worse. Coach sessions that do not consider the overarching system in which recipients work are liable to miss the mark. Systems simply matter (Fixsen et al., 2016; Fullan & Kirtman, 2019; Lewis, 2015).

The challenge for coaches is helping teams and teachers enhance the system. Questions you may ask include the following:

- How does a coach help teachers and teams pinpoint what is and is not working in the system?

- Once issues have been pinpointed, how does a coach help teachers and teams navigate the change process?

- What challenges do teachers and teams face when they realize that systems improvements are necessary?

This chapter lays the groundwork for coaches to support teachers and teams through the difficult process of systems-level change. All the information presented within the chapter is drawn from research from varied fields of study, including implementation science and improvement science. By the end of this chapter, you will be able to answer the previous questions and be equipped to support teachers and teams within the systems they work, be it a classroom or a pre-K program/school. For these reasons, coaches benefit from becoming familiar with the content within this chapter prior to planning, conducting, and reflecting on coaching.

To make the somewhat abstract concept of systems improvement more readily understandable, we take a step-by-step approach to unpacking the information contained within Chapter 4. The first section starts with the basics: defining the term "system," unpacking the components that make up any system, and elaborating on why systems matter to coaches. Grounded with the idea that the role of any coach is to attend to the larger system in which teachers and teams work, the second section explains three key systems-level change principles coaches can use to guide recipients through the work of improving systems. We embed examples throughout the first two sections of the chapter to make some of the more abstract concepts concrete. We end with several resources that can be used to support coaches' work with teachers or teams.

THE BIG PICTURE: WHAT IS A SYSTEM AND WHY DOES IT MATTER?

Defining a System

Let's start with the most basic question: What is a system? In education, a *system* may refer to a classroom, an elementary school, a middle school, or a pre-K program. Spanning out to take a larger view, a *system* could refer to all the schools within one pre-K-12th grade school district. Thus, a system is not one specific entity but may refer to one or more units that are linked together in some way (Foster-Fishman et al., 2007). Often, but not always, the units of the system share a common goal or purpose. For this chapter, we use the term "system" to refer to the context in which coaching is occurring, which could be one or more classrooms or schools/pre-K programs.

Components of a System

Whether *system* refers to one classroom, one school, or 10 districts, every education system is made up of a constellation of parts called *components* (Damschroder et al., 2009; Foster-Fishman et al., 2007; Fullan & Kirtman, 2019). Although different fields of study "slice and dice" these sys-

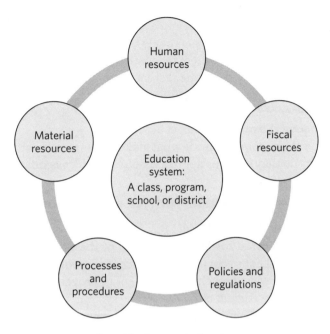

Figure 4.1. Components of a system.

tem components in various ways, there are clear commonalities across these fields. We visually depict components of a system in Figure 4.1 and list them next:

- *Human resources:* The people involved with the system, including their behavior, views, and beliefs (e.g., teacher's self-efficacy, a leadership team)

- *Fiscal resources:* Funding sources and how resources are allocated in the system (e.g., the pre-K or school budget, how much money is allocated toward professional learning)

- *Policies and regulations:* The formal rules, laws, and guidelines of the system (e.g., staffing and student policies)

- *Processes and procedures:* The day-to-day operating approaches of the system (e.g., how decisions are made; how barriers are removed, including who is involved; processes for gaining access to professional learning opportunities)

- *Material resources:* The physical resources of the system (e.g., curricular and assessment materials, the school building, a classroom space)

An example may make each systems component more concrete. Red Leaf Middle School's goal is to improve math outcomes among their sixth-grade students. Five sixth-grade teachers at Red Leaf are expected to implement a new math curriculum with their students to support this goal. It is now several weeks into the implementation effort and three teachers have not received all the curricular materials. As a result, these three teachers cannot fully implement all the lesson components with their student, an issue related to material resources. Human resources are also coming into play in the system's implementation effort: A fourth teacher has all the materials but does not use them because she does not believe students benefit from them. The school procedures (a third system component) are such that the sixth-grade teachers cannot simply request the materials that are needed. They must gain special permission from the principal. But the fiscal resources (a fourth system component) that were required to pay for the needed math materials have now been allocated toward a reading program. Furthermore, the principal is hesitant to request the reading and math materials because the district policies (a fifth system component) state that the principal may receive a poor mark on her formal evaluation for underidentifying the curricular materials needed at the school. All these issues come together to create a system that is getting in the way of students receiving the full benefit of the math instruction.

The previous example illustrates how one system component links to another one. The previous example is somewhat of an oversimplification. In reality, it is much more complex. Each component links to every other component to form a tangled, messy web of parts that come together to form the whole of the system (Foster-Fishman et al., 2007).

The complexity of systems components is what makes them so difficult to understand, leading to the next question: Why do they even matter to a coach? We address this question next.

Why Do Systems Matter in Coaching?

Let's return to the example of Red Leaf Middle School to answer this question. None of the Red Leaf system components supported the implementation of the new math curriculum. It should come as no surprise when Red Leaf's goal for improved math outcomes is not reached. The system components are getting in the way of reaching the goal of improved student outcomes. Thus, systems matter because they shape student outcomes. If the system is not reaching its goals, then we must look to the different system components to tease out why the goal is or is not reached (Bryk, 2015; Foster-Fishman et al., 2007; Freeman et al., 2017; Fullan & Kirtman, 2019).

Moreover, when any system is not producing what it intends to produce, it is time to make a change to one or more of the system components. This may be easier said than done. Although the work of systems-level change does not rest on the shoulders of any single leader, teacher, or team coach, coaches can work with other educators to be a part of systems improvement. Supporting systems-level change is a key activity of the systems coach (see Chapter 2). Yet, even a teacher coach can apply systems-level change ideas to sessions with teachers. The three principles provide guidance for teachers and team coaches when approaching systems improvement. We also illustrate how the principles are applicable to the day-to-day work of both types of coaches. We have compiled these principles from various bodies of research, including implementation science (Damschroder et al., 2009; Fixsen et al., 2016), improvement science (Bryk, 2015; Lewis, 2015), and systems-level change (Adelman & Taylor, 2007; Foster-Fishman et al., 2007).

SYSTEMS-LEVEL CHANGE PRINCIPLES FOR COACHES

Principle 1: Understand the System to Understand Outcomes

Principle 1 states that coaches take a clear look at what is happening in the system (e.g., classroom, school, district) to understand why desired outcomes are or are not achieved. Experts call this *seeing the system* (Bryk, 2015; Lewis, 2015). The coach's job is to help teachers and teams see their classroom, school, pre-K program, or district system. Another way to say this is that the coach works with teachers or teams to assess which components support improved student outcomes and which get in the way. Given that system components constantly interact with each other to shape outcomes, understanding the system strengths and weaknesses can come across as a daunting task. Where do coaches start?

Whether you are a teacher coach or systems coach, use the tool shown in Figure 4.2 (blank versions of this form are available in Appendix H and to download) to understand the system's strengths and weaknesses. This tool lists each system component and more specific factors that make up that system component. Coaches can use this tool with coachees to gather a big-picture view of each system component and whether that component is a strength or weakness.

APPENDIX H   **Understanding the System**

Overview: This tool can be used to understand the strengths and weaknesses that are currently in place in the system. These strengths and weaknesses shape the degree to which system goals are attained. Coaches working with teachers or systems coaches may use this tool in sessions with coachees to pinpoint which system components are problematic and which are not.

Directions:
1. Think about the system goal. Write that goal here: _____
2. Read over each item contained within each column. Ask yourself, "Does this item reflect a strength or a weakness in the system?"
   a. What data will you use to determine if an item is a strength or weakness? List your data sources here: _____
3. Place a checkmark in the box indicating strengths of the system that are in place and support the goal previously listed.
4. Think about all the weaknesses of the system (unchecked boxes).
   a. Which weakness would you like to address first? _____ Why? _____
   b. How will addressing this system component support progress toward the goal? _____
5. Use the Plan-Do-Study-Act tool when you are ready to advance to the next step.

Component 1: Human resources	Component 2: Policies and regulations	Component 3: Procedures and processes	Component 4: Fiscal resources	Component 5: Material resources
❑ Staff believe the goal is important. ❑ Staff believe they have the expertise to achieve the goal. ❑ Staff are receptive to working toward the goal. ❑ Staff are offered networking and learning opportunities with colleagues to learn about the goal and talk about what the goal means for their work at the school. ❑ The culture of the school accepts that there is a learning curve and embraces making mistakes when working toward the goal. ❑ Leaders support the goal in their words and actions. ❑ Other school/pre-K programs champion support of the goal in their words and actions.	❑ District, school, and classroom policies affecting students and/or staff (e.g., attendance, discipline, teacher evaluation) support the goal. ❑ Federal regulations (e.g., IDEA) are used to support the goal. ❑ The vision/mission of the school/classroom aligns to the goal area.	❑ Staff recruitment and selection procedures align to the goal. ❑ Procedures exist for removing barriers to the goal. ❑ Procedures exist for securing and gaining access to professional learning and coaching related to the goal. ❑ There is a process for engaging in Plan-Do-Study-Act cycles to support progress in the goal area.	❑ Costs for the goal area are calculated on a regular (e.g., annual) basis. ❑ Adequate state, district, and school funding is allocated toward the goal.	❑ Evidence-based curricular and assessment materials in the goal area are reviewed and selected according to a coherent process. ❑ Evidence-based curricular and assessment materials in the goal area are available to all staff. ❑ Evidence-based curricular and assessment materials related to the goal area can be adapted to meet the range of student needs within the classroom/school. ❑ Professional learning is provided to all staff to build their knowledge and implementation of the curriculum and assessment materials.

Figure 4.2. Understanding the System. (*Note:* Blank versions of this form are available in Appendix H and to download.)

Applying Principle 1   Let's dig into an example to make Principle 1 clearly applicable to systems coaches who are supporting teams. Imagine that you are a systems coach working with a high school team that is responsible for leading their school's efforts to improve student attendance rates. You introduce the tool to the team at a coaching session and explain how the tool is used. Each member independently completes the tool and shares their completed forms. You facilitate the discussion to ensure that all team members have opportunities to share their insights and the previously established team norms are adhered to during the discussion. At the next session, team members come to agreement on which system components are getting in the way of reaching the system's attendance goals: 1) procedures/processes that currently exist within the school and 2) board-approved policies/regulations. The team works through the tool to produce initial thoughts about what they might do to improve the challenges in the system. The team then shares their insights with the rest of the staff to gain their insights. Once this occurs, you and the team have a clear understanding of which system components are getting in the way of reaching the goal: They can see their system.

Applying Principle 1 is only slightly different for a coach working with teachers than it is for a systems coach. The primary difference is that the system in question is a classroom. This means that the teacher and coach work together to identify which system components (e.g., fiscal, material, and human resources; policies and regulations; procedures and processes) support desired outcomes, which get in the way of those outcomes, and how the components interact to shape outcomes. Just as with a team, the coach works with the teacher to help them see which system components support and which hinder progress toward the desired goal.

An example may make the application of Principle 1 clearer for the teacher coach. Pretend that you are a teacher coach assigned to work with several pre-K teachers at Sunny Vale Elementary School. One of these teachers, Suzhanne, has expressed a concern that her students are not beginning the school day ready to learn. As a result, the children lose nearly 15 minutes of morning literacy instruction, and some of the children are not mastering critical literacy concepts. After running through Steps 1–5 in the Understanding the System tool (see Figure 4.2), the two of you come to understand that Suzhanne has set up several classroom entry procedures that require students to independently complete multistep tasks (e.g., hang up your coat, put away your personal belongings, sit down on your square on the carpet, sit with your hands in your lap until all children arrive). In addition, her classroom policy is that children who do not independently complete the entry task receive three warnings and then cannot participate in free choice time. Instead, the children must complete classroom chores with the paraprofessional. In turn, the paraprofessional cannot work with other children who may need reteaching on the morning's literacy concepts. The Understanding the System tool shows that at least three classroom system components (policies, procedures, and human resources) are shaping what is happening in her classroom. Armed with this information, Suzhanne is ready to address three system barriers so that more children can productively engage in those first 15 precious minutes dedicated to literacy instruction.

These examples suggest that teams and teachers benefit from understanding systems, whether the system is a school, district, or classroom. But keep in mind that whether you are a teacher coach or a systems coach, systems change work does not end at Principle 1. It is not enough to understand the system. Principle 2 offers a strategy for approaching systems change, whether that change occurs at the classroom, school, or district level of the system.

Principle 2: Systems-Level Change Is an Intentional and Continuous Process

If Principle 1 is about understanding what needs to change in the system, then Principle 2 focuses on how systems are changed. This is accomplished through ongoing efforts that are thoughtful and organized rather than haphazard. Using Plan-Do-Study-Act cycles is one common strategy for approaching systems change (Berwick, 1996).

In short, once it becomes clear that a change is needed, Plan-Do-Study-Act cycles begin. A Plan-Do-Study-Act cycle includes developing a plan with specific strategies to address the challenge areas (e.g., What do we need to do?), enacting the plan (i.e., do), examining what happens as a result of that plan—did the challenge improve, stay the same, or get worse? (i.e., study)—and refining the strategies to address the challenge area(s) based on their impact (i.e., act). These steps are repeated until the challenge is resolved. The tool shown in Figure 4.3 illustrates how

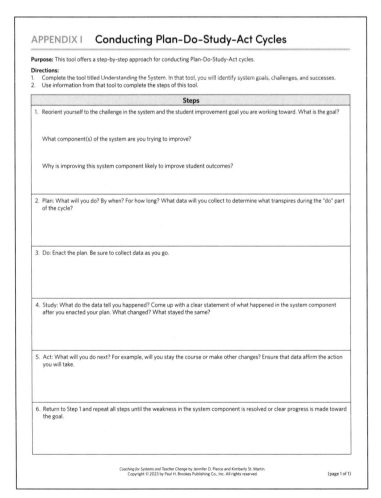

Figure 4.3. Conducting Plan-Do-Study-Act Cycles. (*Note:* Blank versions of this form are available in Appendix I and to download.)

either a teacher or a systems coach can conduct a Plan-Do-Study-Act cycle (blank versions of this form are available in Appendix I and to download).

Applying Principle 2   Principle 2 is central to the work of a systems coach. Recall from Principle 1 that the systems coach worked with a high school leadership team to identify how system components influenced attendance rates. The coach's next step would be to initiate Plan-Do-Study-Act cycles by working with the team.

- The coach and team may recommend revising their high school attendance policies to ensure that students who miss the first 5 minutes of class are not counted as absent because that is a current school policy that has been identified as a barrier to improving student attendance (i.e., plan).

- The coach and team obtain approval and work with the principal (who is also on the team) to use the new draft of the policy for 4–6 weeks (i.e., do), collecting data on how the attendance rates change over that time frame.

- The coach and team examine (i.e., study) the attendance data and determine the impact of the revised attendance policy on overall attendance rates compared with the previous policy.

- The team and the coach revisit their original strategy (revise the attendance policy) to pinpoint what they need to do next (i.e., act). For example, the team may determine further refinements are needed to the attendance policy or the existing revisions are producing positive results, so staying the course with implementing the revised policy is necessary.

The Plan-Do-Study-Act cycle would be used in a recursive way to address other system needs.

Principle 2 may also be applied to the work of a teacher coach. In fact, a teacher coach proceeds through the Plan-Do-Study-Act cycles just as a systems coach does. The only difference is that the coach conducts the Plan-Do-Study-Act cycles with the teacher to help them understand the classroom as a system.

Principle 3: Systems-Level Change Is an Adaptive Challenge

Principle 2 offered the idea that systems change can be approached with a technical strategy (Plan-Do-Study-Act cycles). Principle 3 shows that there is also a nontechnical aspect to systems-level change, which means that transforming systems—from a classroom to an entire school or across multiple pre-K programs—is not only about completing Plan-Do-Study-Act cycles. It is also about helping teachers and teams work through critical barriers to change (e.g., stress, frustration, resistance) that often crop up alongside any systems change effort. Left unaddressed, these human reactions to change can halt the systems change effort (Hall & Hord, 2015).

Why is systems-level change so difficult? Think of systems transformation as a tricky process that typically has more than one possible solution, creating an atmosphere of ambiguity that requires flexible thinking, a shift in beliefs and values, and new ways of working. The issue will not be easy to solve, and some people in the system may not even want to tackle it. Maintaining status quo can be more appealing than making changes, however well-intentioned those changes are for those involved. For these reasons, systems-level changes tend to create stress, anxiety, cognitive dissonance, or even resistance among teachers and teams (Bryk, 2015). To be clear, positive reactions are also possible and may wax and wane with more challenging reactions during the change process (Hall & Hord, 2015). Figure 4.4 summarizes the spectrum of these reactions.

Whether a teacher, hybrid, or systems coach, it is very likely (and understandable) that teachers and teams will show some of these reactions when faced with systems-level change. As a coach, do not push back against these reactions. Your role is to support teachers and teams in addressing

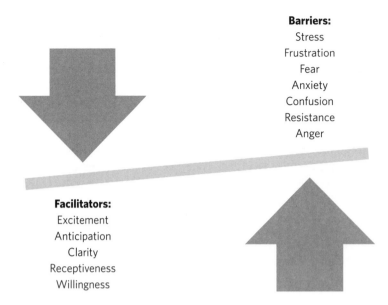

Figure 4.4. Typical reactions to change.

the overall change effort (how to shift low expectations for students) and the difficult human emotional reactions that tend to go hand-in-hand with the change effort. Therefore, when teachers or implementation teams are showing signs of stress, frustration, or disinterest in making a change, work with these reactions in two ways:

1. Systems-level change research suggests that one simple yet profound way to help teachers and teams become more receptive to change is to build in choice about what will change and provide a voice (or input) about the change. Expect to face increased resistance to change when educators have little voice into the overall idea of change (e.g., when to change, how major or minor the change is) or little choice in whether they will change (Hall & Hord, 2015).

2. Incorporating alliance strategies into coaching sessions is another important way to help reduce stressors associated with change. Chapter 5 is dedicated to these strategies.

See Chapter 7 for more information on supporting teachers and teams through systems-level change. That chapter offers several strategies for guiding coachees through change, particularly when there is reluctance.

Applying Principle 3   As with the first two systems-level change principles, we use an example to illustrate how this principle can apply to the work of a coach. Let's pretend that you are a coach supporting a teacher, Ms. Arroyo. Ms. Arroyo's goals are to improve her fourth-grade students' science achievement. Ms. Arroyo recently came to you because several of her students were not completing their daily science homework. None of these students demonstrate proficiency with the concepts included in the homework, and Ms. Arroyo is becoming increasingly worried that they are falling further behind. Ms. Arroyo's past attempts to address the situation focused on talking with the students and contacting parents, but the situation has not yet improved.

After talking with Ms. Arroyo, you realize that she is very frustrated, specifically stating that she does not want to make a change to certain aspects of her homework procedures and policies (e.g., assigning science homework twice a week that has resulted in many student errors, not accepting late homework, assigning a zero for incomplete or late homework). Rather than brushing her frustration aside, assuming this reluctance will fade, or forcing the issue that homework policies and procedures change, you decide to focus on ways to offer voice and choice. First, you and Ms. Arroyo brainstorm other types of changes she could enact to her classroom system.

1. *Changing the human component:* The fourth-grade teacher will meet briefly with groups of students who need some additional scaffolding in the science concepts that are going to be assigned for homework. The teacher will partner struggling students with a homework buddy who is performing well in science and who can aid the struggling student.

2. *Changing the material component:* Prior to assigning homework, determine if the assignment reinforces science concepts of which students have demonstrated mastery. This will reduce the likelihood the students will practice errors and should help increase homework completion.

With these potential changes in mind, you then ensure Ms. Arroyo has voice by asking her to flesh out the details of the change effort (e.g., when will this change occur, what she will do to make this change). Ms. Arroyo now has a clear idea of what she will do that is different and has shifted from frustrated and resistant to change to committed to enacting a change to help improve student outcomes.

If you are a systems or hybrid coach, then you could very easily translate the previous example to your work with a team and with teams and teachers. Offer voice and choice in the change effort when teachers or one or more members of a team is reacting to the change in a negative way.

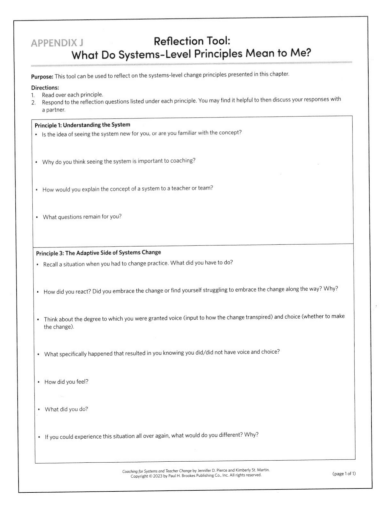

Figure 4.5. Reflection Tool: What Do Systems-Level Principles Mean to Me? (*Note:* Blank versions of this form are available in Appendix J and to download.)

APPENDIX K **Recommendations for Using Understanding the System With Teachers or Teams**

Purpose: This tool presents recommendations for using the Understanding the System tool.

Directions:
1. Read over these recommendations before using the Understanding the System tool.
2. Use the recommendations to present Understanding the System to teachers or teams.

Recommendations
❒ Ensure you understand systems and then develop teacher/team expertise in systems.
❒ Develop an "elevator pitch" on systems components and why systems matter. This will force you to succinctly state system components and why they matter to teachers and teams. You may find it helpful to use Figure 4.1 with the teacher or team to clarify components of a system.
❒ Ask teachers or teams to come up with their own "elevator pitch" on systems components and why systems matter.
❒ If the tool is used with a team, then ensure that the team shares their responses with the entire staff, solicits feedback, and revises their thinking after completing Steps 1-5.
❒ If the tool is used with a teacher, then ask the teacher to share their responses with any other adults working in the classroom, obtain feedback from the other adults, and revise their thinking after completing Steps 1-5.
❒ Understanding the System can be completed more than once. In fact, teachers and teams may want to revisit the tool frequently to assess how strengths and weaknesses have evolved.

(page 1 of 1)

Figure 4.6. Recommendations for Using Understanding the System With Teachers or Teams. (*Note:* Blank versions of this form are available in Appendix K and to download.)

APPENDIX L **Recommendations for Using Conducting Plan-Do-Study-Act Cycles With Teachers or Teams**

Purpose: This tool presents recommendations for using the Conducting Plan-Do-Study-Act Cycles tool.

Directions:
1. Before using the Conducting Plan-Do-Study-Act Cycles tool, read over these recommendations.
2. Use the recommendations when working through Conducting Plan-Do-Study-Act Cycles with teachers or teams.

Recommendations
❒ The "plan" is a brief description of what the teacher or team will do to address the system weakness. The core of this plan contains the change idea, which articulates precisely what the teacher or team will do, by when, and how.
❒ Be sure that the team or teacher identifies the data that will be collected during the "do" part of the cycle. If the teacher or team does not collect data, then they will not know what transpired as a result of enacting the plan.
❒ Try to keep the plan and data collection process simple. Systems change is an ongoing process, and there is no need to try to change everything all at once. In fact, taking on too much or the most complicated systems change endeavor will likely make the work more difficult. Start with a small change that is likely to be successful and know that each change can build toward the next. Quick wins are important in systems-level changes.

(page 1 of 1)

Figure 4.7. Recommendations for Using Conducting Plan-Do-Study-Act Cycles With Teachers or Teams. (*Note:* Blank versions of this form are available in Appendix L and to download.)

SUMMARY

The concept of a system may not at first seem central to the work of a coach, particularly a coach working with teachers to improve their practice and student outcomes. This thinking could not be further from the truth. The overall health of the system is contingent on what happens with policies, regulations, processes, procedures, and resources (including the fiscal, human, and material resources). If you want clarity on why a classroom, school, pre-K program, or district system is or is not reaching its goals, then it will be important to look to these system components to understand what is shaping the system outcomes. The three system-level change principles can and should be applied to your coaching sessions to help teachers and teams improve their systems.

RESOURCES

This section contains several tools to help you apply the content from this chapter to your work with teachers, teams, or teachers and teams. Figure 4.5 (blank versions of this form are available in Appendix J and to download) is a reflection tool you can use to think about and talk with a partner about systems-level change principles. Figures 4.6 and 4.7 (blank versions of these forms are available in Appendices K and L and to download) provide recommendations or guidelines for using two tools presented in prior sections of this chapter: Understanding the System and Conducting Plan-Do-Study-Act Cycles.

REFERENCES

Adelman, H. S., & Taylor, L. (2007). Systemic change for school improvement. *Journal of Educational and Psychological Consultation, 17*(1), 55–77.

Bastable, E., Massar, M. M., & McIntosh, K. (2020). A survey of team members' perceptions of coaching activities related to Tier 1 SWPBIS implementation. *Journal of Positive Behavior Interventions, 22*(1), 51–61.

Berwick, D. M. (1996). A primer on leading the improvement of systems., *BMJ, 312*(7031), 619–622.

Bryk, A. S. (2015). 2014 AERA distinguished lecture: Accelerating how we learn to improve. *Educational Researcher, 44*(9), 467–477.

Damschroder, L. J., Aron, D. C., Keith, R. E., Kirsh, S. R., Alexander, J. A., & Lowery, J. C. (2009). Fostering implementation of health services research findings into practice: A consolidated framework for advancing implementation science. *Implementation Science, 4*(1), 1–15.

Fixsen, D., Blase, K., Van Dyke, M., & Metz, A. (2016). *Implementation for the masses.* National Implementation Research Network, FPG Child Development Institute, University of North Carolina at Chapel Hill.

Foster-Fishman, P. G., Nowell, B., & Yang, H. (2007). Putting the system back into systems change: A framework for understanding and changing organizational and community systems. *American Journal of Community Psychology, 39*(3–4), 197–215.

Freeman, J., Sugai, G., Simonsen, B., & Everett, S. (2017). MTSS coaching: Bridging knowing to doing. *Theory Into Practices, 56*(1), 29–37.

Fullan, M., & Kirtman, L. (2019). *Coherent school leadership: Forging clarity from complexity.* Association for Supervision and Curriculum Development.

Hall, G. E., & Hord, S. M. (2020). *Implementing change: Patterns, principles, and potholes* (5th ed.) Pearson.

Lewis, C. (2015). What is improvement science? Do we need it in education? *Educational Researcher, 44*(1), 54–61.

March, A. L., Castillo, J. M., Daye, J. G., Bateman, L. P., & Gelley, C. D. (2019). Qualitative investigation of RtI coaches roles, responsibilities, and experiences supporting schools participating in a state level RtI implementation project. *Journal of Educational and Psychological Consultation, 30*(2), 210–250.

Strategies and Resources for More Effective Coaching

Using Alliance Strategies

Laying the Foundation for Effective Coaching

KEY QUESTIONS

1. What is alliance, and why is it important in coaching?

2. What strategies can coaches use to build and maintain alliance with coachees?

3. What alliance strategies are used in the three-phase coaching cycle? Why?

CHAPTER TAKE-AWAYS

1. Alliance is the malleable dynamic that creates the foundation for all the other work that occurs between the coach and coachee.

2. Three factors shape alliance: interpersonal skills, collaborative skills, and expertise. Coaches attend to these three factors when building and maintaining alliance.

3. Coaches use specific strategies with teachers and teams to build and maintain alliance. These strategies are used during each phase of the coaching cycle.

CHAPTER OVERVIEW

Chapter 5 brings the concept of alliance into focus: the relational dynamic that is the foundation of all the work that occurs between the coach and coachee(s). We intentionally begin Section II with this focus for one reason. Alliance is one of four coaching practices that form the basis of all coaching sessions. (The remaining three practices are covered in the next chapter.) As you read in Chapter 3, positive alliance enhances a teacher's or team's willingness to engage in coaching sessions (Johnson et al., 2016) and higher fidelity of teacher practice (Wehby et al., 2012). Poor coach–coachee relationships, however, can produce resistance from the coachee to participate in sessions (Johnson et al., 2016) and limits the amount of observable changes to teacher or team practice (Gessnitzer & Kauffeld, 2015). Therefore, positive alliance is a critical part of effective coaching.

Given its importance, it is imperative that you understand what alliance is and how to build and maintain it prior to planning, conducting, or reflecting on coaching cycles. This chapter begins with an overview of the different factors that comprise alliance. Explaining these factors helps coaches understand that even a seemingly intangible concept such as alliance can be made understandable and actionable. By "actionable" we mean that once you understand alliance, you can more thoughtfully build and maintain strong relationships with teachers or teams. The second section of the chapter gets at the heart of what coaches can do to build and maintain positive relationships with teachers or teams to prepare you to take information about alliance and translate it into action. We describe effective alliance strategies coaches can use, whether you are conducting your first coaching session or your 50th. We also specify the value each strategy adds to coaching sessions so that you can make informed decisions about which strategies to use with teachers or teams based on the status of the relationship and the needs of the coaching recipients. We end Chapter 5 with related resources that can be used by novice and expert coaches.

If your goal is to plan, conduct, and reflect on effective coaching sessions with teachers or teams, then take time to deeply familiarize yourself with the content of this chapter. Positive coach–coachee alliance does not happen on its own. Building and maintaining alliance is just as intentional as any other coaching practice.

DEFINING ALLIANCE

"Alliance" may be a newer word in your coaching vocabulary. Indeed, we are rather unique among educational coaching researchers and experts in our preference for the term over the more widely used word "relationship." But we are very intentional with the using the word "alliance" over the word "relationship." For one, "alliance" is the preferred term used by the helping professions (e.g., mental health, psychology) to convey the idea that interpersonal dynamics influence coachee outcomes (Horvath, 2001). We believe that education in general, and coaching in particular, is also a helping profession. Therefore, we use the same term used by other fields to refer to the concept of the coach–coachee dynamic.

Moreover, the definition of our preferred term contains some unique nuances that we think are missing from the more generic word "relationship." Consider these two *Oxford Dictionary* definitions:

1. *Relationship:* The way in which two or more concepts, objects, or people are connected, or the state of being connected. The way in which two or more people or groups regard and behave toward each other.

2. *Alliance:* A union or association formed for mutual benefit, especially between countries or organizations. A relationship based on an affinity in interests, nature, or qualities.

Notice that the word "relationship" centers on the idea of connectedness as evident in how the two people behave, think, or feel about each other. Coaches and coachees are certainly connected, and their connection can be understood in how they interact with each other. The definition of "alliance" conveys the idea that there is a choice in the matter. The two units elect to come together, and the act of coming together is both mutually advantageous and based on a shared purpose. This sounds like coaching, right? Moreover, there is an "affinity" in this union, a word that the *Oxford Dictionary* notes is synonymous with the two other important concepts in coaching: empathy and rapport.

We value the idea that both the coach and the coachee mutually benefit from the partnership, an idea that is not necessarily implied in the term "relationship." We also value the idea that there is a shared purpose in the union, which is not mentioned at all in the word "relationship." Rapport and empathy are also necessary between the coach and coachee, an additional reason why the term resonates so deeply with us. Although the nuances in the two definitions are subtle, the richness in meaning of "alliance" is enough to make it our preferred term.

Let's head toward an even deeper discussion of the concept by drawing on mental health, psychology, and coaching literature. We explain three factors that comprise alliance next, which were briefly introduced to you in Chapter 3.

Factors of Alliance

If you have read Chapter 4, then you understand that some concepts in coaching are multidimensional (e.g., systems). Alliance falls into this category because it is made up of three factors, which are explained next and summarized in Figure 5.1.

Figure 5.1. Factors of alliance. (*Source:* Pierce, 2015.)

Interpersonal Skills The first factor of alliance in part relates to the coach's communication skills, which means that the coach's words, body language, and even tone of voice are overt ways of communicating that influence alliance. Coaches listen more than they talk in situations with strong alliance. They ask clarifying and open-ended questions that focus the conversation around teaching and systems change. They tease out critical implications when coachee's share broad stories or teaching or teaming experiences and explicitly connect those implications to concrete actions the teacher or team may take to improve their work (Dryden, 2017).

Interpersonal skills go beyond simply how a coach communicates. Not surprisingly, a coach's capacity to build a trusting rapport with coachees is another aspect of interpersonal skills. In short, when trust is high, alliance is strong. When trust erodes or is absent, the dynamic suffers. Some researchers even consider trust to be one of the most influential aspects of alliance (Horvath, 2001), and your own experience likely confirms that trust is central to any relationship. The same holds true in coaching.

What does a trusting bond or rapport look like in coaching? According to Safran et al. (2011), trusted coaches

- Are reliable and fulfill commitments

- Make vulnerability acceptable by conveying that teachers and teams can safely make mistakes and feel uncertain about resolving a problem

- Avoid being overly critical or judgmental and instead show empathy

- Create a climate in which coachees feel safe

Collaboration   A second factor of alliance relates to the coach's collaboration skills, which include

- How the coach sets goals with teachers and teams

- How the coach creates a partnership with the coachee(s)

- How the coach and coachee coconstruct agreements about their work together

Let's unpack each of these items, starting with goal setting. When a collaborative dynamic exists, the coach works with the teacher or team to identify what will be gained from coaching and how to focus coaching efforts: how the teacher or team will change, how students will change, and/or how the system will change. A coach who takes a less collaborative approach will set goals *for* the teacher or team, presuming that the coach's vision for improvement is the same as (or better than) the teacher or team vision. The collaborative coach thus prioritizes the expressed needs of the teacher or team. Notice how we specify that these needs are expressed, which means that collaboratively oriented coaches go out of their way to ask teachers and teams how they would like to develop and then treat these needs as paramount. Coaches with a less collaborative approach do not ask or ask but then relegate teacher's and team's needs to the back burner (Horvath et al., 2011; Sonesh et al., 2015). There are times when there is a mismatch between what the coachees see as a need compared with what the coach observes is a need. The skillful coach will strategically design a set of activities that will ultimately accomplish the expressed and observed needs. See the text box for additional information about goal setting.

Goal Setting: A Part of Building and Maintaining Positive Alliance

Goal setting for some coaching experts is considered an effective coaching practice that can stand on its own (Knight, 2015), much like modeling or providing performance feedback. We acknowledge the importance of goal setting in coaching but take a different approach to integrating it into our coaching framework. We embed goal setting within the effective coaching practice of using alliance strategies. Why do we do this rather than separating goal setting out as a stand-alone coaching practice? The answer is simple: the goal-setting process shapes coachee's perceptions of alliance (Gessnitzer & Kauffeld, 2015; Pierce, 2019). See the latter section of this chapter to learn more about goal setting to build and maintain positive alliance.

A collaborative coaching dynamic also emphasizes coach–coachee partnerships. This means that all parties involved are valued for the unique strengths they bring to the table. Recognizing that the coach is not the only bearer of insight and does not hold all the answers encourages teachers and teams to value their own internal insights and realize that they can tackle even the most challenging situations.

Finally, a collaborative dynamic exists when the coach and the teacher or team mutually establish how they will work together. Collaborative coaches clarify what to expect from coaching sessions, outline what each person will do during coaching, establish a process for how they will communicate with each other (e.g., how performance feedback will be shared with the teacher or team), and determine what will and will not be confidential between the partners. Agreeing about the ways in which the coach and coachee work together ensures that coachees know what to expect and are prepared to fully engage in sessions. A coach with a less collaborative stance will spell out the parameters for the partners and expect that the coachees abide by these guidelines, which creates a dynamic that might be preferential to the coach but not to the coachee (O'Broin & Palmer, 2009).

If you are even remotely familiar with coaching, you are probably not surprised by any of the previous ideas. In short, taking a collaborative stance to coaching will support positive alliance. After all, coaching is not about controlling the path of teachers or teams. It is about supporting them.

Expertise   A third factor of alliance relates to the coach's expertise in 1) the content area (e.g., behavioral or reading components of an MTSS framework) and the context in which the coaching occurs (e.g., teaching pre-K students, elementary or secondary schoolwide implementation and systems change) and 2) the act of conducting coaching cycles using effective coaching practices. Coaches and coachees with positive alliance know that the person supporting them deeply understands the day-to-day work of the teacher or team. Practically speaking, this means that coaches should coach in areas in which they have expertise rather than in areas in which they have little experience (Pierce, 2019).

Just as important, the teacher or team recognize that the coach is equipped to help coachees grow professionally. Very few educators want to be coached by someone who does not seem to know what they are expected to coach or how to conduct coaching cycles or does not come across as well versed in effective coaching practices (observing, modeling, providing performance feedback, using alliance strategies). Yet, teachers and teams know that their professional growth is in good hands when a coach clearly holds proficiency in the content and context in which coaching occurs (Horvath, 2001; Pierce, 2019).

Figure 5.2.   Three factors of alliance and alliance strategies. (*Source:* Pierce, 2015.)

ALLIANCE STRATEGIES

Because the prior section focused on the three factors of alliance, one question that might be on your mind is, "What can I do as a coach to show strong interpersonal skills, take a collaborative coaching stance, and demonstrate expertise?" There are observable behaviors—we call them *alliance strategies*—you can actively use when coaching to build and maintain positive alliance (see Figure 5.2; Pierce, 2019; Safran et al., 2011).

If you are naturally adept at establishing and maintaining congenial relationships with other educators, then you may mistakenly assume that you do not need to intentionally incorporate alliance strategies into coaching sessions. Know that there are unique considerations in the coach–coachee dynamic that can derail alliance. For example, some recipients enter the coaching situation with less-than-stellar prior experiences being coached. Others may have the idea that coaching is occurring because of the perception of poor performance. Yet, other teachers or teams may not have a choice in participating in coaching. They also may not have a clear understanding of what occurs in coaching sessions. These are common obstacles that influence how teachers and teams respond to even the friendliest coach. It makes sense for even the most relationally adept coaches to rely on a specific set of strategies to create positive alliance with teachers or teams.

Alternatively, perhaps you feel unprepared or uncertain about building and maintaining alliance with coachees. After all, it can be difficult to know how to help teachers or teams become comfortable with taking professional risks, try out new practices, reflect openly on their own

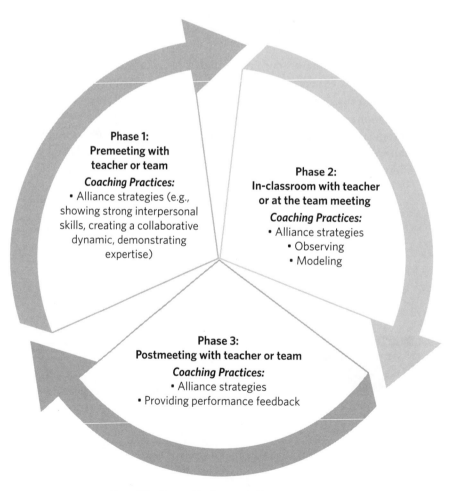

Figure 5.3. The coaching framework. (*Source:* Pierce, 2015.)

capacity, and identify areas of professional growth. These are tricky areas coaches must navigate and can result in either strengthening or weakening relationships. You do not have to pretend to know how to establish a positive coaching dynamic. If you find that you are uncertain about building and maintaining alliance, then these strategies can serve as the foundation of your coaching practice repertoire.

Before we unpack each of the alliance strategies, let's clarify when you may find it useful to integrate them into your work with teachers and teams. Recall from Chapter 2 that coaching occurs in a three-phase recursive cycle. In the first phase of the cycle, coaches conduct a premeeting with the teacher or team (identified members of the team or the entire team). It is important to use alliance strategies during this first phase so that the teacher or team are primed for the next two phases of the cycle. Next, the coach works directly in the classroom or in the team meeting. Continue to use alliance strategies during this phase to ensure teachers or teams are comfortable with coaching. In the third phase of the cycle, the coach conducts a postmeeting with the teacher or team, again using alliance strategies to maintain a positive dynamic. Thus, alliance strategies are used throughout each phase. Figure 5.3 offers a visual refresher of our coaching framework.

APPENDIX M   Alliance Assessment

Purpose: This tool can be used to assess alliance between teachers or teams and coaches.

Directions:
1. This form can be completed by the coach as a self-assessment or may be anonymously completed by coaching recipients.
   - If used by coaching recipients, then first rate the coach in each area of alliance (a 1 reflects a low score while a 5 reflects the highest score). Write down your reasons for each rating and what the coach might do to improve the rating. Return the form to the coach. The coach will use the information to enhance their work with teachers or teams.
   - If used as a self-assessment, then rate yourself in each column. Use the information to continuously improve as a coach.

Factor of alliance		Rating	Reason for rating	Ideas for improving
Interpersonal skills	Communicating effectively	1 2 3 4 5		
	Building trust	1 2 3 4 5		
Collaboration	Setting goals	1 2 3 4 5		
	Creating a partnership	1 2 3 4 5		
	Setting parameters	1 2 3 4 5		
Expertise	Conveying expertise in content and context	1 2 3 4 5		
	Demonstrating expertise in coaching	1 2 3 4 5		

Figure 5.4.   Alliance Assessment. (*Sources:* Pierce, 2015; Wehby et al., 2012.) (*Note:* Blank versions of this form are available in Appendix M and to download.)

How do you know which strategy to use and when to use it? Most of these strategies can be used during any phase of the coaching cycle. If there is a specific phase in which its most helpful to use a specific strategy, then we note that in the following section. It is not necessary to use every strategy over the course of the three phases of the coaching cycle. In fact, there are not any hard and fast rules for pinpointing which strategies to use; it is somewhat of a subjective decision you will need to make based on your interactions with teachers or teams.

With that said, every strategy serves a purpose, so think about what teachers and teams seem to need and then use the strategies that connect to that need. Remember that use of the strategies needs to be flexible. The dynamic between a coach and a coachee will have peaks and valleys because alliance can perpetually be in flux. Be prepared to shift your use of alliance strategies based on the needs of the teacher or team.

If you are still unsure which strategies may be most salient to your work with a teacher or team, then try using the following approaches:

- Integrate a few strategies from each type (interpersonal, collaboration, and expertise) into your cycles of coaching. Adjust your use of the strategies based on how the teacher or team responds to you.

- Ask teachers or teams to anonymously complete the Alliance Assessment and then select the most relevant strategies to use based on teacher or team feedback. The alliance assessment can also be used as a self-assessment to reflect on your strengths and opportunities for growth (see Figure 5.4; blank versions of this form are available in Appendix M and to download).

Demonstrating Strong Interpersonal Skills

Using Effective Communication   Apply these communication strategies to every phase of the coaching cycle to set a positive tenor.

- Listen more than you speak to deepen your understanding of the teacher's or team's work and convey the message their ideas and insights are valued.

- Ask clarifying and/or open-ended questions to confirm you understand the teacher or team, deepen the teacher's or team's thinking, encourage self-reflection, and narrow the focus of the coaching session on the coaching goals.

- Summarize key ideas stated by teachers or teams. Summarizing shows you understand the coachee and can also help focus/refocus the conversation when teachers or teams share overly broad ideas that may not connect to the coaching goals.

- Employ open body language (e.g., face the coachee, avoid crossing arms, put away distractions such as cell phones, be mindful of facial expressions) to convey a climate of safety and show you are mentally present in the current interaction.

Table 5.1.   Communication strategies

Strategy	Purpose	Examples
Listen more than you speak.	• To deepen your understanding of the teacher's or team's work • To convey that their ideas and insights are valued	• Reduce coach talk time. • Increase coachee talk time.
Employ open body language.	• To convey a climate of safety and show you are mentally present in the current interaction	• Face the coachee. • Avoid crossing arms. • Avoid using facial expressions that express disagreement or skepticism. • Put away distractions such as cell phones or computers.
Summarize key ideas teachers or teams state.	• To show you understand the coachee • To help focus/refocus the conversation when teachers or teams share overly broad ideas that may not link to the coaching	• "I heard the teacher or team say. . . ." • "It seems that _____ is a harder team task and _____ is going well."
Ask clarifying and/or open-ended questions.	• To either better understand or confirm you understand the teacher or team • To deepen the teacher's or team's thinking • To encourage self-reflection • To narrow the focus of the coaching session on the coaching goals	• "How did the lesson go?" • "What did you hope to accomplish with students?" • "Can you tell me more about what you just said?" • "What worked today and what could have gone better? Why?" • "How does today's experience show progress toward your goal?"
Nod your head and/or occasionally verbally confirm.	• To show you are actively listening • To affirm you are receptive to the ideas of the coachee	• State affirmations such as, "Uh-huh," "Yes," or "Right."

Source: Pierce (2015).

- Nod your head and occasionally verbally confirm (e.g., "Uh-huh," "Yes") to show you are actively listening and receptive to the ideas of the coachee(s).

Table 5.1 provides an at-a-glance list of communication strategies for coaches. The table also clarifies the purpose for each strategy and offers specific examples of each strategy that can be used in coaching sessions.

Building Trust   Trust building should occur throughout each phase of the coaching cycle. Although it may seem obvious, two of the most effective things you can do to build trust include 1) fulfilling commitments and 2) showing empathy (Kemp 2011). Regarding the former, we suggest you align your words and actions: If you say you will do something, then do it. The bottom line here is that coachees need to know that you are reliable. Regarding the second strategy, show empathy by using nonjudgmental language, even when teachers or teams hold different views than you.

Other alliance strategies can be used to address other aspects of coaching (Dryden, 2017). To clarify, you are also building a trusting bond with coachees when you listen more than you speak, set goals based on the needs of recipients, and create equitable partnerships. Scenario 1, which is included in the Resources section at the end of this chapter, shows how using different kinds of alliance strategies supports trust between a coach and the coachee(s).

Demonstrating That Coaching Is Collaborative

Setting Goals With Teachers or Teams Based on Their Needs   Goal setting typically occurs during the premeeting phase of the coaching cycle. Keep in mind a few important tips when setting goals with coachees. For one, while alliance is just beginning to be established, avoid telling the teacher or team what the goal should be without gathering more information from the coachee(s). Instead, ask teachers or teams what they want to accomplish from coaching and then come to agreement about that goal. If teachers or teams request that you set their goal, then ask recipients to talk about what is working well and what has been difficult with teaching or systems change. Next, offer a few suggestions for goals that connect to areas of difficulty. Finally, ask teachers or teams to select the goal that resonates the most with what they would like to accomplish. Because a coach has expertise in the content and context, it is likely the coach has a good idea about what the goal should be for a specific situation. Gathering more information from the coachee(s), however, can either confirm the goal and/or help to shape the steps that will need to be taken to achieve the goal.

Another tip for goal setting relates to the level of difficulty to achieve the goal. It may seem obvious, but help the teacher or team set a realistic goal. The idea is the coachee(s) benefits from setting a goal that allows them to achieve a "quick win," particularly during initial coaching sessions when coachees may not understand the value of coaching. In addition, quick wins encourage high self-efficacy, or the belief that the coachee(s) have the capacity to achieve a valued goal (McKenna & Davis, 2009). If the teacher or team wants to set a goal that is extremely complicated or difficult to achieve, then help the coachee set smaller goals that lead up to the more complicated change. This type of step-by-step approach to goal setting also creates a continuity to the coaching work in which initial sessions clearly connect to what will occur in later sessions.

Creating Partnerships   Creating a coach–coachee partnership that is based on equity is one strategy for demonstrating that coaching is collaborative. These partnerships convey that the coach and teacher or team are

- On equal footing, such that one partner does not hold more power or authority than the other

- Equally valued for their contributions, insights and expertise, such that one partner is not viewed as the central bearer of knowledge or experience

- Mutually benefitting from the partnership, such that one partner is expected to grow while the other partners are viewed as fully developed professionally

Coaches can take specific steps to create equitable partnerships. Use these strategies throughout each phase of the coaching cycle, particularly during the pre- and postmeeting phases.

- Share experiences when you professionally struggled and made mistakes. Talking about your own teaching or team challenges shows coachees that everyone engages in continuous improvement.

- When teachers or teams are struggling, focus on the positive while honoring difficulties. For example, remind them of specific ways in which they have grown or experienced a success. Find ways to say, "We're in this together!" or "Look at how much we have already accomplished!" Teaching and leading systems change efforts can be extremely difficult. We all need a champion in our corner to help us get through the difficult times.

Setting Parameters for Partnership

Agreeing how the coach and coachees will work together is a final strategy for creating a collaborative coaching environment. For example, the coach and coachee should mutually agree on

- What will transpire in coaching sessions (e.g., what the coachee will do and what the coach will do)

- How often and when the partners will work together

- What will be kept confidential between the coach and coachee and what can be shared with others outside of the partnership, particularly with leaders who are responsible for evaluation

A few notes are important to consider when setting these parameters. Regarding the first two items in this list, we recommend that you work with the coachee to create a written coaching agreement (or coaching compact) (see Figure 5.5; blank versions of this form are available in Appendix N and to download). This compact is a written agreement about what happens during coaching interactions and is generated based on the input from both the coach and the coachee(s) (teachers or teams). Ideally, this compact is created during the first phase of coaching (i.e., the initial premeeting) so that there is an agreed-on way of working together from the onset of the partnership. This compact can then be reviewed or even adjusted during subsequent phases of the coaching cycle. See Chapter 6 for more guidance on this compact, including a script you can use to set up the compact in partnership with teachers or teams and detailed information about observing, modeling, and providing performance feedback to teachers and teams.

Regarding confidentiality, know that some schools have guidelines about what information remains between the coach and coachee and what can be communicated outside of the partnership, especially with leaders who are responsible for evaluation. Sometimes these guidelines are formally written into policies. Other times the guidelines are unwritten but firmly a part of a school's culture. Other schools do not address confidentiality at all (i.e., decisions about what will and will not be shared are completely at the discretion of the partners).

We strongly suggest that coaches, coachees, and evaluators (e.g., principals, other administrators) discuss confidentiality during the initial premeeting at the beginning of the partnership. Specifically, clarify which specific coaching data will and will not be shared with evaluators. Then, ensure that these parameters are adhered to during the subsequent phases of the cycle so that alliance is not compromised. The bottom line is that recipients need to know if their work with coaches will be used to evaluate their teaching (Pierce, 2019). Violating the agreed-on confidentiality norms can erode alliance.

Demonstrating Expertise

Establishing Content Area Capacity Showing capacity in the content area in which coaching occurs is the next strategy for building and maintaining alliance. To do this, convey to teachers and teams that you know what you are talking about and have deep content knowledge in the area in which you coach. You should respond succinctly and clearly to their questions, share information and resources that are relevant but easy to understand, and help the teacher or team gain access to critical information they would not otherwise have at their disposal. These strategies can be used at any phase of the coaching cycle.

Conveying Capacity in Coaching Conveying competence in conducting coaching sessions is a final alliance strategy. This means there is an established consistency and a pattern to your coaching sessions that makes sense to coachees. Your pattern should be to conduct the three-phase recursive coaching cycles. Take time to plan and reflect on your work with teachers and teams so that you can conduct these three phases with ease and competence. Figure 5.6 (blank versions of this form are available in Appendix O and to download) offers a tool for planning, conducting, and reflecting on coaching sessions. You will see this tool again in Chapter 6.

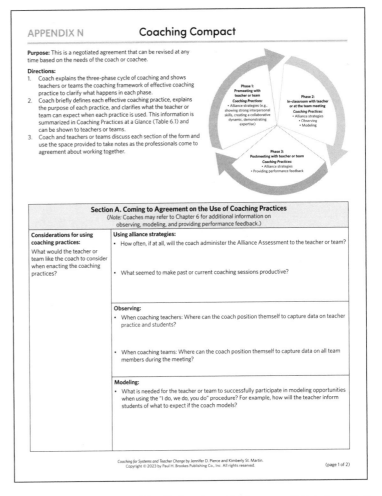

Figure 5.5. Coaching Compact. (*Note:* Blank versions of this form are available in Appendix N and to download.)

SUMMARY

Coaches often enter their line of work with some of the soft relational skills required for providing the just-in-time support needed by teachers and teams. But fractures in the coach–coachee alliance are not uncommon, and simply sharing a congenial relationship with colleagues will likely be insufficient for addressing such fractures (Pierce, 2019; Safran et al. 2011). We hope that this chapter showed you that every coach can take an intentional approach to building and maintaining alliance. We also hope you learned that alliance does not have to be an intangible concept that defies logic. Even though building and maintaining alliance may not always be clear-cut work, every coach can create that strong foundation with teacher and teams because it is crucial for all the other work that occurs among professionals.

APPENDIX O **Planning, Conducting, and Reflecting on Coaching Sessions: A Focus on Alliance**

Directions:
1. Complete the Planning section of the tool prior to working with teachers or teams.
2. Then, complete the Conducting and Reflecting sections of the tool after working with teachers or teams.

Planning	Imagine that you are planning for upcoming coaching sessions with teachers or teams. 1. What will you do during the **premeeting phase** of the coaching cycle to build alliance? 2. What will you do when observing in the **classroom or at the team meeting** to build alliance? 3. What will you do during the **postmeeting phase** of the coaching cycle to build alliance?
Conducting	1. What did you do during the **premeeting** to build alliance? How did the teacher or team react? 2. What did you do during **the team meeting/when in the teacher's classroom** to build alliance? How did the teacher or team react? 3. What did you do during the **postmeeting** to build alliance? How did the teacher or team react?
Reflecting	1. Think about building alliance across the three phases of the coaching cycle (e.g., premeeting, observation, postmeeting). What worked well for the teacher or team? Why? 2. How could alliance building go better across the three phases? Why? 3. What will you do to enhance alliance building across each phase of the coaching cycle? Why?

 (page 1 of 1)

Figure 5.6. Planning, Conducting, and Reflecting on Coaching Sessions: A Focus on Alliance. (*Note:* Blank versions of this form are available in Appendix O and to download.)

RESOURCES

This section contains three scenarios and one discussion guide (see Figure 5.7; blank versions of this form are available in Appendix P and to download). The discussion guide can be completed after reading each scenario. Use what you have learned from this chapter and prior chapters to respond to each question in the guide.

Scenario 1

Katarina is a coach working with pre-K teachers in a large school district to improve their use of shared book reading practices. Some of the teachers have never worked with a coach before, but all the teachers have expressed an interest in improving their shared book reading practices. The pre-K director recommended that Katarina begin by organizing a professional learning workshop on the specific book reading practices, followed by opportunities for teachers to participate in coaching sessions to support the implementation of these practices in their classrooms.

After teachers completed the professional learning workshop, Katarina provided teachers with lesson guides and a book reading schedule and described how the coaching process was designed to support teachers as they used new instructional strategies during whole- and small-group read-aloud activities. Katrina explained that teachers could choose to participate in bimonthly meetings with a group of other teachers to discuss implementation and share tips for using the new practices effectively, or they could choose to have Katrina observe their classrooms weekly and meet with her individually afterward to discuss how things were going. She noticed that some of the teachers seemed unsure about whether they wanted to participate in the one-to-one coaching sessions. Two of the teachers said that they did not know if they currently had time to dedicate to receiving coaching. As Katarina listened to the teachers, she wondered, "How can I build a strong alliance with teachers who seem hesitant to participate in coaching?"

Scenario 2

Marta, a district-employed coach, has been working with the teachers at Lands View Elementary School for several years on math instruction and PBIS, but she recently also began to support teachers' implementation of culturally responsive classroom management practices. Even though Marta has successfully coached teachers at the school in PBIS and math, several told Marta that they were not ready to participate in coaching in a new area. One teacher, Frank, told her, "I'm worried that I'm going to make a lot of implementation missteps, and I just don't feel like I'm ready to be observed." As Frank spoke, Marta nodded and said, "Yes, it can be difficult to try out new practices. I can hold off on observing a lesson. Would you be more comfortable just touching base after school one day so that we can talk more about implementation? Or, would you like me to model a lesson for you?" Frank reluctantly agreed to meet with Marta in a few days.

As Marta prepared for her meeting, she decided she would use a few strategies to build alliance with Frank. The following list shows some strategies Marta considered employing.

- Asking Frank and other teachers to complete a new Coaching Compact. Completing a new version of the compact could be a low-stakes entry point for supporting teachers with the management practices

- Asking open-ended questions about implementation and teaching in general, including, "What has been going well for your students lately? What's been a challenge?" "Have you identified any new management practices to implement? How has that gone for you and your students?"

- Sharing her own struggles as a teacher to create an even playing field with teachers reticent to participate in coaching sessions

The steps seemed productive, but Katarina also wondered, "What could I do to create stronger alliance with Frank and other teachers on their journey to implement new culturally responsive management practices?"

APPENDIX P **Discussion Guide: Alliance Scenarios**

Purpose: This guide can be used to reflect on the two scenarios presented in Chapter 5 and discuss reflections with a partner.

Directions:
1. Read the questions that relate to the scenarios included in Chapter 5.
2. Record your responses to each question.
3. Finally, share your responses with a partner.

Scenario 1 Questions
1. Think about Katarina's professional learning options for teachers: participating in bimonthly meetings or participating in one-to-one coaching sessions. Would you offer both types of supports to teachers? Why or why not?
2. How could you use alliance strategies to increase teachers' interest in coaching?

Scenario 2 Questions
1. Why do you think teachers seem reluctant to work with Marta?
2. What do you think about Marta's plan to use the three strategies with Frank? What does and does not make sense to you about the plan? Why?
3. What alliance strategies could Marta use with teachers? Why?

Scenario 3 Questions
1. What are your reactions to the information Esta shared with Carlos?
2a. Read over the requests Esta made of Carlos (shown next). • Set goals for the team. • Report to Esta what occurs at team meetings. • Create and follow an annual plan for what occurs at team meetings. What are the pros and cons of meeting each of Esta's requests in relation to building and maintaining alliance?
2b. Should Carlos adhere to each request? Why or why not?
2c. How would you talk with Esta about her requests?
3. How would you begin to work with the team based on what you know from Esta?

Figure 5.7. Discussion Guide: Alliance Scenarios. (*Note:* Blank versions of this form are available in Appendix P and to download.)

Scenario 3

Carlos was just hired to serve as the systems coach for Cherrywood Middle School. Carlos's primary job is to support the school's leadership team through their second year of implementing schoolwide MTSS. A few weeks before school began, he met with the school principal, Esta. At the meeting, she reminded Carolos that she had been the coach prior to Carlos and had a great deal of familiarity with each teacher on the team. She said, "I want you to know that the teachers tend to distrust new faculty members. Don't take it personally if they seem disengaged." She also said, "I'd like to meet with you every week to talk about what you are seeing during the team meetings. I want to know which teachers are on board, which are not, and what you plan to do to get teachers on board. Maybe you can set goals for the team so that you can be sure to make greater MTSS implementation progress. I'd also like to see your annual plan for facilitating team meetings for the team." As Esta finished speaking, the phone rang and interrupted their conversation. After it became clear that Esta could not continue the meeting, Carlos left and set up an appointment with her to follow up on the conversation.

REFERENCES

Dryden, W. (2017). *The coaching alliance: Theory and guidelines for practice*. Routledge.

Gessnitzer, S., & Kauffeld, S. (2015). The working alliance in coaching: Why behavior is the key to success. *Journal of Applied Behavioral Science, 51*(2), 177–197.

Hemmeter, M. L., Hardy, J. K., Schnitz, A. G., Adams, J. M., & Kinder, K. A. (2015). Effects of training and coaching with performance feedback on teachers' use of Pyramid Model practices. *Topics in Early Childhood Special Education, 35*(3), 144–156.

Horvath, A. O. (2001). The alliance. *Psychotherapy: Theory, Research, Practice, Training, 38*(4), 365–372.

Horvath, A. O., Del Re, A. C., Flückiger, C., & Symonds, D. (2011). Alliance in individual psychotherapy. *Psychotherapy, 48*(1), 9–16.

Johnson, S. R., Pas, E. T., & Bradshaw, C. P. (2016). Understanding and measuring coach–teacher alliance: A glimpse inside the 'black box'. *Prevention Science, 17*(4), 439–449.

Kemp, T. (2011). Building the coaching alliance: Illuminating the phenomenon of relationship in coaching (pp. 149–176). In G. Hernez-Broome, L. A., Boyce, & I. Kraut (Eds.), *Advancing Executive Coaching*. Wiley.

Knight, J. (2015). *The most important part of instructional coaching? Setting a goal*. https://www.instructional coaching.com/important-part-instructional-coaching-setting-goal/

McKenna, D. D., & Davis, S. L. (2009). Hidden in plain sight: The active ingredients of executive coaching. *Industrial and Organizational Psychology, 2*(3), 244–260.

O'Broin, A., & Palmer, S. (2009). Co-creating an optimal coaching alliance: A cognitive behavioural coaching perspective. *International Coaching Psychology Review, 4*(2), 184–194.

Pierce, J. D. (2015). *Teacher–coach alliance as a critical component of coaching: Effects of feedback and analysis on teacher practice*. http://hdl.handle.net/1773/33786

Pierce, J. D. (2019). How good coaches build alliance with teachers. *Educational Leadership, 77*(3), 78–82.

Safran, J. D., Muran, J. C., & Eubanks-Carter, C. (2011). Repairing alliance ruptures. *Psychotherapy, 48*(1), 80–87.

Sonesh, S. C., Coultas, C. W., Lacerenza, C. N., Marlow, S. L., Benishek, L. E., & Salas, E. (2015). The power of coaching: A meta-analytic investigation. *Coaching: An International Journal of Theory, Research and Practice, 8*(2), 73–95.

Wehby, J. H., Maggin, D. M., Partin, T. C. M., & Robertson, R. (2012). The impact of working alliance, social validity, and teacher burnout on implementation fidelity of the good behavior game. *School Mental Health, 4*(1), 22–33.

Moving Beyond Alliance

Observing, Modeling, and Providing Performance Feedback

---

1. How does a coach apply the remaining three coaching practices of observing, modeling, and providing performance feedback to teachers and teams within a three-phase coaching cycle?

2. What are some important tips to keep in mind when observing, modeling, and providing performance feedback?

CHAPTER TAKE-AWAYS

1. We define *effective coaching* as ongoing cycles of the four most effective coaching practices: using alliance strategies (discussed in detail in the previous chapter), observing, modeling, and providing performance feedback.

2. The four practices contained with our coaching framework provide a structure for coaching, not a lock-step process for working with teachers or teams.

3. Enacting the four coaching practices takes planning and reflection because each practice is nuanced.

CHAPTER OVERVIEW

Chapter 6 shifts toward the remaining three effective practices that comprise our framework of coaching teachers and teams: observing, modeling, and providing performance feedback. Subsequently, in the sections that follow you will learn how to use each coaching practice, when to use them in the three-phase recursive cycle, and why. We also give specific guidance for integrating observations, modeling, and performance feedback into your work with teachers and teams. Chapter 6 concludes with several resources that can be used by new and experienced coaches to make the application of coaching cycles more effective and efficient.

We offer two notes before turning to the core content of this chapter. We acknowledge that other coaching frameworks may not be constructed around a core set of observable practices in the way that we have done. Some coaching models also suggest that coaching is more of an art than a science. This line of thinking suggests that effective coaching can neither be precisely defined nor explicitly taught and learned. Perhaps you might even find yourself sharing this view.

First, although we embrace the idea that coaching can be somewhat nebulous (e.g., the amount of time a coach works with teachers and teams varies, alliance strategies are tailored to specific coaching situations), we recognize research shows what the most effective coaches do with teachers and teams (Kraft et al., 2018). Therefore, our coaching framework extrapolates research findings so that real-world coaches and coachees can benefit from this information. Coaching that results in improved outcomes is not accidental and unexplainable. Effective coaches have clear patterns, and these patterns are the observable behaviors we aim to clarify.

Second, coaches who are well versed in other coaching frameworks remain unsure about what they are supposed to explicitly do when working with teachers or teams and why. Therefore, it seems coaching frameworks *not* centered on observable practices can leave coaches at a loss for what to do, when, and why. Some questions we have been asked by coaches demonstrate this confusion:

- How do I run a teacher or systems coaching session? What do I do first and why? Is there a sequence I should follow?

- Why is it necessary to observe teachers and teams? What do I exactly do when I observe, and does every teacher need about the same amount of this coaching practice? Does it matter if I am watching a video and am not face to face with the teacher or team?

- What is the added value of modeling for experienced teachers and teams? How do I approach modeling so that I do not step on other people's toes?

- How do I provide performance feedback that does not cause teachers, teams, or even me anxiety? Do teachers and teams miss out on anything if I elect to not provide feedback?

The questions indicate that coaches are hungry to know concrete information about how to enact effective coaching sessions with teachers and teams. This chapter is designed to provide this much needed information to coaches.

EFFECTIVE COACHING PRACTICES IN THE THREE-PHASE RECURSIVE CYCLE

We define *effective coaching* as ongoing cycles of using alliance strategies, observing, modeling, and providing performance feedback. When should you observe, model, and provide performance feedback in the three-phase cycle? Glance through Figure 6.1 to refresh your memory of our coaching framework.

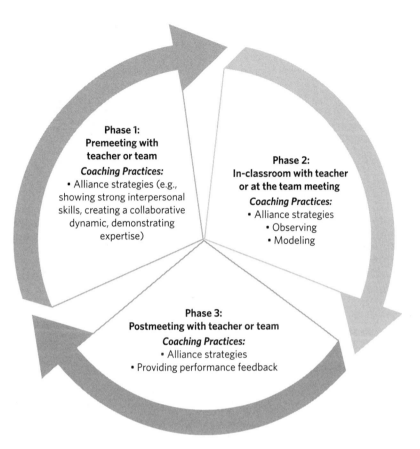

Figure 6.1. Effective coaching practices in a three-phase recursive cycle. (*Source:* Pierce, 2015.)

Now, review what happens in each of the three phases. After reading over the synopsis of each phase, check out the text box to get additional insight into our coaching framework.

- Phase 1: The premeeting

  - Coaches emphasize alliance strategies in this phase of the cycle. Alliance strategies are crucial at this point because coaching needs to get off on the right foot. Coaches may also model and provide performance feedback to teachers and teams during this phase, but it typically happens after some cycles of coaching have already occurred.

- Phase 2: In the classroom or at the team meeting

  - Although coaches will continue to use alliance strategies in this second phase, observation is the central practice for this part of the coaching cycle. Modeling and perhaps occasional performance feedback may also occur here; however, the performance feedback will be quite brief and unobtrusively provided to not disrupt the teaching or team meeting.

- Phase 3: The postmeeting

  - When conducting the postmeeting meetings with teachers and teams, coaches primarily use alliance strategies and provide performance feedback. As with Phase 1, coaches may also model for teachers and teams to help them better understand the feedback and note changes to practice that should be made in the classroom or team meeting.

Table 6.1. Coaching practices at a glance

Coaching practice	Definition	When used	Purpose of practice	What teachers and teams can expect
Using alliance strategies (described in Chapter 5)	The use of strategies to build and maintain a positive working relationship between the coach and coachee	All phases, but particularly important in Phases 1 and 3	To create a solid foundation for all the work that occurs between the professionals (coach and coachee)	Coach may ask the teacher or team to complete an Alliance Assessment (Figure 5.4) and/or Coaching Compact (Figure 5.5).
Observing	The process of viewing the teacher or team in their setting and collecting data on teacher or team practice	Phase 2	To ensure the coach understands teacher practice or team practice To collect data on teacher or team practice	Coach will take data on the teacher or team practice (and student-related data if applicable). Duration and frequency of observation may vary.
Modeling	The act of demonstrating how to use a specific teaching or team practice (e.g., analyzing data) for coachees	Primarily Phase 2 Occasionally Phases 1 and 3	To support the teacher's or team's correct use of a practice or activity in their setting	Modeling will only occur after it is agreed on by the teacher or team and only when the teacher or team incorrectly uses a practice or makes implementation errors. Coach will use an "I do, we do, you do" procedure that includes active teacher or team participation. Modeling may or may not occur during each observation.
Providing performance feedback	The act of sharing concrete and actionable data on teacher or team practice	Primarily Phase 3 Occasionally Phases 1 and 2	To help teachers or teams monitor progress toward their goal(s) and continue to grow in their use of practices	Performance feedback is specific, positive, corrective, if necessary, and timely. Performance feedback will identify what the teacher or team did and how it benefitted students or the school implementation effort (i.e., the rationale). Data may be presented in a variety of ways (e.g., structured notes, verbal statements, visual summaries such as graphs, charts, or tallies). Data may be presented to assist coachees' self-reflection and identify next steps.

Source: Pierce and Buysse (2014).

A Flexible Coaching Framework

This framework indicates when coaches are most likely to use each coaching practice, why these practices are used, and how to successfully enact each practice. But know that coaching is not a lock-step process. We suggest you treat this framework as a structure for your work with teachers or teams rather than as a set of rigid expectations. Flexibly employ the four effective practices included in the framework and the guidance offered for each practice.

DEFINING EFFECTIVE COACHING PRACTICES

Next, we unpack each of these coaching practices by highlighting more detailed information coaches need to know about each practice. This information is also summarized in Table 6.1.

Observing

By now you know that observing is the process of seeing a teacher or team in action in the classroom or at a team meeting. The purpose of an observation is for the coach to have a clear understanding of how the teacher works with students or how the team is managing implementation efforts (Dunst et al., 2015; Garbacz et al., 2015; Kraft et al., 2018; Kretlow & Bartholomew, 2010; Polly et al., 2013). Therefore, observing is the dominant practice used in the second phase of the coaching cycle and is critical to coaching. You cannot model or provide performance feedback if you do not know precisely what the teacher is doing when working with students or what the team does during an implementation team meeting.

The primary activity while observing is to gather simple data on what transpires with the teacher or team practice by focusing on the practices that are the greatest interest to the teacher or team and accomplishing the intended outcomes. You will use that data in the postmeeting to 1) construct positive (or affirmative) and potential corrective performance feedback you will offer to the teacher or team and 2) consider how to encourage the teacher or team to reflect on the teaching or meeting. If you do not collect data, then you run the risk of conveying to teachers and teams that coaching sessions are based on subjective judgments rather than concrete information about what transpired in the classroom or during the meeting. If you collect data in an area that is not of interest to the teacher or team, however, then you also run the risk of sending a signal to the coachee(s) that their needs are not a priority. Avoid these issues by asking the teacher or team during the premeeting what they would like for you to focus on during the observation.

You might be curious about what teachers or teams may want you to observe. Review Figure 6.2, which offers areas in which you might collect coaching data and also explains how you can collect such information. Note that some of the data collection methods are quantitative, whereas other methods are qualitative. Both of these methods may be helpful to the teacher or team. The key ideas here are to ensure that the data you collect are on the practices that are of interest to the teacher or team and that your data collection method allows you to readily gather information on the desired area.

There are times when the teacher's or team's interests may not align with the interests of the school or pre-K program (e.g., the teacher would prefer to be coached in math, but the school is implementing a reading program). Such requests can happen when buy-in for an implementation effort is either fragile or not yet well established. Fall back on alliance strategies in such cases. For example, try using open-ended questions to gather information from the coachee(s) to coconstruct a goal that is of mutual interest. Or, keep in mind a goal in mind that could become of interest to the teacher or team in the future and try to shape coachees toward that goal over several coaching cycles.

Examples of Data Collection Methods and Areas
Coaching Teachers
• Fidelity assessments related to the specific practice the teacher is implementing
• Tallies of open- and closed-ended questions and number of correct student responses
• Tallies of whole-group, small-group, and individual student questions and number of correct student responses
• Ratio of positive and corrective statements (e.g., 4:1)
• Duration of each type of learning activity observed (e.g., whole class lecture, small-group activities, partner activities, independent learning) and amount of time students are actively engaged in each activity
• Number of transitions (e.g., entering the room, sitting down, engaging in entry task, switching from one learning activity to another), duration of each transition, and what students did during each transition
Coaching Teams
• Fidelity assessments related to the school/pre-K program implementation effort
• Type and/or number of meeting structures in place: notetaker, meeting facilitator, agenda, timekeeper, and so forth.
• Total number of agenda items, number of items on the agenda that are relevant to the implementation effort, and amount of time allocated to each item
• Number and clarity of next steps team members will need to assign to other team members at the conclusion of the meeting; degree to which these next steps relate to an implementation issue
• Number of previously identified action steps that have been completed in the expected time frame and degree to which the action steps resolved an implementation issue
• Type and/or duration of engagement of each team member during the meeting
• Number, type, and quality of decisions made by the team to resolve implementation issues
• Degree to which and/or number of times the implementation plan is referenced at the meeting and/or in the agenda items; comments made by team members about the implementation plan in relation to the meeting
• If data interpretation is the area of interest and focus: number and type of question(s) asked during data analysis; degree to which data compilations can answer the questions asked; and accuracy of precise problem statements, contributing factors, and conclusions drawn from the data analysis
• If conducting a Plan-Do-Study-Act cycle: degree to which each step of the cycle is used, fluency with each step of the cycle, engagement of team members in the cycle, and clarity in conclusions drawn by the team when participating in the cycles

Figure 6.2. Examples of data collection methods and areas.

Modeling

Modeling is the act of demonstrating how to use a specific teaching or teaming practice. Modeling most commonly occurs during the second phase of the coaching cycle because its purpose is to help coachees learn how to correctly implement a practice when it would be occurring naturally in a context (e.g., Kretlow & Bartholomew, 2010; Simonsen et al., 2014). For example, a coach might model how to use a reading strategy during regularly scheduled reading instruction. A systems coach might model how to use a Plan-Do-Study-Act cycle during a team meeting when the team is attempting to enact Plan-Do-Study-Act.

Modeling can also occur during a pre- or postmeeting, however. In these cases, think of modeling as a form of a professional learning workshop for teachers or teams in which the coachees receive additional opportunities to practice implementation in a decontextualized situation. Keep in mind that when modeling occurs outside of Phase 2, the teacher or team may not be able to implement the practice in their own setting.

Regardless of the phase of the cycle in which modeling occurs, if modeling does not occur but is needed, then the teacher or team may continue to incorrectly implement a practice. Undoing incorrect learning can be challenging for coaches and coachees, so it is better to try to avoid this from happening. Alternatively, if a teacher or team implements a given practice, then modeling may be safely omitted from the entire cycle of coaching (Dunst et al., 2015; Garbacz et al., 2015).

You might be wondering what a coach precisely does when modeling. The central purpose of modeling is to help the teacher or team better understand how to use the practice that is of greatest interest to them. The good news is that coaches have a few ways of modeling. For example, if teachers and teams have already indicated they are comfortable with you modeling in their context, then you could use an "I do, we do, you do" approach with teachers or teams (Archer & Hughes, 2010), which includes the following:

- The coach shows the teacher or team how to implement the practice correctly.

- The coach implements the practice in tandem with the teacher or team.

- The coach offers the teacher or team opportunities to independently use the practice.

If electing to use this type of approach, then it will be important for some preparation work to be done before the modeling begins. First, if modeling for a teacher, then ask the teacher to talk to their students in advance so that they are prepared for what will occur. After all, we do not want students to be caught off guard or get the impression that the modeling act is an indicator that the teacher is not skilled. (We have seen teachers talk to their students about modeling, likening it to what a sports coach may do when helping athletes advance their skills in a certain area.) If coaching a team, ensure all team members know that modeling may occur during a meeting. Second, it is important to provide a correct demonstration of the teacher or team practice. Models need to be accurate so that teachers or teams can witness the given practice in their setting and understand what it means to properly implement that practice (Kretlow & Bartholomew, 2010). Practically speaking, seeing a coach incorrectly use a practice does not help the coachees know how to implement it correctly.

If the "I do, we do, you do" approach seems a bit too structured, intensive, or not palatable for the teacher or team, then consider making some adjustments. For example, omit the "I do" or "we do" (rather than both) portions of the modeling process, which may make the modeling process more streamlined so that the teacher or team can more quickly resume the lesson or meeting. If modeling during the observation is simply undesirable, then provide teachers and teams with video exemplars of the practice. Coaches and coachees can watch the videos, discuss how the practice of interest was used, and even try using the practice together at that moment. The downside to this approach is that the practice may not be aligned to the teacher's or team's context, making it hard for the coachee(s) to understand how to enact the practice in their setting. Another idea is for coaches to provide explicit written guidelines or resources on the use of the practice of interest coupled with potentially using the "I do, we do, you do" approach to help the teacher or team successfully enact the practice.

Providing Performance Feedback

Providing performance feedback is another critical practice in the coaching framework. Although performance feedback is typically shared with teachers or teams during the postmeeting phase (i.e., Phase 3), it can be offered during every other phase of coaching once the first coaching premeeting has occurred (more on this in the next section of the chapter). Regardless of the phase in which it is offered, coaches provide performance feedback so that teachers and teams have concrete, actionable data that helps them reflect on their practice and advance their goal areas (Cavanaugh, 2013; Dunst et al., 2015; Garbacz et al., 2015; Kretlow & Bartholomew, 2010; Polly et al., 2013).

What makes performance feedback actionable and concrete? This type of feedback is

- *Specific,* such that the data provided to the teacher or team objectively describes what transpired in the classroom or at the meeting. It is not general.

- *More affirmative (positive) than corrective,* such that the teacher or team receive about four times (or more) behavioral-specific praise about the successes that were observed during the lesson or team meeting.

- *Corrective when necessary,* such that when the coachee(s) make teaching or team practice missteps, the coach communicates that information to the coachee(s).

- *Timely* (as much as possible), such that the teacher or team receive the feedback shortly after the observation so that the lesson or team meeting is fresh in the minds of the coach and coachees (Randolph et al., 2019).

In addition to the previous features, we also recommend that performance feedback clearly states what transpired in the classroom or at the meeting that benefitted students or the school implementation effort. We call this feature of performance feedback the *rationale.* Although research on performance feedback does not necessarily highlight this nuance, we have found that teachers and teams need to know why the feedback is so important for their practice.

Coachee's description of classroom events

During today's small-group reading lesson, students chorally read the paragraph and then reread it to a partner. Choral reading and rereading are research-based ways to engage all learners in repeated reading, which is important for building overall reading proficiency. All students participated in this activity and used the partner reading procedures correctly. Then, you asked each at least one open-ended question. Each student responded correctly to the question they were asked. At the end of the lesson, students had to write a summary of the paragraph on their own. Five of the six students were engaged during this part of the lesson. You gave these students affirmations at the end of the lesson by praising them for meeting the small-group expectations. One student had her head down on the table during the writing portion of the lesson and was assigned one tally mark per minute she was not engaged. What are your reactions, and how would you like to use this information in relation to your teaching goals?

Coachee's description of classroom events with coach's performance feedback

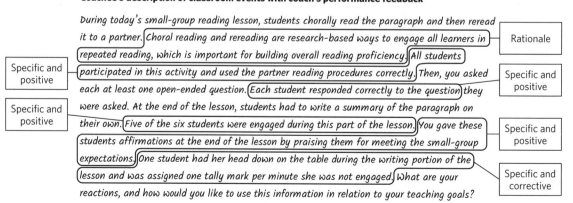

Figure 6.3. Concrete and actionable performance feedback.

Figure 6.3 provides examples of performance feedback that are constructed based on the features previously listed. Assume that it was provided to a teacher whose goals were to 1) increase their use of positive behavior strategies and 2) incorporate evidence-based reading strategies into small-group instruction with struggling readers. Also assume the feedback was provided within a few days of the observation, making it timely as well. Finally, notice that the performance feedback contains a rationale, which signals to the teacher why the information shared by the coach is important for student improvement.

You may have noticed from the example that the performance feedback was clearly based on data the coach collected during the observation, making it concrete. The feedback starts with a statement of what was observed, offers a rationale to signal to the teacher why the teaching practice is important for students, and includes four specific statements that are primarily focused on what was successful during the lesson. Then it includes one corrective feedback statement. Just as important, you may have noticed that the coach ends with open-ended questions (i.e., alliance strategies) that orient the teacher toward self-reflection and action.

With a basic understanding of what each practice is, when it is used, why, and the primary activities of the practice, we offer tips for successfully observing, modeling, and providing performance feedback. Some of the tips relate to each coaching practice, whereas others offer guidance for one specific coaching practice. Whether coaching teachers or teams in person, through a video recording, or even virtually, use these tips to help you more successfully enact each coaching practice.

TIPS FOR ENACTING COACHING PRACTICES

Using Alliance Strategies When Observing, Modeling, and Providing Performance Feedback

Our first tip relates to using alliance strategies when enacting other coaching practices during any phase of the coaching cycle. We recommend enacting strategies that suit specific teachers and teams when observing, modeling, or providing performance feedback. You can reference the information gathered from the Alliance Assessment (see Figure 5.4). In addition, use one of your initial premeetings to coconstruct a Coaching Compact (see Figure 5.5) with teachers or teams. The purpose of the tool is to ensure that coaches and coachees agree about what will transpire during each phase of coaching, including what happens during an observation (e.g., when it will occur, for how long, if there is a specific area of interest for you to focus on during the observation), when you may model (e.g., use the full "I do, we do, you do" procedure or another approach), and how you will collect and deliver performance feedback (e.g., outlining when data be shared and if it be presented verbally, in writing, or both).

Although teachers and teams may be accustomed to being observed, participating in modeling, or receiving performance feedback, different coaches often do different things. The variation in prior coaching experiences can leave recipients uncertain about what to expect from their coach, what to do during the coaching session, and what the teacher or team will gain from each coaching practice. Avoid this confusion by specifying the details of each coaching practice in the Coaching Compact. You may even find it helpful to use the script shown in the text box to structure your Coaching Compact conversation with teachers or teams.

Sample Script for Creating the Coaching Compact With Teachers or Teams

"I'd like to use our time during today's premeeting to set up a Coaching Compact. The compact serves as a way for us to clarify what happens during each phase of the coaching cycle, talk about the different coaching practices I'll use during the cycle, and clarify what you can expect to do when I enact the practices. I'd also like to hear your reactions and preferences related to the practices so that we can create a safe culture for our work together. We can use this template to capture our ideas about our partnership."

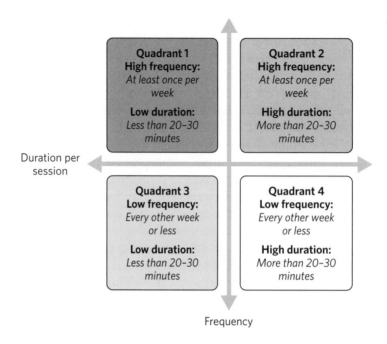

Figure 6.4.   2 × 2 matrix for dosage of observations and modeling.

Determining Dosage for Observing and Modeling

If you have read Chapter 3, then you know that the dose (e.g., frequency and duration) of an observation or modeling is not formulaic. Is it best to observe for an hour for each teacher or team or for 20 minutes? Should you model for every teacher or team who requires it or only on an occasional basis? Unfortunately, research simply has not clarified answers to these questions (Kraft et al., 2018). Some teachers and teams may show improved teaching or team practice after receiving a higher coaching dosage: 20-minute (or longer) observations occurring every week or from weekly opportunities to participate in modeling with the coach (Pas et al., 2015; Sutherland et al., 2015). Other teachers and teams, however, may show improved teaching and team practice with shorter,

Table 6.2.   Dosage decision tree

Teacher or team needs	Suggested decision (in order of recommendation)
This is a complex practice, the coachee needs to make a lot of growth and is interested in making the change.	Quadrant 1, 2, or possibly 4
This is a complex practice, the coachee needs to make a lot of growth and is not interested in making the change.	Quadrant 3 or 1
This is a complex practice, the coachee does not need to make a lot of growth and is interested in making the change.	Quadrant 1 or 3
This is a complex practice, the coachee does not need to make a lot of growth and is not interested in making the change.	Quadrant 3
This is not a complex practice, the coachee needs to make a lot of growth and is interested in making the change.	Quadrant 1, 2, or possibly 4
This is not a complex practice, the coachee needs to make a lot of growth and is not interested in making the change.	Quadrant 3 or 1
This is not a complex practice, the coachee does not need to make a lot of growth and is interested in making the change.	Quadrant 3 or 1
This is not a complex practice, the coachee does not need to make a lot of growth and is not interested in making the change.	Quadrant 3

less frequent sessions, such as 10- to 15-minute observations occurring every other week and with few opportunities to participate in modeling with the coach (Kraft et al., 2018). Adding to this ambiguity, the amount of desired teacher or team growth (e.g., minimal to significant changes to teaching or team practice), the type of desired growth (e.g., improvement in a simple task or in a complicated teacher or team practice), and even teacher or team interest in making the change (e.g., low interest in changing to high desire to change) can influence decisions about dosage (Kraft et al., 2018). Indeed, pinpointing optimal dosage of observations and modeling opportunities for teachers and teams can be tricky.

Our second tip is that coaches use the 2 × 2 matrix shown in Figure 6.4 and the decision rules shown in Table 6.2 to guide decisions about dosage. Two caveats are important. First, we rarely suggest high-frequency, high-dosage observations or models because high frequency and high dosage of coaching can be overwhelming to the coachees and even the coach. It can also begin to develop dependency on the coach, which makes it challenging for the coach to know when and how to fade the coaching supports. Second, expect to adjust observation and modeling dosage by always circling back to asking yourself the question, "Is the teacher or team making progress?" If the answer is yes, then proceed. If the answer is no, then make some adjustments to either the frequency or the duration (or both).

Optimizing Observations

Our third tip relates to the second phase of coaching, when you observe teachers or teams. Although it might seem mundane, we suggest you think about where you will physically position yourself when observing coachees. Whether observing teachers in person, virtually, or after the fact (via a recording), be sure you can capture what occurs between the teacher and students. Positioning the camera (or yourself) is important because you will want to notice and record data about what the teacher does and what students do in response to the teacher. For this reason, some coaches find it helpful to sit off to the side of the classroom when observing a teacher live, knowing that exact positioning depends on the layout of the room.

Similarly, in the case of observing a team in person, virtually, or after the fact (via a recording), you will want to take data on several (if not each) team members. Students will not be present at a team meeting, but you do want to be able to capture what each team member does or does not do and how members interact with each other. The rationale here is that team meetings differ greatly: some team members may remain silent for the meeting, others may speak extensively, another member may try to speak but find themselves unable to contribute for some reason. Furthermore, the team members may engage in many tasks in the meeting, and you will need to collect data on who is involved and in what ways. These are all pieces of information you will want to see and note (mentally or as brief notes). Therefore, try to position yourself or the camera so that you can view all the members.

Providing Performance Feedback When Enacting Other Coaching Practices

A final tip relates to the use of performance feedback when enacting other coaching practices. We offer four suggestions:

1. If the teacher or team is comfortable receiving in-the-moment feedback, then offer very brief snippets of information to coachee(s) when observing or modeling, particularly if the teacher or team seems uneasy or discouraged. It is important to offer positive (affirmative) in-the-moment feedback. Corrective feedback should be reserved for the postmeeting so that information can be presented with sensitivity. One easy way to offer in-the-moment feedback is to

use sticky notes to jot down a few brief, positive comments on teacher practice/team practice. Hand it to the teacher or leave it in a spot readily seen by the coachee. Framing in-the-moment feedback around positive statements shows the teacher or team that their strengths are recognizable and coaching will focus on strengths, not areas of growth.

2. Before providing performance feedback during the postmeeting, ask the teacher or team to share their reflections about the observation. The point here is to honor the insights of the coachees and ensure that their reflections are at the forefront of the coaching session. Share the data collected on teacher or team practice, making connections between what their reflections were and the data you collected.

3. If working virtually with a teacher or team, then use the same guidelines for constructing and providing feedback as you would use when working face to face with coachees (Rodgers et al., 2019).

4. Ask teachers or teams to react to the data you share by asking them open-ended questions. Chapter 5 contains a series of these questions (see Figure 5.5).

SUMMARY

The most critical work of a teacher coach or a systems coach is to conduct recursive cycles of effective coaching practices. This chapter aimed to explain how to conduct such cycles, acknowledging that effective coaching is just as intentional as high-quality teaching. Similar to teaching, these coaching practices will soon become a routine over time, guiding your work so that the goals of coaching can be achieved—improved teacher practice, improved team practice, improved systems, and even improved student outcomes. If you are ready to translate the information on the coaching framework into your work, then take a look at a new version of a tool you have seen in Chapter 5 (see Figure 6.5; blank versions of this form are available in Appendix Q and to download). Use the tool to ensure your coaching role includes effective coaching practices.

RESOURCES

This section contains two scenarios, a discussion guide (see Figure 6.6; blank versions of this form are available in Appendix R and to download), and three coaching protocols (see Figures 6.7, 6.8, and 6.9; blank versions of these forms are available in Appendices S, T, and U and to download). Read over the two scenarios, both of which are a continuation of scenarios presented in Chapter 5. Then, complete the discussion guide, using what you have learned from this chapter and prior chapters to respond to each question in the guide. Finally, use the coaching protocols to plan, conduct, and reflect on each phase of the coaching cycle—conducting premeetings, observing the teacher or team, and conducting postmeetings.

Scenario 1

Marta has been working with Frank and several other teachers at Lands View Preschool to advance their implementation of culturally responsive classroom management practices. Frank was initially uncomfortable with being coached in this area because the practices were new for him. He and Marta created a Coaching Compact during a premeeting, however, which spelled out how Marta could observe, model, and provide performance feedback to Frank. Creating that compact helped Frank become comfortable with participating in coaching. Then, Marta completed two complete cycles of coaching (e.g., had two pre- and postmeetings and two observations

Appendix Q — Planning, Conducting, and Reflecting on Four Coaching Practices

APPENDIX Q — **Planning, Conducting, and Reflecting on Four Coaching Practices**

Purpose: This tool is used by coaches to **plan, conduct,** and **reflect** on coaching cycles.

Directions:
1. Complete the Planning section of the tool prior to working with teachers or teams.
2. Complete the Conducting and Reflecting sections of the tool after working with teachers or teams.

Planning	Coach: Coachee: 1. What initiated the request for coaching? 2. What will you do during the **premeeting phase** of the coaching cycle to build **alliance**? If the need arises to **model and/or provide performance feedback**, then how will this be accomplished? 3. When working directly **in the classroom or at the team meeting**, how will you build **alliance, observe, and model?** If the need arises to provide in-the-moment teaching/team meeting **performance feedback**, then how will this be accomplished? 4. What will you do during the **postmeeting phase** of the coaching cycle to provide **performance feedback?** If the need arises to model, then how will this be accomplished?
Conducting	1. What did you do during the **premeeting** to build **alliance**? How did the teacher or team react? 2. What did you do during **the team meeting/when in the teacher's classroom** to build **alliance, observe, and model?** How did the teacher or team react? If you provided **performance feedback**, then what did you do, and how did the teacher or team react? 3. What did you do during the **postmeeting** to build **alliance** and provide **performance feedback?** How did the teacher or team react? If you also modeled, what did you do, and how did the team react?
Reflecting	1. What worked well during **each part of the coaching cycle** (e.g., premeeting, team meeting/teacher observation, postmeeting)**?** Why? 2. What could go better next time during **each phase?** Why? 3. What will you do to enhance **each phase** of the coaching session? Consider how you can improve in each practice: **using alliance strategies, observing, modeling, and providing performance feedback.**

Figure 6.5. Planning, Conducting, and Reflecting on Four Coaching Practices. (*Note:* Blank versions of this form are available in Appendix Q and to download.)

Appendix R — Discussion Guide

APPENDIX R — **Discussion Guide**

Purpose: This discussion guide can be used to reflect on the two scenarios presented in Chapter 6 and discuss reflections with a partner.

Directions:
1. Read the questions.
2. Record your responses to each question in the space provided. Finally, share your responses with a partner.

Scenario 1 Questions
1. Imagine you are Marta. What would you do during the postmeeting session to best support Frank? Consider how you would provide performance feedback and how you would use alliance strategies.

2. What are some things you would avoid doing at the postmeeting if you were Marta? Why?

3. What would you do to prepare for another round of coaching with Frank, assuming the next step would be to conduct a premeeting with him after conducting the postmeeting?

Scenario 2 Questions
1. Imagine you are Carlos. What would you do to help the team become more self-reliant? Be specific by stating how you could begin conducting coaching cycles using the four practices from this book's coaching framework.

2. What do you think is important for you to avoid doing if you were Carlos? Why?

3. How would you work with Esta if you were Carlos? What would you do and why?

Figure 6.6. Discussion Guide. (*Note:* Blank versions of this form are available in Appendix R and to download.)

in Frank's classroom). Frank responded positively to each phase of the coaching cycle and even reported that he wanted to try implementing one new management practice with students in the upcoming week. Hearing this, Marta conducted an additional premeeting with Frank to support his use of that new practice. At that meeting, Frank and Marta decided she would observe him in his classroom in a few days.

The day of the observation, Marta collected data on Frank's use of the practice and noted how students responded to his use of the new practices. She found that he struggled a great deal and that most students did not respond positively to what he was trying out. A few students were disengaged, with a few putting their heads down and refusing to participate in the lesson. Marta ended the observation with a brief note on Frank's desk highlighting a few of the positive moments of the lesson but left wondering what she should do during the postmeeting session to best support Frank.

Scenario 2

Carlos was just hired to serve as the systems coach for Cherrywood Middle School. Carlos's primary job is to support the school's leadership team through their second year of implementing schoolwide MTSS. In his initial work with the team, he developed an MTSS implementation action plan, co-led team meetings, and provided team members with student-level academic and behavioral data compilations. He also led the team through the analysis of the student data. Although

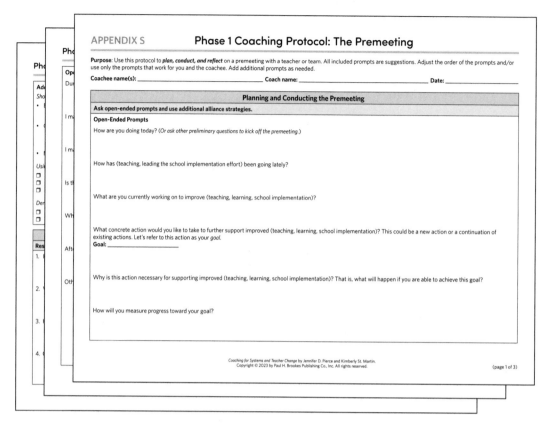

Figure 6.7. Coaching Protocol for Premeetings. (*Note:* Blank versions of this form are available in Appendix S and to download.)

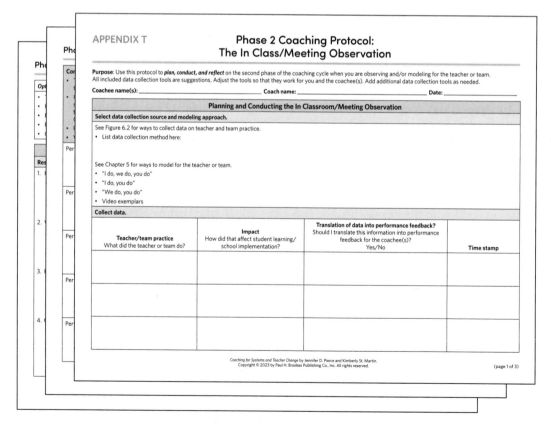

Figure 6.8. Coaching Protocol for the in Class/Meeting Observation. (*Note:* Blank versions of this form are available in Appendix T and to download.)

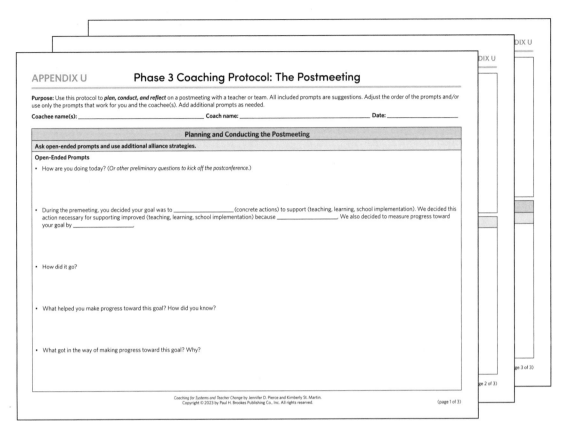

APPENDIX U **Phase 3 Coaching Protocol: The Postmeeting**

Purpose: Use this protocol to *plan, conduct, and reflect* on a postmeeting with a teacher or team. All included prompts are suggestions. Adjust the order of the prompts and/or use only the prompts that work for you and the coachee(s). Add additional prompts as needed.

Coachee name(s): _____ Coach name: _____ Date: _____

Planning and Conducting the Postmeeting

Ask open-ended prompts and use additional alliance strategies.

Open-Ended Prompts

• How are you doing today? (*Or other preliminary questions to kick off the postconference.*)

• During the premeeting, you decided your goal was to _____ (concrete actions) to support (teaching, learning, school implementation). We decided this action necessary for supporting improved (teaching, learning, school implementation) because _____. We also decided to measure progress toward your goal by _____.

• How did it go?

• What helped you make progress toward this goal? How did you know?

• What got in the way of making progress toward this goal? Why?

Coaching for Systems and Teacher Change by Jennifer D. Pierce and Kimberly St. Martin.
Copyright © 2023 by Paul H. Brookes Publishing Co., Inc. All rights reserved. (page 1 of 3)

Figure 6.9. Coaching Protocol for Postmeetings. (*Note:* Blank versions of this form are available in Appendix U and to download.)

the team members voiced appreciation for his efforts, he recently began to think that he took too much responsibility for completing team tasks. That is, other team members seemed to rely on him completely to set the agendas, lead each meeting, and share updates with the rest of the school staff about MTSS implementation. Just as concerning was that team members remained unsure how to analyze the student data provided to them. They would regularly ask Carlos to identify key take-aways. He realized that he had taken these actions because of his conversation with Esta, the school principal. She seemed to expect him to run these meetings, and he was worried about not meeting her expectation.

After talking over his concerns with an MTSS coach working at another school, he realized the team would never have the opportunity to grow if he continued to do the work for them. The other coach suggested he apply specific coaching practices with the team rather than doing the work for the team. Carlos wondered what he could do to help the team become more self-reliant in leading MTSS implementation. He also wondered how he could work with Esta to shift his coaching in this new direction.

REFERENCES

Archer, A. L., & Hughes, C. A. (2010). *Explicit instruction: Effective and efficient teaching.* Guilford Press.

Cavanaugh, B. (2013). Performance feedback and teachers' use of praise and opportunities to respond: A review of the literature. *Education and Treatment of Children, 36*(1), 111–137.

Dunst, C. J., Bruder, M. B., & Hamby, D. W. (2015). Metasynthesis of in-service professional development research: Features associated with positive educator and student outcomes. *Educational Research and Reviews, 10*(12), 1731–1744.

Garbacz, S. A., Lannie, A. L., Jeffrey-Pearsall, J. L., & Truckenmiller, A. J. (2015). Strategies for effective classroom coaching. *Preventing School Failure: Alternative Education for Children and Youth, 59*(4), 263–273.

Kraft, M. A., Blazar, D., & Hogan, D. (2018). The effect of teacher coaching on instruction and achievement: A meta-analysis of the causal evidence. *Review of Educational Research, 88*(4), 547–588.

Kretlow, A. G., & Bartholomew, C. C. (2010). Using coaching to improve the fidelity of evidence-based practices: A review of studies. *Teacher Education and Special Education, 33*(4), 279–299.

Pas, E. T., Bradshaw, C. P., Becker, K. D., Domitrovich, C., Berg, J., Musci, R., & Ialongo, N. S. (2015). Identifying patterns of coaching to support the implementation of the Good Behavior Game: The role of teacher characteristics. *School Mental Health, 7*(1), 61–73.

Pierce, J. D. (2015). *Teacher–coach alliance as a critical component of coaching: Effects of feedback and analysis on teacher practice.* http://hdl.handle.net/1773/33786

Pierce, J. D. (2019). How good coaches build alliance with teachers. *Educational Leadership, 77*(3), 78–82.

Pierce, J. D., & Buysse, V. (2014). *National Center for Systemic Improvement. Effective Coaching: Improving teacher practice & outcomes for all learners.* https://ncsi-library.wested.org/resources/57

Polly, D., Mraz, M., & Algozzine, R. (2013). Implications for developing and researching elementary school mathematics coaches. *School Science and Mathematics, 113*(6), 297–307.

Randolph, K. M., Duffy, M. L., Brady, M. P., Wilson, C. L., & Scheeler, M. C. (2019). The impact of iCoaching on teacher-delivered opportunities to respond. *Journal of Special Education Technology, 35*(1). https://doi.org/10.1177/0162643419836414

Rodgers, W. J., Kennedy, M. J., VanUitert, V. J., & Myers, A. M. (2019). Delivering performance feedback to teachers using technology-based observation and coaching tools. *Intervention in School and Clinic, 55*(2), 103–112.

Safran, J. D., Muran, J. C., & Eubanks-Carter, C. (2011). Repairing alliance ruptures. *Psychotherapy, 48*(1), 80–87.

Simonsen, B., MacSuga-Gage, A. S., Briere III, D. E., Freeman, J., Myers, D., Scott, T. M., & Sugai, G. (2014). Multi-tiered support framework for teachers' classroom-management practices: Overview and case study of building the triangle for teachers. *Journal of Positive Behavior Interventions, 16*(3), 179–190.

Sutherland, K. S., Conroy, M. A., Vo, A., & Ladwig, C. (2015). Implementation integrity of practice-based coaching: Preliminary results from the BEST in CLASS efficacy trial. *School Mental Health, 7*(1), 21–33.

Facing the Complexities of Change

Resources and Tools to Enhance Forward Movement

7

KEY QUESTIONS

1. Why is readiness important when teachers or teams are expected to make a change?

2. How can coaches quickly and accurately measure teacher and team readiness?

3. How do coaches build readiness when teachers or teams are ambivalent to make a change?

4. How can coaches maintain a positive mindset about teacher and team readiness?

CHAPTER TAKE-AWAYS

1. When teachers or teams are expected to change but are reluctant or unwilling to do so, the change effort may not be achieved.

2. Readiness to change is neither a permanent state nor is it 100% present or 100% absent. Rather, readiness is often experienced along a continuum. Teacher and team placement on this continuum shifts. Coaches can quickly understand a teacher's and team's readiness for change by using an informal measure provided in this text.

3. When readiness to change is at the low end (e.g., below 70%–80% on the informal measure), coaches can use several strategies to build teacher or team readiness to change, including a) creating a communication protocol, b) networking teachers and teams, and c) conducting motivational interviews.

CHAPTER OVERVIEW

Chapter 7 builds on the ideas addressed primarily in Chapter 4—supporting teachers and teams with systems-level change. In this chapter, however, we narrow our conversation to those educators who may not be quite ready to make a change that is expected of them. In the following sections, we remind coaches why change can be so difficult for coachees and offer strategies for productively assisting teachers and teams through the change. We reference tools throughout the chapter to ensure coaches have access to things that can readily be integrated into coaching cycles with teachers and teams. We conclude with a resource to help coaches synthesize this chapter's contents with the information addressed in previous chapters. Overall, we hope that you can rely on this chapter for working productively with teachers and teams facing change.

At the end of the chapter, we include a brief discussion of readiness "do's and don'ts" for coaches because we have found that coaches typically encounter teachers and teams who are not quite ready to change. Even the most seasoned coaches find reluctance to change difficult to work through. The "do's and don'ts" section offers several reminders for maintaining positive views about readiness, which may come in handy when supporting teachers or teams who are not ready to make a change. After all, facing the need to change is not just challenging for teachers and teams; it can be hard on coaches, too.

THE CHALLENGE OF CHANGE

Implementation teams and teachers often find making changes to their practice can be difficult because it typically requires coaches to learn how to do something new or in a different way while dealing with the emotional ups and downs of doing something in a new way that may feel unfamiliar or even risky (see Chapter 4). Therefore, change packs a one-two punch, often making teachers and teams prefer the status quo, signaling they may not be ready to make a change (Hall & Hord, 2015).

THE IMPORTANCE OF READINESS

To be clear, the degree to which teachers and teams are ready to change is more than a cursory consideration by the coach. When teachers and teams are expected to change but are ambivalent or unwilling to do so, the end goal of the change effort (e.g., implementation of a new socioemotional practice by a teacher, use of Plan-Do-Study-Act cycles by a leadership team) might not be achieved (Helfrich et al., 2011; Kondakci et al., 2017; Weiner, 2009; Zimmerman, 2006). Readiness is not an either-or in which teachers or teams will either be ready or not ready. Rather, teachers and teams fall somewhere along a readiness continuum. Furthermore, level of readiness typically fluctuates depending on many factors, including the degree to which individual teachers or teams believe 1) the change is needed, 2) they have the skills necessary to make the change, and 3) they have leadership support for making the change (Holt et al., 2007; Weiner, 2009).

These points suggest that coaches need not wait for teachers and teams to reach a minimum level of readiness before working with them to make a change. If coaches wait for teachers or teams to reach an arbitrary readiness level or assume that teachers and teams will not ever be ready, then coaches can lose valuable time supporting the coachees (Anello et al., 2017). Instead, the coach's role is to determine where teachers and teams fall along the readiness continuum and, when needed, help foster their readiness for that change (McCamish et al., 2015). The next section offers a brief method of measuring readiness to help coaches understand teacher or team readiness. We outline three strategies that can be used to assist teachers and teams in developing their readiness to change.

MEASURING READINESS

The purpose of measuring readiness is to better understand the degree to which teachers and teams are prepared to make a change. Coach perceptions about others' readiness may not be accurate. Once teacher or team readiness data are collected, coaches can use the information to determine which coachees need additional support in developing readiness and which teachers or teams are already primed to undertake a change effort. Measuring readiness need not be a time- or labor-intensive undertaking. In fact, readiness can be measured in less than 10 minutes during a pre- or postmeeting. Moreover, readiness can be measured with any teacher or team. For example, coaches may administer the brief readiness assessment when

- Teachers or teams seem on the fence about making a change

- Teachers or teams send mixed signals about being ready to make a change

- Coaches are unsure about teachers' or teams' readiness to make a change

If teachers or teams are visibly not ready to make a change, then they likely will verbally and nonverbally articulate disinterest or unwillingness to change. In this scenario, it is not necessary to administer the readiness measure because you already have observable, describable behavior indicating readiness is on the lower end of the continuum.

Figure 7.1 contains a readiness measure along with directions for administration and data interpretation (blank versions of this form are available in Appendix V and to download). This very brief measure is based on a variety of readiness tools, including measures from Holt et al. (2007) and Shea et al. (2014), as well as the larger body of readiness research (Choi & Ruona, 2011; Helfrich

---

APPENDIX V   **Readiness Measure**

Purpose: Use this assessment to gauge teachers' or teams' readiness to change.

Directions for Administration:
1. Ask individual teachers or each team member to rate themselves on a scale of 1 to 10 for each question (1 = *completely disagree* and 10 = *completely agree*). Coaches may ask the questions verbally and record teacher or team scores. Alternatively, the form can be completed by the teacher or team and then provided to the coach. The Notes column can be used to record any teacher or team comments or questions.
2. Calculate the mean of all the ratings. The mean is the final readiness score. *Note:* For teams, include every score from each person. The total group mean is the final score for the team, which should be used with coaching groups.

Interpretation Guidance: Teachers or teams scoring at 70%–80% can be considered ready to change.

Teacher or team self-rating	Ratings 1 = *completely disagree* 10 = *completely agree*	Notes
This change is clearly needed.	1 2 3 4 5 6 7 8 9 10	
I have the skills that are needed to make this change work.	1 2 3 4 5 6 7 8 9 10	
This organization's most senior leader(s) is/are committed to this change.	1 2 3 4 5 6 7 8 9 10	

(page 1 of 1)

Figure 7.1   Readiness Measure. (*Note:* Blank versions of this form are available in Appendix V and to download.)

et al., 2011; Turri et al., 2016; Weiner, 2009). Interpreting data from the readiness measure is fairly straightforward. After asking teachers or teams the three questions, the coach calculates the mean score and translates that score to a percentage. When working with teams, each person's readiness score is calculated. Then, a group average is calculated, and that score represents the team's readiness. Research suggests that teachers or teams scoring around 70%–80% or higher are ready to make a change (Office of Special Education Programs Technical Assistance Center on Positive Behavior Interventions Supports, 2015; Tyre et al., 2012).

STRATEGIES FOR ASSISTING TEACHERS AND TEAMS THROUGH CHANGE

Creating and Using a Communication Protocol

Creating and using a communication protocol about the change effort is the first strategy for building readiness (Damschroder & Lowery, 2013; National Implementation Research Network, n.d.). The purpose of the protocol is twofold. First, the protocol creates a pathway of ongoing communication about the change effort among the educators involved in that effort. Such protocols are useful because change efforts rarely afford people directly involved the opportunity to talk with each other about what is and is not working. Therefore, the protocol spells out how and when the educators involved will talk to each other about the change effort. The protocol also spells out what information will be shared—the challenges and the successes. With such a clearly defined communication process established, information about the change (why the change is needed, who is affected, the goals of the change effort, how people will be supported along the implementation process) is shared with teachers or teams and with leaders working in the system.

The second purpose of the protocol is to ensure there is a structured, collaborative process in place for *continually improving* the implementation effort. Thus, after determining the critical information about the change, involved parties (e.g., teachers or teams and the formal leaders of the school and district) meet on a reoccurring basis (e.g., monthly) and share concrete information with each other about what is and is not working with the change effort. Solutions are identified for barriers, and the people involved in removing the barriers agree how and when the solutions will be enacted.

Increased readiness among those not ready to make a change is a typical byproduct of a communication protocol (National Center for Systemic Improvement, 2017). Why?

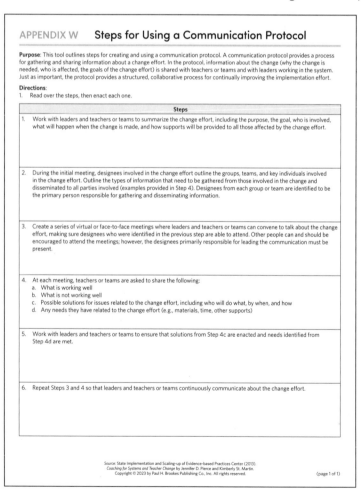

APPENDIX W   Steps for Using a Communication Protocol

Purpose: This tool outlines steps for creating and using a communication protocol. A communication protocol provides a process for gathering and sharing information about a change effort. In the protocol, information about the change (why the change is needed, who is affected, the goals of the change effort) is shared with teachers or teams and with leaders working in the system. Just as important, the protocol provides a structured, collaborative process for continually improving the implementation effort.

Directions:
1. Read over the steps, then enact each one.

Steps
1. Work with leaders and teachers or teams to summarize the change effort, including the purpose, the goal, who is involved, what will happen when the change is made, and how supports will be provided to all those affected by the change effort.
2. During the initial meeting, designees involved in the change effort outline the groups, teams, and key individuals involved in the change effort. Outline the types of information that need to be gathered from those involved in the change and disseminated to all parties involved (examples provided in Step 4). Designees from each group or team are identified to be the primary person responsible for gathering and disseminating information.
3. Create a series of virtual or face-to-face meetings where leaders and teachers or teams can convene to talk about the change effort, making sure designees who were identified in the previous step are able to attend. Other people can and should be encouraged to attend the meetings; however, the designees primarily responsible for leading the communication must be present.
4. At each meeting, teachers or teams are asked to share the following: a. What is working well b. What is not working well c. Possible solutions for issues related to the change effort, including who will do what, by when, and how d. Any needs they have related to the change effort (e.g., materials, time, other supports)
5. Work with leaders and teachers or teams to ensure that solutions from Step 4c are enacted and needs identified from Step 4d are met.
6. Repeat Steps 3 and 4 so that leaders and teachers or teams continuously communicate about the change effort.

Figure 7.2   Steps for Using a Communication Protocol. (*Source:* State Implementation and Scaling-up of Evidence-based Practices, 2013.) (*Note:* Blank versions of this form are available in Appendix W and to download.)

So often implementation efforts happen as if in a vacuum: Someone determines a change is needed, the change is brought to the school, and educators are expected to adapt to the quick quickly and with little involvement. Creating and using the communication protocol embeds a *structured, collaborative process* into the school for continually improving the implementation effort. Use the steps listed in Figure 7.2 to enact a communication protocol (blank versions of this form are available in Appendix W and to download).

Networking Teachers and Teams

Creating a community or network of teachers and teams who are going through a similar change with each other is the second strategy for boosting readiness (Damschroder & Lowery, 2013). Teachers and teams who are connected to others going through similar change efforts can talk about the change landscape, learn how others are dealing with the situation, and gain insight into what may (or may not) transpire when the change is made. Furthermore, these networked communities allow coaches to talk about what is and is not working with the change effort, therein helping teachers or teams more deeply understand and plan for the pending change. It also provides the coaches opportunities to work with people who have experienced the change in a productive way (Bryk et al., 2015).

Networking teachers and teams does not need to be a formal endeavor. Nevertheless, some coaches may find it helpful to apply some tips to structure networking opportunities so they are focused on building readiness for the change effort. Read through the tips shown in Figure 7.3 (blank versions of this form are available in Appendix X and to download). They highlight the point that the purpose of the networked community is not to make the experience punitive to teachers and teams by making them to feel they are being forced to get on board with the change effort. Instead, the purpose is to offer teachers and teams with ongoing opportunities to connect with others experiencing similar professional experiences. Increased readiness to make a change is an eventual byproduct of participating in such a networked group (Bryk et al., 2015).

Motivational Interviewing

Motivational interviewing, which is a series of questions that coaches can ask teachers or teams to increase readiness for change, is the final strategy for building readiness. Motivational interviewing is a well-documented, research-based technique used by therapists to support clients through a change (Hettema et al., 2005; Miller & Rollnick, 2012). The questions reflect the idea that helping teachers or teams build readiness is not about convincing them to do something but is about asking them the right questions so that they can better understand their own reactions to

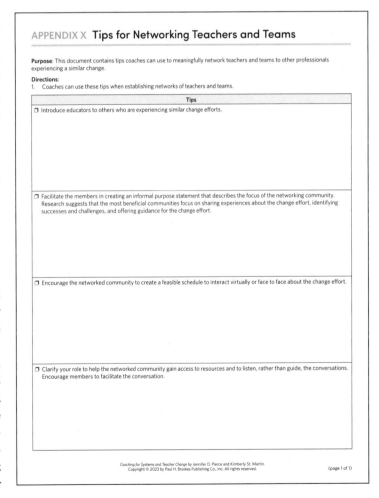

APPENDIX X Tips for Networking Teachers and Teams

Purpose: This document contains tips coaches can use to meaningfully network teachers and teams to other professionals experiencing a similar change.

Directions:
1. Coaches can use these tips when establishing networks of teachers and teams.

Tips
❑ Introduce educators to others who are experiencing similar change efforts.
❑ Facilitate the members in creating an informal purpose statement that describes the focus of the networking community. Research suggests that the most beneficial communities focus on sharing experiences about the change effort, identifying successes and challenges, and offering guidance for the change effort.
❑ Encourage the networked community to create a feasible schedule to interact virtually or face to face about the change effort.
❑ Clarify your role to help the networked community gain access to resources and to listen, rather than guide, the conversations. Encourage members to facilitate the conversation.

Figure 7.3 Tips for Networking Teachers and Teams. (*Note:* Blank versions of this form are available in Appendix X and to download.)

APPENDIX Y   Motivational Interviewing for Change

Purpose: This resource contains critical questions that coaches can ask teachers and teams when coachees are not ready to make a change. The overarching purpose of motivational interviewing is to offer teachers and teams opportunities for thinking and talking about their own insights about the change effort.

Directions:
1. Familiarize yourself with the questions below.
2. Ask coachees the questions when discussing the change area. The four questions can be asked during a pre- or postmeeting. Coaches may verbally ask the teacher or team to respond to each question and take notes on their responses.
3. It is often helpful to provide the prompts to the teacher or team so that they can reflect on them on their own and then share their responses with you.

Questions
1. Why would you want to make this change?
2. How might you go about it in order to succeed?
3. What are the three best reasons for you to do it?
4. How important is it for you to make this change, and why?

Figure 7.4   Motivational Interviewing for Change. (*Source:* Miller & Rollnick, 2012.) (*Note:* Blank versions of this form are available in Appendix Y and to download.)

the change effort (see Figure 7.4; blank versions of this form are available in Appendix Y and to download).

The four questions can be asked during a pre- or postmeeting. Coaches may verbally ask the teacher or team to respond to each question and take notes on their responses. It is often helpful to provide the prompts to the teacher or team so that they can reflect on them on their own and then share their responses with you. With that said, the overarching purpose of motivational interviewing is to offer teachers and teams opportunities for thinking and talking about their own insights about the change effort. As with every other readiness strategy, the objective is not to convince or relentlessly chip away at ambivalence but to help teachers and teams gain self-insight about the change. Deeper insight can unlock reasons for reluctance to change (Miller & Rollnick, 2012).

READINESS DO'S AND DON'TS

Now that coaches have several strategies in mind for supporting teachers and teams through change, we offer a few words of advice. First, do expect to work with teachers and teams reluctant to change. Change is often the only constant in education (as in other fields), and it is unrealistic for coaches to expect that teachers and teams will always be ready for every change that comes their way.

Related to this point, do view those who are not quite ready to make a change in a positive light and with empathy. Building readiness to change will be difficult—potentially even downright impossible— if teachers or teams perceive that their coach is frustrated with a lack of readiness (Grafmann et al., 2019).

Third, do use alliance strategies (see Chapter 5) when teachers or teams are not quite ready to make a change. As you may have noticed as you read this chapter, many of the things that you do to build alliance with teachers or teams can also help build readiness. For example, talking with teachers or teams, building a strong rapport with them, and centering all coaching activities on their needs can set the stage for high levels of readiness.

Finally, do not enact readiness strategies with the expectation that teachers and teams will reach readiness at the same time or at the same pace. Every teacher or team comes to a given situation with their own experiences, views, needs, and expectations. As a result, some teachers or teams will reach readiness sooner than others. Some will need very little support, and some will need extensive support. Therefore, apply readiness strategies with the understanding that the pathway to readiness is an individual one—teachers and teams will vary when they reach readiness and how long it will take to get to that point.

SUMMARY

Coaches can conduct recursive cycles of effective coaching practices; however, teachers or teams may still not be ready to make some changes to their practice. A lack of readiness for change does not have to stop coaches in their tracks. Although alliance strategies go a long way toward building readiness, sometimes coaches need additional tools in their toolboxes for guiding teachers and teams through change. This chapter aimed to show coaches how to measure readiness and build readiness when reluctance reigns. Apply these strategies to help teachers and teams reach readiness for making changes to their practice.

RESOURCES

Read over the tool shown in Figure 7.5 (blank versions of this form are available in Appendix Z and to download). If it looks familiar, you are correct. It is a tool we presented in Chapter 3. This version can be used to connect what you learned from this chapter to your role as a coach. You may find it helpful to share and discuss your responses with a partner.

APPENDIX Z — Connecting the Dots: Readiness for Change, the Coaching Framework, and Your Coaching Role

Purpose: Use this tool to reflect on what you learned about readiness to change and this text's coaching framework.

Directions:
1. Complete each section of this tool so that you can integrate what you learned from Chapter 7 to your coaching practice.
2. You may find it helpful to discuss your responses with a partner and record any notes.

	Questions
Phase 1: The premeeting	1. What did you learn about readiness that could be applied to Phase 1 of the coaching cycle? 2. What questions remain for you? 3. What are you most excited to apply to your coaching practice? What do you think will be tricky? Why?
Phase 2: In the classroom or at the team meeting	1. What did you learn about readiness that could be applied to Phase 2 of the coaching cycle? 2. What questions remain for you? 3. What are you most excited to apply to your coaching practice? What do you think will be tricky? Why?
Phase 3: The postmeeting	1. What did you learn about readiness that could be applied to Phase 3 of the coaching cycle? 2. What questions remain for you? 3. What are you most excited to apply to your coaching practice? What do you think will be tricky? Why?

Figure 7.5 Connecting the Dots: Readiness for Change, the Coaching Framework, and Your Coaching Role. (*Note:* Blank versions of this form are available in Appendix Z and to download.)

REFERENCES

Anello, V., Weist, M., Eber, L., Barrett, S., Cashman, J., Rosser, M., & Bazyk, S. (2017). Readiness for positive behavioral interventions and supports and school mental health interconnection: Preliminary development of a stakeholder survey. *Journal of Emotional and Behavioral Disorders, 25*(2), 82–95.

Bryk, A. S., Gomez, L. M., Grunow, A., & LeMahieu, P. G. (2015). *Learning to improve: How America's schools can get better at getting better.* Harvard Education Press.

Choi, M., & Ruona, W. E. (2011). Individual readiness for organizational change and its implications for human resource and organization development. *Human Resource Development Review, 10*(1), 46–73.

Damschroder, L. J., & Lowery, J. C. (2013). Evaluation of a large-scale weight management program using the consolidated framework for implementation research (CFIR). *Implementation Science, 8*(1), 1–17.

Grafmann, C., Schölmerich, F., & Schermuly, C. C. (2019). The relationship between working alliance and client outcomes in coaching: A meta-analysis. *Human Relations.* https://doi.org/10.1177/0018726718819725

Hall, G. E., & Hord, S. M. (2015). *Implementing change: Patterns, principles, and potholes* (4th ed.). Pearson.

Helfrich, C. D., Blevins, D., Smith, J. L., Kelly, P. A., Hogan, T. P., Hagedorn, H., Dubbert, P. M., & Sales, A. E. (2011). Predicting implementation from organizational readiness for change: A study protocol. *Implementation Science, 6*(1), 1–12.

Hettema, J., Steele, J., & Miller, W. R. (2005). Motivational interviewing. *Annual Review Clinical Psychology, 1,* 91–111.

Holt, D. T., Armenakis, A. A., Feild, H. S., & Harris, S. G. (2007). Readiness for organizational change: The systematic development of a scale. *Journal of Applied Behavioral Science, 43*(2), 232–255.

Kondakci, Y., Beycioglu, K., Sincar, M., & Ugurlu, C. T. (2017). Readiness of teachers for change in schools. *International Journal of Leadership in Education, 20*(2), 176–197.

Lewis, C. (2015). What is improvement science? Do we need it in education? *Educational Researcher, 44*(1), 54–61.

McCamish, C., Reynolds, H., Algozzine, B., & Cusumano, D. (2015). An investigation of characteristics, practices, and leadership styles of PBIS coaches. *Journal of Applied Educational and Policy Research, 1*(1), 15–34.

Miller, W. R., & Rollnick, S. (2012). *Motivational interviewing: Helping people change.* Guilford Press.

National Implementation Research Network. (n.d.). *Practice: Policy feedback loops.* https://nirn.fpg.unc.edu/module-5/topic-3-practice-policy-feedback-loops

Office of Special Education Programs Technical Assistance Center on Positive Behavioral Interventions and Supports. (2015, October). *Positive behavioral interventions and supports (PBIS) implementation blueprint: Part 1: Foundations and supporting information.* University of Oregon.

Shea, C. M., Jacobs, S. R., Esserman, D. A., Bruce, K., & Weiner, B. J. (2014). Organizational readiness for implementing change: A psychometric assessment of a new measure. *Implementation Science, 9*(1), 1–15.

State Implementation and Scaling-up of Evidence-based Practices Center. (2013). *Communication protocols.* The National Implementation Research Network (NIRN). https://nirn.fpg.unc.edu/sites/nirn.fpg.unc.edu/files/resources/AI%20Hub%20Handout%208%20Communication%20Protocols%20.pdf

Turri, M. G., Mercer, S. H., McIntosh, K., Nese, R. N., Strickland-Cohen, M. K., & Hoselton, R. (2016). Examining barriers to sustained implementation of school-wide prevention practices. *Assessment for Effective Intervention, 42*(1), 6–17.

Tyre, A. D., Feuerborn, L., Beisse, K., & McCready, C. (2012). Creating readiness for response to intervention: An evaluation of readiness assessment tools. *Contemporary School Psychology, 16*(1), 103–114.

Weiner, B. J. (2009). A theory of organizational readiness for change. *Implementation Science, 4*(1), 1–9.

Zimmerman, J. (2006). Why some teachers resist change and what principals can do about it. *NASSP Bulletin, 90*(3), 238–249.

Let's Make It Real

Applying Coaching to Critical Issues

8

KEY QUESTIONS

1. How can you translate the content and resources from the book to the scenarios presented in this chapter?

2. How can you use the scenarios in this chapter to enhance your work as a coach?

CHAPTER TAKE-AWAYS

1. Numerous challenges are expected to arise while coaching, and these challenges are not necessarily unique to one specific coaching situation (e.g., team coaching at the pre-K level, coaching teachers at the middle or high school level).

2. Coaches apply the core knowledge they have developed and use various tools to meaningfully respond to these challenges.

3. Coaches reflect on and work through case studies on their own and with colleagues to continually enhance their interactions with teachers and teams.

CHAPTER OVERVIEW

Chapter 8 returns to the everyday challenges coaches can expect to experience in their work with teachers and teams. We originally presented these challenges in Chapter 2. In this chapter, you will read about some of those challenges hypothetical coaches have experienced when serving as a teacher, system, or hybrid coach in pre-K, elementary, and secondary settings. Therefore, each scenario centers on a specific challenge and contains a series of questions that prompt you to integrate resources and information from prior chapters into your responses.

Although you may find it particularly helpful to work through the case examples that align to your specific coaching role, we suggest you read and address all the scenarios. After all, the challenges that arise in these case examples are not necessarily unique to one type of coaching situation. A challenge from the scenario on coaching a team at the pre-K level may resonate with coaches working with elementary school teachers, or vice versa.

It may be helpful to work through these case examples with one or more coaching colleagues. Nearly every question embedded within the scenarios could be answered in various ways; there are rarely definitive, clear-cut responses to the prompts. Some coaches may respond differently from you, and your conversations with colleagues about these scenarios can only enrich your knowledge and skill as a coach.

Finally, we recommend that you revisit these case examples on multiple occasions as you plan, conduct, and reflect on the sessions you conduct with teachers or teams. Why? You may find that your responses to the prompts change over time as you refine your knowledge and skill as a coach. Coaches who understand such nuances of coaching will be well prepared to improve teaching, team practice, the systemwide implementation of educational programs, and student outcomes.

COACHING PRE-K TEACHERS

Sheila's Dilemma: Coaching Teachers in the Use of New Curriculum Materials

Sheila, a veteran coach, was assigned to provide support to the 10 pre-K teachers in a district working to implement a new early literacy curriculum. These teachers had never gained access to coaching supports before. The program director met with Sheila to discuss the teachers' lack of readiness to implement a more comprehensive and evidence-based early literacy program. The program director shared some of the comments that had been made by the teachers when the curriculum adoption process was underway. Statements such as, "The children are not developmentally ready to learn how to identify letters, some sounds, print concepts, and engage in basic levels of phonological awareness." The district's data suggest the community would benefit from a more literacy-rich early childhood program because the children are coming to pre-K with very limited vocabulary. The expectation is the teachers will begin using the new materials at the start of the school year, which is only 10 weeks away.

Sheila is preparing for the initial meetings with the teachers. She is worried about how receptive people will be to coaching and to the prospect of learning how to use the new curriculum resources.

Imagine that you are Sheila and respond to the following questions.

- Given the lack of readiness for coaching and using a new curriculum resource, how should Sheila structure her coaching premeetings with the teachers?

- What resources and tools from this book could be helpful in this situation? Why?

- How can Sheila support teachers who are not be interested in being coached? What should she do first? Come up with a sequence of events that outlines in detail some of Sheila's crucial next steps and why she needs to take these actions.

- How can Sheila help the teachers thrive and improve under the current conditions?

COACHING ELEMENTARY TEACHERS

Ahren's Dilemma: Coaching Teachers on Formal Improvement Plans

Ahren, a first-year coach, was recently assigned to provide support to a small group of teachers working at several elementary schools in three different districts. At his supervisor's suggestion, Ahren first met one to one with the principals of the schools so that he could introduce himself, learn more about the teachers on his caseload, and identify days and times he might visit the various schools.

Although Ahren was confident that these initial meetings had been productive, he was now concerned and even a bit overwhelmed. The main information he had gleaned about the teachers he was assigned to coach was all were on improvement plans due to poor performance evaluations. His coaching sessions were to be used to shape future evaluations of the teachers. Moreover, all the teachers were required to participate in coaching as a part of their improvement plans, although Ahren did not know yet if the teachers welcomed it. Despite the fact that Ahren was a new coach, he knew that requiring coaching could add some challenges to his work with the teachers. He wondered, "How can I make the most of this coaching situation?"

Imagine that you are Ahren and respond to the following questions.

- Pretend that Ahren wants to enlist support from the school principals and his supervisor to help him be productive as a coach. What might he do? Why?

- What resources and tools from this book could be helpful in this situation? Why?

- How can Ahren support teachers who may or may not be interested in being coached? What should he do first? Come up with a sequence of events that outlines in detail some of Ahren's crucial next steps and why he needs to take these actions.

- How can Ahren help the teachers thrive and improve under the current conditions?

COACHING MIDDLE OR HIGH SCHOOL TEACHERS

Lydia's Dilemma: Customizing Support for Many Teachers Using Face-to-Face and Virtual Coaching

Lydia is a math coach for 50 teachers at 10 different middle schools in a large urban school district. She formerly taught math at one of the district middle schools and just started her second year as a coach.

Lydia and the other coaches in her district were recently given the option to coach in person and virtually. Lydia welcomed this change for a few reasons. One potential benefit was technology might help her conduct more regular sessions with the many teachers on her caseload. In addition, she was virtually coached when she was a teacher and had a positive experience. Yet, Lydia was not sure how teachers would respond to the use of virtual coaching or if she even knew how to translate face-to-face coaching practices to the virtual world. Some questions running through her mind included, "Were teachers excited about the idea of virtual coaching, or would they prefer to maintain face-to-face coaching supports?" Most concerning was how she could use technology to ensure that her coaching was customized for each teacher based on their unique needs and goals. Offering customized coaching was one specific piece of feedback teachers had given her on the anonymous survey she had given teachers last spring. At the time, she planned to observe, model, provide performance feedback, and use alliance strategies face to face, not virtually.

As Lydia considered her upcoming coaching role, she wondered, "How can I best offer coaching to the teachers I will support?"

Imagine that you are Lydia and respond to the following questions.

- What do you think Lydia should do to customize her coaching practice so that the needs of the 50 teachers are met while still using effective coaching practices? Develop a sequence of events that outlines some of Lydia's crucial next steps and why she needs to take these actions.

- Make a list of the pros and cons of virtual coaching and face-to-face coaching given Lydia's coaching situation. If you were Lydia, how would you balance the use of these two coaching formats? Why?

- What resources and tools from this book would you use if you were Lydia? Why?

COACHING PRE-K IMPLEMENTATION TEAMS

Dominique's Challenge: Supporting an Implementation Team in a Program Without a Strategic Approach to Coaching

Dominique is a pre-K coach who was just hired to support the implementation leadership team at a local pre-K program. It is the first time that the team has participated in coaching, and Dominique is eager to make a positive first impression and productively kick off the work. During Dominique's first visit to the school, however, she found that the individual team members she met with and even the program director had little idea what her role might look like and why coaching might be an important addition to the school's program. Even more concerning was that some of the team members voiced a disinterest in coaching, saying that the overall implementation effort was a passing fancy of the program director that would not last more than a couple of years at the most. One team member even shared that she did not think it was wise to allocate so many resources toward coaching because the funding required for the role was not likely to last long term. As Dominique left her first day on the job, the program director reminded Dominique that she was counting on her to quickly fix the issues at the school.

Imagine that you are Dominique and respond to the following questions.

- The pre-K program where Dominique works does not have a plan for enacting coaching. What do you think Dominique should do to enact coaching more strategically? Come up with a sequence of events that fleshes out some of Dominique's crucial next steps and why these actions are necessary.

- How should Dominique work with the program director to make coaching a more coherent and meaningful part of the pre-K program? Why?

- What resources and tools from this book would you use if you were Dominique? Why?

COACHING ELEMENTARY IMPLEMENTATION TEAMS

Jarron's Challenge: Moving Beyond the Role of Trainer to Enact Systems Coaching

Jarron is a system coach for the MTSS implementation teams at six elementary schools in his local region. He, along with the other MTSS coaches in his area, are expected to provide professional learning workshops on MTSS and work directly in schools with implementation teams. Other than that general guidance, Jarron has a great deal of flexibility in his work with schools. In the past, he followed the lead of many of his MTSS system coach colleagues by primarily providing professional learning workshops to the team members. He also occasionally attended implementation team meetings at his assigned schools, but he found that it was extremely challenging to fit in school visits because he was conducting so many workshops. Unfortunately, when he did visit schools, he saw that most of the teams struggled to skillfully facilitate their team meetings (e.g., some teams did not follow a structured agenda, some tried to do so but were missing key parts such as a data review) and key features of MTSS did not appear to be in place (e.g., students were gaining access to intervention on an irregular basis, screening and progress monitoring were not in place across all grade levels). He knew that the teams were trying to implement what he had trained them to do, but a lot of what was covered in the professional learning workshops seemed to be getting lost in the day-to-day work at the schools.

After realizing that many of the implementation teams were struggling to enact MTSS, Jarron decided to switch gears in how he used his time. He immediately scheduled reoccurring visits to each school so that he could begin actively coaching the implementation teams. Although satisfied with this first step, he knew he had some important next steps. For example, he wanted to

- Communicate his role switch (from being primarily a trainer to providing more coaching) so that he did not catch teams off guard

- Identify the needs of the different teams beyond what he had already observed so that he could target his coaching to those specific needs

- Plan his upcoming coaching cycles

   Imagine that you are Jarron and respond to the following questions.

- In addition to the action steps previously listed, what else do you think Jarron should do to begin coaching more frequently? Come up with a sequence of events that fleshes out some of Jarron's crucial next steps and why he needs to take these actions.

- What resources and tools from this book would you use if you were Jarron? Why?

COACHING MIDDLE OR HIGH SCHOOL IMPLEMENTATION TEAMS

Coaching Teams New to Leading an Implementation Effort

Yung recently began coaching a high school team. This team is responsible for leading the school's newly adopted practices to improve on-time graduation rates. After attending several workshops focused on on-time graduation practices, Yung and the team are quite optimistic about potential at the school. After the professional learning workshops, Yung and the team members developed a comprehensive plan to implement the practices, shared that plan with the rest of the staff members, and adjusted it based on staff feedback. Then, Yung and the team kicked off implementation by conducting a workshop for the entire school staff on the practices. They also shared the school's new graduation rate improvement goals and conducted a community introductory session so that parents, students, and other interested community members could learn about the school's efforts.

Despite the positive energy of the team and their productive first steps, a growing number of teachers at the school seem to be quickly overwhelmed with using the practices. Within a few weeks, some teachers asked for more workshops and for implementation team members to help them in their classes. Other teachers directly approached Yung and asked her to help them enact the practices in their classrooms. A few teachers even decided that they were not going to implement at all, telling Yung that the kick off was happening too quickly and without enough guidance from the team.

As Yung and the implementation team members reflect on the current state of implementation, they realize that they need to adjust their course of action. The team was beginning to lose their enthusiasm for the graduation efforts and was becoming frustrated with the reactions from some of the teachers.

In her own reflections, Yung realized that she needed to take some immediate actions to help the team and the rest of the school staff through the difficult experience of implementing the new practices.

Imagine that you are Yung and respond to the following questions:

- What do you think Yung should do to support the team and the school staff through this phase of implementation? Come up with a sequence of events that fleshes out some of Yung's crucial next steps and why she needs to take these actions.

- Reflect on the steps the team and Yung took to kick off implementation. If you were Yung, how would you have supported the leadership team through these activities? Why?

- What resources and tools from this book would you use if you were Yung? Why?

COACHING IN A HYBRID ROLE

Justine's Challenge: Balancing the Hybrid Role

Justine has been coaching teachers and the implementation team overseeing the use of PBIS in classroom settings for about 2 years. Up to this point, much of Justine's coaching support has focused on the individual teachers at the school in classroom PBIS. Focusing on coaching teachers allowed her to complete at least one coaching cycle for nearly every teacher at the school. As a result, nearly every staff member has become proficient in the fundamentals of PBIS.

With a new school year just about to start, Justine would now like to ensure the implementation team receives more systems coaching in their efforts to apply PBIS to nonclassroom settings. This is not to say that in prior years she did not support the leadership team. On the contrary, Justine always made sure to attend the weekly team meetings, provide suggestions when the team asked for guidance, and offer insight into some of the main successes and challenges teachers had with classroom PBIS implementation. But Justine did not view her support to the team as coaching because she had not completed coaching cycles with the team in the same way she had with teachers.

As Justine thought about the upcoming school year, she realized that she needed to create a feasible and productive schedule of coaching teachers and the PBIS team. She also realized that she was ready to make the shift but wondered if the team was ready to participate in coaching cycles. This would be a different type of support for the team, and she was not sure if they would react positively to such a change. She also wondered how teachers would react to receiving fewer coaching cycles per week. Would they view a reduction in coaching cycles in a positive light? What would she do if the teachers started to lose ground in their PBIS implementation? She asked herself, "How can I juggle the demands of teacher coaching and team coaching?"

Imagine that you are Justine and respond to the following prompts:

- What do you think Justine should do to balance the work of coaching teachers and teams? Come up with a sequence of events that fleshes out some of Justine's crucial next steps and why she needs to take these actions.

- How would you talk with the members of the implementation team and the individual teachers about the upcoming changes to coaching? Why?

- How would you enlist the help of the building principal and your supervisor (if they are two different people) to balance the role of the hybrid coach? Why?

- What resources and tools from this book would you use if you were Justine? Why?

SUMMARY

The challenges of coaching are many, but do not let that fact get in the way of your success as a coach. Review the content and tools discussed in this book when you are faced with a pressing coaching challenge. Talk with some colleagues, and reflect on what you know. We firmly believe that any coach can break through sticky coaching situations by applying what they have learned. Although we have provided you with some hypothetical scenarios to practice applying what you have learned, you will inevitably have your real scenarios. You can use the questions we embedded within each scenario to help you reflect on your best next step, regardless of the nature of the challenge. Your coaching practice with teachers and teams can only enhance their implementation efforts.

III

Implementing an Effective Coaching Framework

Coaching That Sticks

Resources and Tools

1. Why does strategic coaching implementation matter?

2. What are the critical factors of implementation, and how do they relate to the five components of every system?

3. How can coaches use the tools contained within this chapter to take a strategic approach to implementing coaching?

1. Coaching that is enacted strategically is more likely to lead to the end goals of improving teacher and team practice, systems, and student outcomes.

2. Research has uncovered many critical factors that play a make-it-or-break-it role in implementation. These factors are "housed" in the five components of the system—human, fiscal, and material resources; policies/regulations; and processes/procedures. If you want to embed coaching into a pre-K/school program so that it can achieve its goals, then you will need to address these system components and their related critical implementation factors at one time or another.

3. Coaches can use the tools contained within this chapter to help them address many of the factors of implementation, therein taking a strategic approach to implementing coaching.

CHAPTER OVERVIEW

Chapter 9 turns to a frequently ignored idea that the strategic implementation of coaching matters. If this sentence seems like it is too heady and not readily applicable to your day-to-day work with teachers and teams, then consider that it is likely that you have already encountered this idea that the implementation of coaching matters. For example, if you have ever 1) wondered what a pre-K/school leader's vision for coaching was, 2) been hired as a coach without being fully prepared to support teachers or teams, or 3) found out that there is not a way to measure your coaching practice so that you can continuously develop, then you have experienced how issues related to implementation interact with the daily work of coaches.

To be clear, implementation issues are not insignificant. The bottom line is that when implementation barriers are present and go unaddressed, coaching is less likely to reach its goals (e.g., improved teacher or team practice, systems outcomes, student outcomes) (Pierce et al., 2019). In turn, the value of coaching becomes questioned, with pre-K programs and schools more likely to abandon it as the chosen approach for supporting teachers and teams (Kraft et al., 2018) in favor of another form of professional learning (e.g., professional learning communities) with the hopes that the same implementation barriers will not arise.

Sadly, such hopes tend to be futile because unresolved implementation barriers do not go away because one innovation (coaching) is swapped out for another innovation (professional learning communities). Thus, how coaching is enacted—how we hire and support coaches, how we measure coaching practice and use the data for continuous improvement, and how leaders communicate the vision for coaching—all influence the degree to which coaching can reach its goals of improving teacher and team practice, systems, and student outcomes.

With the premise that the implementation of coaching matters as the foundation of the chapter, we begin with a brief explanation of some implementation basics, including why the implementation of any innovation (e.g., coaching) is so difficult and what the most critical factors of implementation are. We then discuss what you need to know about making adjustments to these critical factors, and how the factors connect to the components of systems (i.e., human, material, and fiscal resources; policies and procedures; processes and procedures) discussed in Chapter 4.

The second section of the chapter focuses on what you and your colleagues can do to take a strategic approach to implementing coaching. We offer several resources, all of which can be used with a variety of educators (e.g., principals) as road maps for taking a systematic approach to implementing coaching. The idea behind these resources is that coaches need tools when the activity at hand is to ensure a research-informed coaching framework is sustainable in the pre-K/school program and achieves its intended goals (see the text box).

Research Informed Coaching Framework: The Innovation to Implement

The information in this chapter assumes the coaching framework being implemented is informed by research. It would be unwise (not to mention a potential waste of resources) to implement a coaching framework that was not research informed. Chapters 2, 3, 5, and 6 include information about the most effective, powerful practices coaches can use with teachers and teams. Use the information from those chapters to ensure that you implement coaching practices with a documented track record of success.

IMPLEMENTATION BASICS

The Science of Implementation

Let's start off with a difficult truth: Implementing anything for the long term is hard (Damschroder et al., 2009; Fixsen et al., 2005). In fact, implementation is now considered a science (Eccles & Mittman, 2006), highlighting that the processes involved with implementation can be so puzzling that they warrant formal examination and study. You can even find numerous lay-person books, journals, and web sites dedicated to the science of implementation (see the text box).

What Is the Difference? Improvement Science and Implementation Science

If you dig into implementation science research, then you may encounter other terms that relate to the idea of rooting innovations into systems to improve adult and child outcomes, especially the term *improvement science*. What is the difference between implementation science and improvement science? Although an entire line of literature exists on the commonalities and distinctions between these two bodies of research (see Bauer et al., 2015; Djulbegovic, 2014; Koczwara et al., 2018), we offer the following suggestions. When the objective is to learn how to enact coaching (e.g., considering the stages of implementation to enact the coaching process) in one or more pre-K/school programs, then gain access to the implementation science literature while still keeping improvement science concepts in mind. When the objective is to improve the use of coaching once it is enacted, then draw on the improvement science literature, especially because its key strategy is the use of the Plan-Do-Study-Act cycle, while still circling back to implementation science concepts.

Implementation Frameworks and the Critical Factors of Implementation

Hundreds of worldwide implementation researchers tend to agree on what factors shape successful implementation (Nilsen, 2015), with several researchers organizing the factors into frameworks or research articles to depict the nature of implementation. Implementers in real settings can familiarize themselves with these frameworks and corresponding articles to better understand what comes into play when seeking to productively root coaching into a system. See Table 9.1 for a listing of prominent implementation frameworks or articles that capture these factors of implementation.

Implementation research has also started to uncover which factors play a make-it-or-break-it role in implementation (e.g., leadership support) (Damschroder et al., 2009; Fixsen et al., 2005; Nilsen, 2015). Look again at Table 9.1. The table presents these make-it-or-break-it factors and for simplicity excludes other factors that may play a more ancillary role in successful implementation. Note that much of this research aligns with what is known about implementing a coaching model (i.e., leadership support for coaching is crucial for rooting it into the system) (Aarons & Sommerfeld, 2012). The take-away here? Even when implementation research is applied to things that fall outside of coaching, we can still glean insights into what is critical to have in place when implementing coaching.

Table 9.1. Select implementation frameworks and research that distill the critical factors of implementation

Implementation framework or key research article	Critical factors of implementation
Consolidated Framework of Implementation Research (CFIR) **Field: Health services** This framework delineates numerous factors and subfactors of implementation and presents those variables into a framework. Several studies and scholarly articles have been conducted on the framework. There is also a web site dedicated to the framework, which contains information on the CFIR constructs, measures, and research articles and guides for designing an evaluation using the framework (https://cfirguide.org). **i-Promoting Action on Research Implementation in Health Services (PARIHS)** **Field: Health services** The PARIHS is an early implementation heuristic that captured the idea that the implementation context was central to innovation uptake. The framework has been revised at least once based on research findings, with the latest version referred to as *i-PARIHS*. Authors now refer to the i-PARIHS as an implementation framework and distill key ideas into a formula that communicates the nature of successful implementation. **Diffusion of Innovations** **Field: Social sciences** Considered to be an early seminal text on the spread and uptake of ideas and innovations, this early text presents the idea that uptake is a social process. Many, if not all, of the factors central to successful uptake presented in this text have been integrated into other implementation frameworks. **National Implementation Research Network (NIRN) Active Implementation (AI) Frameworks** **Field: Education and child services** NIRN presents five frameworks that guide users through a structured process of implementing innovations. Each framework represents a critical factor of implementation and has been extensively discussed and applied in research, gray literature, and practice. In addition to the online resources offered to NIRN (https://nirn.fpg.unc.edu/ai-hub) and the 2005 research synthesis on implementation, the frameworks are central to the work of educators in the technical assistance center called *SISEP*, or the State Implementation and Scaling up of Evidence-Based Practices (https://sisep.fpg.unc.edu). **Factors Affecting Implementation** **Field: Psychology and community settings** This literature review and meta-analysis presents two key ideas: 1) The level of implementation affects the outcomes of the innovation and 2) the numerous factors that shape the quality of the implementation effort. This article is widely cited in implementation research, highlighting critical ideas about the nature of implementation, including near perfect implementation quality is not necessarily desirable or necessary to see desired innovation outcomes; there are different aspects of implementation (e.g., fidelity, sustainability, program reach); different ways to measure implementation (e.g., direct observation, self-report); and adaptations to innovations during the implementation process are expected due to contextual variations of implementation sites and users.	• Leader support • Champions for coaching • Coach competency • Coach access to development opportunities • Coach self-efficacy • Staff beliefs about coaching • Adaptability of coaching framework to local contextual needs while retaining the most effective coaching practices • Easy-to-use information about coaching that distills current and seminal research • Core competencies of coaching exist • Communication of the vision, purpose, and goals of coaching • Alignment of coaching with the pre-K/school program's overall values and goals • How coaching fits within existing workflows and processes (e.g., how and when teachers or teams will gain access to coaching) • Beliefs about the importance of coaching, especially in relation to other professional learning opportunities • Process for measuring coach practice • Use of Plan-Do-Study-Act cycles to improve coaching practice • Process for linking coaching to changes in teacher or team practice, the system, and student outcomes • Costs of coaching (e.g., long-term investment requirements, return on investment) • Available resources for coaching (e.g., time, funding, personnel) • Phases of implementing coaching (engaging, planning for coaching, initial implementation, continuous improvement of implementation)

112

Diffusion of Innovations in Service Organizations: Systematic Review and Recommendations

Field: Psychology, sociology, and organizational theory

This literature review, also considered to be a seminal article, presents salient factors of implementation. Authors present an implementation framework, which, in turn, undergirds numerous other implementation frameworks created by different researchers.

Institute for Healthcare Improvement (IHI)

Field: Health Care

The IHI model employs Plan-Do-Study-Act cycles to help systems improve, therein improving outcomes of clients served by the system. PDSA cycles are one of the most important tools in the IHI model. Teams working in the system identify a goal, or aim, establish how to measure progress toward the aim (e.g., system changes) and client outcomes (e.g., improved client satisfaction), select one or more strategies for progressing toward the aim, and then test the change idea. After the change idea is tested, the team uses the data they collected to determine if progress was made toward the goal. If progress was achieved, then the team stays the course of their work. If progress was not achieved, then the team identifies a different change idea to test. The process of testing change ideas, analyzing data, and making adjustments to change ideas is continual so the system and client outcomes continually improve.

IHI offers numerous in-depth face-to-face and virtual learning opportunities, including institutes. The IHI web site also contains many tools, research reports, publications, videos, case studies, and improvement stories (http://www.ihi.org /resources/Pages/HowtoImprove/default.aspx).

Carnegie Model of Improvement Science

Field: Education

The Carnegie Model of Improvement Science is based off the work of the IHI. Thus, the Carnegie Model of Improvement Science is a process for conducting Plan-Do-Study-Act cycles to improve educational systems and the outcomes of students served within those systems. In addition, it relies on teams called *network improvement communities* to continually employ the PDSA cycles to make gains, therein improving the system and outcomes of students in the system. The Carnegie Model of Improvement has a web site (https://www.carnegiefoundation.org/our-ideas/), annual conference, numerous books, and publicly available literature, all of which can be used to help users employ the model.

Adjusting the Critical Implementation Factors

Now that you are familiar with critical factors of implementation, consider this question: How can you adjust implementation factors to optimize the use of coaching? More specifically, if leadership support is crucial for sustaining the implementation of coaching, then how can you best gain support and retain it, particularly when there is high leadership turnover? What is the most productive way leaders can communicate their support for coaching? How often do leaders need to communicate that support? Researchers are still working to answer such questions, which means implementers using innovations in real settings may simply have to work through such questions in their own contexts while accepting ambiguity still exists.

Making Meaningful Adjustments to Critical Implementation Factors

A word of caution is necessary at this juncture. Willy-nilly manipulation or occasional adjustment to factors of implementation is not enough to fully embed coaching into the pre-K/school program. Instead, there will be the need to regularly attend to critical factors of implementation so that adjustments do not upend coaching (Braithwaite et al., 2018; Pierce et al., 2019). See the text box.

The Downside of One-and-Done Adjustments

Imagine you have worked as a coach at a school for the past 5 years. In your first 3 years of your role, you worked hard to ensure that staff were on board with coaching. Over time, teachers, paraprofessionals, Ms. Simonsen the principal, and even parents and caregivers championed coaching. Although there were some bumps in the road, those first 3 years at the school were quite successful. The teachers were enthusiastically engaged with coaching, and it became a part of the school's culture. Most important, coachees showed improvements in their teaching, and students in their classrooms showed steady gains.

Unfortunately, after 3 years, several of these coaching champions moved to other schools. Even Ms. Simonsen was replaced by a new principal, Mr. Hines. Although you shared with Mr. Hines that coaching had been widely supported, he seemed somewhat disinterested in your work with teachers. Just as concerning, Mr. Hines reduced the time teachers could participate in coaching. He even created new and more cumbersome procedures for teachers to participate in coaching—requiring teachers get his permission first before meeting with you. It became a struggle to coach teachers, and you worried that the dwindling number of coaching champions bode poorly for your continued work at the school.

As you reflected on your 5 years at the school, you acknowledged that you no longer felt confident that coaching was helping teachers improve their practice. Your other reflection was that support from coaching champions was not permanent but temporary. You have experienced the downside of one-and-done adjustments of an implementation factor.

Adjusting the Critical Implementation Factors Within Each System Component

Now look at Figure 9.1. Note that every critical factor of implementation is housed *within* a system component. (Chapter 4 outlines the following system components: human, material

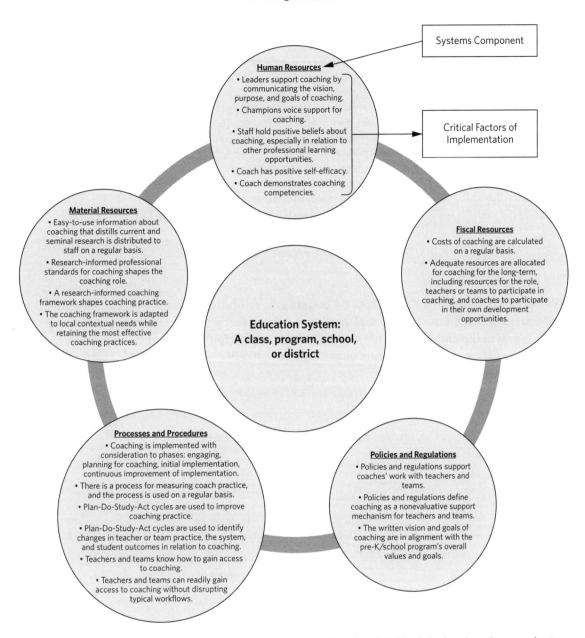

Figure 9.1. Critical factors of implementation within system components. (*Note:* For each circle, bold underlined words are the names of systems components, and bulleted items within each circle are the critical factors of implementation.)

and fiscal resources; processes and procedures; and policies and regulations.) For example, the critical factors of leader support and coaching champions are housed within the human resources system component. Within the material resources system component, you will find several implementation factors, including research-informed coaching core competencies.

You might be wondering why it is important that each critical factor of implementation is housed within one system component. If you want to root coaching into pre-K/school programs so it can achieve its intended goals, then you will need to address system components and their related critical implementation factors at one time or another. In short, we must

Table 9.2. Matrix of resources

System component	Applicable resources
Human resources	Implementation Checklist (Chapter 9, Figure 9.2)
	Coaching Competencies (Chapter 9, Table 9.3)
Fiscal resources	Implementation Checklist (Chapter 9, Figure 9.2)
	Calculating the Fiscal Costs of Coaching (Chapter 9, Figure 9.3)
Material resources	Implementation Checklist (Chapter 9, Figure 9.2)
	Coaching Competencies (Chapter 9, Table 9.3)
	Coaching Framework (Chapters 3, 5, and 6; various figures)
Policies/regulations	Implementation Checklist (Chapter 9, Figure 9.2)
Processes/procedures	Implementation Checklist (Chapter 9, Figure 9.2)
	Plan-Do-Study Act cycles (Chapter 4, Figure 4.3; Chapter 4, Figure 4.7)
	Measures of Coach Practice (Self-Assessment: Chapter 9, Figure 9.5; Direct Observation of Coaching Fidelity: Chapter 9, "Measuring Fidelity of Coaching Practice With a Direct Observation Approach" text box)

look at the big picture of the factors by constantly attending to each system component on a reoccurring basis and the critical implementation factors that fall within those components. If you make one-time adjustments to implementation factors *or* focus just on the factors in one system component, then coaching is not likely to become a permanent part of the system.

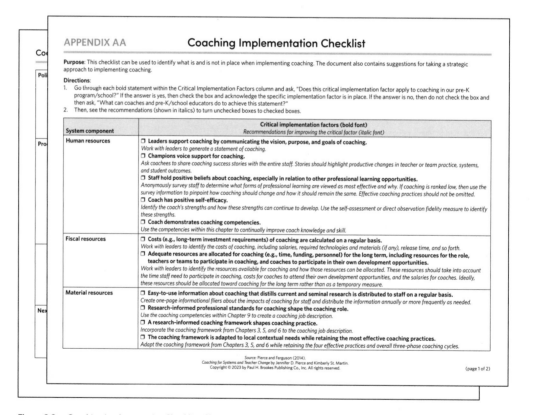

Figure 9.2. Coaching Implementation Checklist. (*Source:* Pierce & Ferguson, 2014.) (*Note:* Blank versions of this form are available in Appendix AA and to download.)

RESOURCES FOR TAKING A STRATEGIC APPROACH TO IMPLEMENTING COACHING

With the fundamental information that was just presented in mind, this next section includes several resources coaches can use to strategically implement coaching. Most of these resources are within in this chapter; however, as you will see in Table 9.2, one or two are included in prior chapters. We have included at least one tool per system component so coaches (and leaders) have access to a comprehensive set of resources and ideas for strategically implementing coaching.

Implementation Checklist

Figure 9.2 translates the critical factors of implementation into a checklist that can be used at least one or twice a year to reflect on the strategic implementation of coaching (blank versions of this form are available in Appendix AA and to download). As you look over this figure, notice that every driving factor is listed as a statement in bold. Each statement reflects what needs to be in place so that the factor facilitates successful implementation of coaching. Go through these statements one by one and ask yourself, "Does this apply to coaching in this pre-K program and/or school?" If the answer is yes, then acknowledge that the specific factor facilitates the successful implementation of coaching. If the answer is no, then ask, "What can coaches and pre-K/school colleagues do to achieve this statement?" The ideas listed in italics under each factor offer ways to translate an unchecked box to a checked box. Finally, use the bottom part of the checklist to record action steps so unchecked boxes become checked boxes.

APPENDIX AB

Calculating the Fiscal Costs of Coaching

Purpose: Use this tool to calculate the costs of coaching. You may need to enlist the help of your school principal or someone from the district finance department.

Directions:
1. Use the top portion of this form to calculate the cost of teacher coaching.
2. Use the bottom half of the form to calculate the costs of coaching teams.

Coaching Teachers			
Column A: Costs	*Column B: Salary cost per session*	*Column C: Number of sessions annually*	*Column D: Cost per row (for each row, multiply Column B times Column C)*
Coach			
Teacher			
Materials			
Other staff (e.g., substitute)			
To calculate the total cost of teacher coaching, add each number from Column D. Record that cost here:			

Coaching Teams			
Column A: Costs	*Column B: Salary cost per session*	*Column C: Number of sessions annually*	*Column D: Cost per row (for each row, multiply Column B times Column C)*
Coach			
Team members (include costs for all team members)			
Leader			
Materials			
Other staff (e.g., include total costs for substitutes for each team member, if required)			
To calculate the total cost of team coaching, add each number from Column D. Record that cost here:			

(page 1 of 1)

Figure 9.3. Calculating the Fiscal Costs of Coaching. (*Note:* Blank versions of this form are available in Appendix AB and to download.)

Identifying the Fiscal Costs of Coaching

The next resource is from the cost-effectiveness research (Knight, 2012; Levin & Belfield, 2015) and allows coaches and other key colleagues (pre-K/school program leaders) to answer the following question: What are the financial costs of teacher or team coaching? Answering this question is important because some implementers may mistakenly view coaching as a short-term professional learning investment (Kraft & Hogan, 2018). Avoid this implementation error by calculating the costs of coaching so that resources can be allocated to coaching for the long-term. (see Figure 9.3; blank versions of this form are available in Appendix AB and to download).

Understanding the Impact of Coaching

Figure 9.4 offers a way to understand the relationship between coaching and changes to teacher or team practice, systems, and student outcomes (blank versions of this form are available in Appendix AC and to download). We do not mean to imply that causal links can be identified among coaching and improvements to coachee practice, systems, and student outcomes. Yet, some conclusions can and should be drawn. The essential questions to ask follow:

- What are the qualitative and quantitative changes from coaching on teacher practice, team practice, systems, and student outcomes?
- What are the big take-aways from coaching?
- What is working well, and what needs to change?
- What can we do to improve the impact of coaching on teacher or team practice, systems, and student outcomes?

When using Figure 9.4, note that the far-left column allows the user to record information about coaching practice so that other changes are identified in relation to what transpired with coaching. After all, the practices coaches use influence what teachers and teams do. As with the prior tool, the top form can be used with teacher coaching, whereas the bottom portion can be used with team coaching.

APPENDIX AC

**Connecting the Dots:
Changes in Teacher/Team Practice,
System Outcomes, and Student Outcomes**

Purpose: Use this tool to identify the impact of coaching.

Directions:
1. Use the top portion of this form to identify the impact of teacher coaching.
2. Use the bottom half of the form to identify the impact of team coaching.

Teacher Coaching			
Data on coaching	*Changes to teacher practice*	*Changes to student outcomes*	*Implications*
Use of coaching framework:			
Information from coaching self-assessment:			
Information from direct observation measure of coach practice:			

Team Coaching				
Data on coaching	*Changes to team practice*	*Changes to system outcomes*	*Changes to student outcomes*	*Implications*
Use of coaching framework:				
Information from coaching self-assessment:				
Information from direct observation measure of coach practice:				

(page 1 of 1)

Figure 9.4. Connecting the Dots: Changes in Teacher/Team Practice, System Outcomes, and Student Outcomes. (*Note:* Blank versions of this form are available in Appendix AC and to download.)

Core Coaching Competencies

One of the critical factors of implementation is that coaches hold the necessary knowledge and skills they need to work effectively with teachers and teams. Therefore, it should not be surprising that the overarching purpose of the prior chapters was to build your coaching competency. We have created a set of competencies for coaching because competency can be one of those make-it-or-break-it factors in the successful implementation of coaching. These competencies can be used by coaches to help themselves and others better understand what coaches need to know and do when working with teachers and teams (see Table 9.3).

Measuring Coach Fidelity of Practice

This next set of tools offers two ways coaches can measure their practice. We first point to a suite of materials that uses a direct observation approach to measuring coaching fidelity. With this approach, the coach will recruit another person (referred to as the *observer*) to observe coach practice, collect data on coach practice, and share that data with the coach.

Table 9.3. Core competencies for coaching teachers and teams

Competency area	Coaching teachers	Coaching teams
Research on coaching	**KNOW:** Coaches hold a foundational knowledge of coaching research, including seminal studies and current examinations. **APPLY:** Coaches integrate their knowledge of research to ensure support for teachers is current and based on research evidence.	**KNOW:** Coaches hold a foundational knowledge of coaching research, including seminal studies and current examinations. **APPLY:** Coaches integrate their knowledge of research to ensure support for teams is current and based on research evidence.
Historical perspective on coaching	**KNOW:** Coaches understand how past and current research and policy have influenced coaching to become a prominent part of the professional learning landscape. **APPLY:** Coaches use research and policy to inform their work with teachers.	**KNOW:** Coaches understand how past and current research and policy have influenced coaching to become a prominent part of the professional learning landscape. **APPLY:** Coaches use research and policy to inform their work with teams.
Goals of coaching	**KNOW:** Coaches understand the broad goals of coaching teachers: to improve teacher practice and student outcomes. **APPLY:** Coaches communicate the goals of coaching teachers and conduct coaching cycles to help teachers achieve these goals.	**KNOW:** Coaches understand the broad goals of coaching to teams: to improve team practice, system outcomes, and student outcomes. **APPLY:** Coaches communicate the goals of coaching teachers and conduct coaching cycles to help teams achieve these goals.
Systems	**KNOW:** Coaches understand what a system is, the components of every system, why systems matter when coaching teachers, and key systems change principles. **APPLY:** Coaches apply systems change principles to help teachers improve practice.	**KNOW:** Coaches understand what a system is, the components of every system, why systems matter when coaching teams, and key systems change principles. **APPLY:** Coaches apply systems change principles to help teams improve practice.
Critical implementation factors	**KNOW:** Coaches understand what the critical factors of implementation are and why these factors matter when coaching teachers. **APPLY:** Coaches identify which implementation factors are and are not in place and apply recommendation to improve the implementation of coaching.	**KNOW:** Coaches understand what the critical factors of implementation are and why these factors matter when coaching teams. **APPLY:** Coaches identify which implementation factors are and are not in place and apply recommendation to improve the implementation of coaching.
Planning, conducting, and reflecting on coaching cycles	**KNOW:** Coaches understand that supporting teachers requires time for planning, conducting, and reflecting on coaching cycles. **APPLY:** Coaches plan, conduct, and reflect on coaching cycles with teachers.	**KNOW:** Coaches understand that supporting teams requires time for planning, conducting, and reflecting on coaching cycles. **APPLY:** Coaches plan, conduct, and reflect on coaching cycles with teams.
Three-phase coaching cycles using effective coaching practices	**KNOW:** Coaches understand that coaching occurs in a three-phase recursive cycle. In the first phase of the cycle, coaches conduct a premeeting with the teacher. In the second phase, coaches work directly in the classroom with the teacher. In the third phase, coaches conduct a postmeeting with the teacher. **APPLY:** Coaches use coaching practices in the three-phase cycle. In the first phase of the cycle, coaches use alliance strategies to build rapport (e.g., setting a goal, coming to consensus about how to engage with each other). In the second phase of the cycle, coaches observe the teacher to gain information about implementation, may model if the teacher struggles with implementation, and continue to use alliance strategies to further develop trust between educators and coaches. In the third phase, coaches provide performance feedback (e.g., sharing checklists or charts). Alliance strategies are also used in this phase of the cycle to ensure that the bond between the teacher and coach is continually developed.	**KNOW:** Coaches understand that coaching occurs in a three-phase recursive cycle. In the first phase of the cycle, coaches conduct a premeeting with the team. In the second phase, coaches work directly with the team at the team meeting. In the third phase, coaches conduct a postmeeting with the team. **APPLY:** Coaches use coaching practices in the three-phase cycle. In the first phase of the cycle, coaches use alliance strategies to build rapport (e.g., setting a goal, coming to consensus about how to engage with each other). In the second phase of the cycle, coaches observe the team to gain information about implementation, may model if the team struggles with implementation, and continue to use alliance strategies to further develop trust between educators and coaches. In the third phase, coaches provide performance feedback (e.g., sharing checklists or charts). Alliance strategies are also used in this phase of the cycle to ensure that the bond between the team and coach is continually developed.

(continued)

Table 9.3. *(continued)*

Competency area	Coaching teachers	Coaching teams
Using alliance strategies	**KNOW:** Coaches understand what alliance is, why it is important, the three factors that shape alliance, and strategies for building and maintaining alliance with teachers. **APPLY:** Coaches flexibly use alliance strategies with teachers during the three-phase coaching cycle.	**KNOW:** Coaches understand what alliance is, why it is important, the three factors that shape alliance, and strategies for building and maintaining alliance with teams. **APPLY:** Coaches flexibly use alliance strategies with teams during the three-phase coaching cycle.
Observing	**KNOW:** Coaches know what observing is, when to observe, and how to observe teachers. **APPLY:** Coaches conduct observations to understand teacher practice and collect data on that practice.	**KNOW:** Coaches know what observing is, when to observe, and how to observe teams. **APPLY:** Coaches conduct observations to understand team practice and collect data on that practice.
Modeling	**KNOW:** Coaches understand what modeling is, when to model, and how to model for teachers. **APPLY:** Coaches use an "I do, we do, you do" modeling procedure when teachers do not know how to correctly implement a practice or activity in their setting.	**KNOW:** Coaches understand what modeling is, when to model, and how to model for teams. **APPLY:** Coaches use an "I do, we do, you do" modeling procedure when teams do not know how to correctly implement a practice or activity in their setting.
Providing performance feedback	**KNOW:** Coaches know what providing performance feedback is, when to provide feedback, and how to do so. **APPLY:** Coaches provide performance feedback in a variety of ways (e.g., structured notes, verbal statements, visual summaries such as graphs, charts, or tallies) that is specific, timely, positive, and corrective if necessary, so that teachers can reflect on practice and advance in their goal areas.	**KNOW:** Coaches know what providing performance feedback is, when to provide feedback, and how to do so. **APPLY:** Coaches provide performance feedback in a variety of ways (e.g., structured notes, verbal statements, visual summaries such as graphs, charts, or tallies) that is specific, timely, positive, and corrective if necessary, so that teams can reflect on practice and advance in their goal areas.
Building readiness for change	**KNOW:** Coaches understand that readiness influences teachers' decisions to make changes to their practice and strategies for building teacher readiness to change. **APPLY:** Coaches use readiness strategies when teachers are reluctant to make a change.	**KNOW:** Coaches understand that readiness influences teams' decisions to make changes to their practice and strategies for building team readiness to change. **APPLY:** Coaches use readiness strategies when teams are reluctant to make a change.

APPENDIX AD   **Coaching Self-Assessment**

Purpose: Use this tool to assess your coaching practice.

Directions:
1. Think about each area of coaching.
2. Check the boxes that accurately describe how you coach.
3. Rate yourself in each area on the 5 point scale. Provide a rationale for each score and note how you can improve in the future.
4. Calculate your global score by adding up each rating, dividing the total by 3, and multiplying that decimal number by 100 to get a percentage.
5. Record your overall percentage here: _____.
6. Complete this assessment at least annually and compare your results over time.

Area	What did I do?	What is my score? 1 = Low 5 = High Why? What will I do to continuously improve?
Using coaching practices	☐ I used alliance strategies with teachers or teams. ☐ I observed teachers or teams and collected data on teacher or team practice. ☐ I modeled for teachers or teams (if needed). ☐ I provided performance feedback that was specific, timely, affirmative (positive), and corrective (if warranted). • What went well? • What could go better?	Circle your score: 1 2 3 4 5 Why? What will I do to improve?
Planning and reflecting on coaching cycles	☐ I planned coaching cycles. ☐ I reflected on coaching cycles. *Note:* The next section self-assesses the act of conducting the coaching cycle. • What went well? • What could go better?	Circle your score: 1 2 3 4 5 Why? What will I do to improve?
Using the three-phase coaching cycle	☐ I held a premeeting with teacher or team. ☐ I worked with the teacher in the classroom or I worked with the team in the team meeting. ☐ I held a postmeeting with the teacher or team. • What went well? • What could go better?	Circle your score: 1 2 3 4 5 Why? What will I do to improve?

Coaching for Systems and Teacher Change by Jennifer D. Pierce and Kimberly St. Martin.
Copyright © 2023 by Paul H. Brookes Publishing Co., Inc. All rights reserved.   (page 1 of 1)

Figure 9.5.   Coaching Self-Assessment. (*Note:* Blank versions of this form are available in Appendix AD and to download.)

Coaches use the data to identify coaching "glows" (strengths) and "grows" (areas for improvement). These direct observation materials were created for the National Center for Systemic Improvement (NCSI), an Office of Special Education Programs (OSEP) funded technical assistance center focused on improving outcomes among students with disabilities (see the text box).

Measuring Fidelity of Coaching Practice With a Direct Observation Approach

The materials listed are used to measure coaching practice and were created for the National Center for Systemic Improvement (NCSI), an Office of Special Education Programs (OSEP) funded technical assistance center focused on improving outcomes among students with disabilities. The suite of materials consists of the following:

- A blank worksheet of the fidelity measurement tool, which can be completed when measuring coaching practice (https://www.air.org/sites/default/files/NCSI_Coaching-Fidelity-Tool_Worksheet-508.pdf)
- A scoring rubric, which offers directions on how an observer will score coaching practice (https://www.air.org/sites/default/files/NCSI_Coaching-Fidelity-Tool_Rubric-508.pdf)
- A completed sample of the tool to offer a hypothetical illustration of how the fidelity tool can be completed by an observer (https://ncsi-library.wested.org/resources/189)
- A brief online module that explains why measuring the fidelity of coaching practice is important and how to use the aforementioned tools (https://ncsi-library.wested.org/resources/247)

It is important to know that direct observation fidelity tools are not intended to be a quick way of measuring coaching practice. However, the process is important to use because it yields highly detailed and specific information about the coach's use of alliance strategies, observations, modeling, and performance feedback. We suggest coaches think of the direct observation process as akin to what a coach does when observing teachers or teams and providing performance feedback for the sake of improving practice. The difference here is that the coach is now being observed and is the recipient of the feedback.

Nevertheless, there will be times when the coach wants to measure their practice. Therefore, we have created a self-assessment that can be used as a quick way for a coach to understand their coaching practice. Coaches can alternate between using the NCSI tools with the self-assessment, particularly when access to an observer poses a challenge or when coaches simply want quicker and/or additional insight into their own practice (see Figure 9.5; blank versions of this form are available in Appendix AD and to download).

SUMMARY

Congratulations! You are likely better prepared to strategically enact coaching! As this chapter shows, the work will not be easy; nor will it be a solo undertaking that falls on the shoulders of the coach. It will be a long-term process that requires partnerships between coaches and leaders. It may also require a potential shift in thinking—moving away from the idea that coaching is a quick-fix solution to improving teacher or team practices, system outcomes, and student outcomes. The work can be worth it if the idea is to make coaching stick within your pre-K/school so that it achieves its intended outcomes. If you use the information and resources in this chapter to take an intentional approach to enact coaching, then the promise of coaching can be a reality.

REFERENCES

Aarons, G. A., & Sommerfeld, D. H. (2012). Leadership, innovation climate, and attitudes toward evidence-based practice during a statewide implementation. *Journal of the American Academy of Child and Adolescent Psychiatry, 51*(4), 423–431.

Bauer, M. S., Damschroder, L., Hagedorn, H., Smith, J., & Kilbourne, A. M. (2015). An introduction to implementation science for the non-specialist. *BMC Psychology, 3*(1), Article 32.

Braithwaite, J., Churruca, K., Long, J. C., Ellis, L. A., & Herkes, J. (2018). When complexity science meets implementation science: A theoretical and empirical analysis of systems change. *BMC Medicine, 16*(1), Article 63.

Bryk, A. S., Gomez, L. M., Grunow, A., & LeMahieu, P. G. (2015). *Learning to improve: How America's schools can get better at getting better.* Harvard Education Press.

Damschroder, L. J., Aron, D. C., Keith, R. E., Kirsh, S. R., Alexander, J. A., & Lowery, J. C. (2009). Fostering implementation of health services research findings into practice: A consolidated framework for advancing implementation science. *Implementation Science, 4*(1), 1–15.

Djulbegovic, B. (2014). A framework to bridge the gaps between evidence-based medicine, health outcomes, and improvement and implementation science. *Journal of Oncology Practice, 10*(3), 200–202.

Durlak, J. A., & DuPre, E. P. (2008). Implementation matters: A review of research on the influence of implementation on program outcomes and the factors affecting implementation. *American Journal of Community Psychology, 41,*327–350.

Eccles, M. P., & Mittman, B. S. (2006). Welcome to implementation science. *Implementation Science, 1,* Article 1.

Fixsen, D., Naoom, S., Blase, K., Friedman, R., & Wallace, F. (2005). *Implementation research: A synthesis of the literature.* University of South Florida, Louis de la Parte Florida Mental Health Institute, National Implementation Research Network.

Greenhalgh, T., Robert, G., Macfarlane, F., Bate, P., & Kyriakidou, O. (2004). Diffusion of innovations in service organizations: systematic review and recommendations. *The Milbank Quarterly, 82*(4), 581–629.

Harvey, G., & Kitson, A. (2015). PARIHS revisited: From heuristic to integrated framework for the successful implementation of knowledge into practice. *Implementation Science, 11*(1), Article 33

Kitson, A., Harvey, G., & McCormack, B. (1998). Enabling the implementation of evidence based practice: a conceptual framework. *BMJ Quality & Safety, 7*(3), 149–158

Knight, D. S. (2012). Assessing the cost of instructional coaching. *Journal of Education Finance, 38*(1), 52–80.

Koczwara, B., Stover, A. M., Davies, L., Davis, M. M., Fleisher, L., Ramanadhan, S., Schroeck, F. R., Zullig, L. L., Chambers, D. A., & Proctor, E. (2018). Harnessing the synergy between improvement science and implementation science in cancer: A call to action. *Journal of Oncology Practice, 14*(6), 335–349.

Kraft, M. A., & Blazar, D. (2018). Taking teacher coaching to scale. *Education Next, 18*(4).68–74.

Kraft. M. A., Blazar, D., & Hogan, D. (2018). The effect of teacher coaching on instruction and achievement: A meta-analysis of the causal evidence. *Review of Educational Research, 88*(4), 547–588.

Levin, H. M., & Belfield, C. (2015). Guiding the development and use of cost-effectiveness analysis in education. *Journal of Research on Educational Effectiveness, 8*(3), 400–418.

Lewis, C. (2015). What is improvement science? Do we need it in education? *Educational Researcher, 44*(1), 54–61.

Nilsen, P. (2015). Making sense of implementation theories, models and frameworks. *Implementation Science, 10*(1), Article 53.

Pierce, J. (2018). *Measuring the fidelity of coaching.* https://ncsi-library.wested.org/resources/247

Pierce, J. D., & Ferguson, A. (2014). *Implementation guide for effective coaching of teachers.* National Center for Systemic Improvement. https://ncsi-library.wested.org/resources/60

Pierce, J., & Ferguson, A. (2015a). *Effective coaching of teachers: Fidelity tool completed sample.* https://ncsi-library.wested.org/resources/189

Pierce, J., & Ferguson, A. (2015b). *Effective coaching of teachers: Fidelity tool worksheet.* https://ncsi-library.wested.org/resources/58

Pierce, J., & Ferguson, A. (2019). *Effective coaching of teachers: Fidelity tool rubric.* https://ncsi-library.wested.org/resources/59

Pierce, J. D., Irby, M., & Weber-Mayrer, M. (2019, December). How coaching takes root. *The Learning Professional, 40*(6). 20–23.

Rogers, E. M. (2010). *Diffusion of innovations.* Simon & Schuster.

Rycroft-Malone, J. (2010). Promoting action on research implementation in health services (PARIHS). In J. Rycroft-Malone & T. Bucknall (Eds.), *Models and frameworks for implementing evidence-based practice: Linking evidence to action* (pp. 109–136). Wiley-Blackwell.

Appendices

CHAPTER 6

CHAPTER 7

CHAPTER 9

Reflecting on My Coaching Role

Purpose: Use this reflection sheet to think about your past, present, and future coaching role and how educational research and policy has shaped that role.

Directions:
1. Read Chapter 1.
2. Respond to the following questions about your coaching role.
3. If you can, share your reflections with a partner.

Questions	Reflections
1. What type of role did you have in the past? In what ways has educational research and policy shaped the nature of that role?	
2. How would you describe your current coaching role? Are you a coach for individual teachers, a team or systems coach, or a hybrid coach? In what ways has educational research and policy shaped the nature of that role?	
3. Think about your future coaching role. In what ways might educational research and policy shape the nature of that role?	

Categorizing Common Activities for Coaching Teachers

Directions:
1. Read over the list of common coaching activities.
2. Place each activity into either Column A or Column B. Items placed in Column A are most closely linked by experimental research to improved teaching and student outcomes. Items placed in Column B are not linked to improved teaching and learning, less likely to lead to improved teaching and student outcomes than the items listed in Column A, or not yet confirmed by research as linked to improved teaching and learning.
3. Check your answers against the answer key.

Common activities for coaching teachers
• Teaching students
• Assessing students
• Planning and conducting professional learning workshops for teachers on content directly related to areas of student needs
• Conducting coaching sessions for teachers that consist of ongoing cycles of observing, modeling, providing performance feedback, and using alliance strategies
• Planning and reflecting on coaching sessions
• Meeting with administrators
• Leading grade-level/content area teacher meetings
• Coordinating curricular programs (e.g., ordering and distributing materials, setting assessment and/or instructional schedules)
• Writing proposals to obtain additional funding for instructional programming
• Advocating for improvements in school policies and/or procedures
• Coplanning with teachers
• Substituting for teachers or other personnel
• Supervising students during noninstructional time (e.g., recess, lunch, passing periods)

Column A: Activities most closely linked with improved teacher practice and student outcomes.	Column B: Activities not linked or less closely linked with improved teacher practice and student outcomes than those listed in Column A. Activities without sufficient research indicating links to improved teaching and learning.

Planning for Enacting Critical Coaching Activities

Purpose: Use this form to determine how you will allocate your time toward the most critical coaching activities. You may also use the tool to communicate to other educators (e.g., principals, teachers) why you will allocate the bulk of your time toward specific activities and less time toward other activities.

Directions:

1. Complete the template either on your own or with colleagues.

Coaching activities linked to improved teaching and student learning	Percentage of time/day
Observing, modeling, providing performance feedback to teachers	
Other common coaching activities	
•	
•	
•	
•	
•	
•	
•	
•	
•	
•	
•	
•	
•	
•	
•	

Blank Template for Categorizing Systems Coaching Activities

Directions:

1. Read over the list of common systems coaching activities.
2. Place each task into either Column A or Column B. Items placed in Column A are hypothesized to lead to improved team practice, systems, and student outcomes. Items placed in Column B are not linked to these improvements, less likely to lead to these improvements than the activities listed in Column A, or not yet confirmed by research as linked to improved teaching and learning.
3. Check your answers against the answer key.

Common Systems Coaching Activities:
• Planning and conducting professional learning workshops for teachers and/or the leadership team
• Conducting coaching sessions for the leadership team that consist of ongoing cycles of observing, modeling, providing performance feedback, and using alliance strategies
• Planning and reflecting on coaching sessions
• Meeting with administrators outside of the leadership team meeting
• Facilitating leadership team meetings
• Coordinating materials (e.g., ordering and distributing materials, setting assessment and/or instructional schedules)
• Writing proposals to obtain additional funding for the ongoing implementation of the selected innovation
• Advocating for improvements in school policies and/or procedures related to the innovation

Column A: Activities hypothesized to be linked to improved team practice and systems (e.g., use of Plan-Do-Study-Act cycles, staff buy-in for implementation effort, improved student outcomes).	**Column B:** Activities hypothesized as unlinked or less closely linked with improved team practice and systems than those listed in Column A. Activities with insufficient research indicating links to improved team practice and systems.

Coaching for Systems and Teacher Change by Jennifer D. Pierce and Kimberly St. Martin.

Discussion Guide:
Preparing for Coaching Barriers

Purpose: Use this tool to prepare for coaching barriers.

Directions:
1. On your own, read over the following graphic that displays common coaching barriers.
2. Read the prompts in the section called "Reflections and Reactions." Write down your reactions to these questions in that same section.
3. Share your reactions with a partner.
4. With a partner, discuss the prompts in the section called "Partner Reflection and Next Steps."
5. Record the action steps you plan to take next.

Coaching Challenges:

Minimal opportunities for formal preparation	Overly broad scope of work	Lack of leadership support	Lack of professional standards and competencies	Nonsystematic implementation of coaching

Reflections and Reactions:

- Think about your coaching role as a systems, teacher, or hybrid coach; the goals of that role; and the challenges previously presented.
  - Which of these challenges do you think are most likely to affect your work with teachers or teams?
  - Why?
  - How might these challenges get in the way of coaching reaching its goals?

- What are your experiences with these barriers? What happened as a result of these barriers, and how did you move past these issues?

Partner Reflection and Next Steps:

- Compare your reflections with your partner's reflections. What were the similarities? What were the differences?

- Identify some important action steps to take, when you will take these actions, and who you may need to communicate with to reduce coaching barriers. Use the Action Planning Tool to ensure you follow through with critical next steps.

Action Planning Tool

Purpose: Use this tool to identify what you will do to overcome coaching barriers. You may update this form as you read other chapters of this book.

Directions:

1. List the coaching barriers you currently face or may face.
2. In the next column, identify what action steps you may need to take to offset barriers. List who you need to communicate with to offset the challenge (e.g., principal, pre-K director).
3. In the third column, identify what happened when you took the actions steps.
4. List ideas for what you need to do next.
5. Use the final column to record any other information or comments.

Barrier	What do I need to do (action steps to take to offset barriers)? With whom do I need to communicate?	What happened?	What is next?	Other comments

Connecting the Dots: Research, the Coaching Framework, and Your Coaching Role

Purpose: Use this tool to reflect on what you learned about the four effective coaching practices used during the three-phase coaching cycle.

Directions:
1. Complete each section of this tool so that you can integrate what you learned from the chapter into your coaching practice.
2. You may find it helpful to discuss your responses with a partner and record any notes in the space provided.

Questions	
Phase 1: The premeeting	1. What did you learn about using coaching practices that could be applied to Phase 1 of the coaching cycle?
	2. What questions remain for you?
	3. What are you most excited to apply to your coaching practice? What do you think will be tricky? Why?
Phase 2: In the classroom or at the team meeting	1. What did you learn about using coaching practices that could be applied to Phase 2 of the coaching cycle?
	2. What questions remain for you?
	3. What are you most excited to apply to your coaching practice? What do you think will be tricky? Why?
Phase 3: The postmeeting	1. What did you learn about using coaching practices that could be applied to Phase 3 of the coaching cycle?
	2. What questions remain for you?
	3. What are you most excited to apply to your coaching practice? What do you think will be tricky? Why?

Understanding the System

Overview: This tool can be used to understand the strengths and weaknesses that are currently in place in the system. These strengths and weaknesses shape the degree to which system goals are attained. Coaches working with teachers or systems coaches may use this tool in sessions with coachees to pinpoint which system components are problematic and which are not.

Directions:

1. Think about the system goal. Write that goal here: _____
2. Read over each item contained within each column. Ask yourself, "Does this item reflect a strength or a weakness in the system?"
   a. What data will you use to determine if an item is a strength or weakness? List your data sources here: _____
3. Place a checkmark in the box indicating strengths of the system that are in place and support the goal previously listed.
4. Think about all the weaknesses of the system (unchecked boxes).
   a. Which weakness would you like to address first? _____ Why? _____
   b. How will addressing this system component support progress toward the goal?
5. Use the Plan-Do-Study-Act tool when you are ready to advance to the next step.

Component 1: Human resources	Component 2: Policies and regulations	Component 3: Procedures and processes	Component 4: Fiscal resources	Component 5: Material resources
☐ Staff believe the goal is important.	☐ District, school, and classroom policies affecting students and/or staff (e.g., attendance, discipline, teacher evaluation) support the goal.	☐ Staff recruitment and selection procedures align to the goal.	☐ Costs for the goal area are calculated on a regular (e.g., annual) basis.	☐ Evidence-based curricular and assessment materials in the goal area are reviewed and selected according to a coherent process.
☐ Staff believe they have the expertise to achieve the goal.		☐ Procedures exist for removing barriers to the goal.	☐ Adequate state, district, and school funding is allocated toward the goal.	☐ Evidence-based curricular and assessment materials in the goal area are available to all staff.
☐ Staff are receptive to working toward the goal.	☐ Federal regulations (e.g., IDEA) are used to support the goal.	☐ Procedures exist for securing and gaining access to professional learning and coaching related to the goal.		☐ Evidence-based curricular and assessment materials related to the goal area can be adapted to meet the range of student needs within the classroom/school.
☐ Staff are offered networking and learning opportunities with colleagues to learn about the goal and talk about what the goal means for their work at the school.	☐ The vision/mission of the school/classroom aligns to the goal area.	☐ There is a process for engaging in Plan-Do-Study-Act cycles to support progress in the goal area.		☐ Professional learning is provided to all staff to build their knowledge and implementation of the curriculum and assessment materials.
☐ The culture of the school accepts that there is a learning curve and embraces making mistakes when working toward the goal.				
☐ Leaders support the goal in their words and actions.				
☐ Other school/pre-K programs champion support of the goal in their words and actions.				

APPENDIX I   Conducting Plan-Do-Study-Act Cycles

Purpose: This tool offers a step-by-step approach for conducting Plan-Do-Study-Act cycles.

Directions:
1. Complete the tool titled Understanding the System. In that tool, you will identify system goals, challenges, and successes.
2. Use information from that tool to complete the steps of this tool.

Steps
1. Reorient yourself to the challenge in the system and the student improvement goal you are working toward. What is the goal? What component(s) of the system are you trying to improve? Why is improving this system component likely to improve student outcomes?
2. Plan: What will you do? By when? For how long? What data will you collect to determine what transpires during the "do" part of the cycle?
3. Do: Enact the plan. Be sure to collect data as you go.
4. Study: What do the data tell you happened? Come up with a clear statement of what happened in the system component after you enacted your plan. What changed? What stayed the same?
5. Act: What will you do next? For example, will you stay the course or make other changes? Ensure that data affirm the action you will take.
6. Return to Step 1 and repeat all steps until the weakness in the system component is resolved or clear progress is made toward the goal.

Reflection Tool:
What Do Systems-Level Principles Mean to Me?

Purpose: This tool can be used to reflect on the systems-level change principles presented in this chapter.

Directions:
1. Read over each principle.
2. Respond to the reflection questions listed under each principle. You may find it helpful to then discuss your responses with a partner.

Principle 1: Understanding the System

- Is the idea of seeing the system new for you, or are you familiar with the concept?

- Why do you think seeing the system is important to coaching?

- How would you explain the concept of a system to a teacher or team?

- What questions remain for you?

Principle 3: The Adaptive Side of Systems Change

- Recall a situation when you had to change practice. What did you have to do?

- How did you react? Did you embrace the change or find yourself struggling to embrace the change along the way? Why?

- Think about the degree to which you were granted voice (input to how the change transpired) and choice (whether to make the change).

- What specifically happened that resulted in you knowing you did/did not have voice and choice?

- How did you feel?

- What did you do?

- If you could experience this situation all over again, what would do you different? Why?

Recommendations for Using
Understanding the System With Teachers or Teams

Purpose: This tool presents recommendations for using the Understanding the System tool.

Directions:
1. Read over these recommendations before using the Understanding the System tool.
2. Use the recommendations to present Understanding the System to teachers or teams.

Recommendations
❏ Ensure you understand systems and then develop teacher/team expertise in systems.
❏ Develop an "elevator pitch" on systems components and why systems matter. This will force you to succinctly state system components and why they matter to teachers and teams. You may find it helpful to use Figure 4.1 with the teacher or team to clarify components of a system.
❏ Ask teachers or teams to come up with their own "elevator pitch" on systems components and why systems matter.
❏ If the tool is used with a team, then ensure that the team shares their responses with the entire staff, solicits feedback, and revises their thinking after completing Steps 1–5.
❏ If the tool is used with a teacher, then ask the teacher to share their responses with any other adults working in the classroom, obtain feedback from the other adults, and revise their thinking after completing Steps 1–5.
❏ Understanding the System can be completed more than once. In fact, teachers and teams may want to revisit the tool frequently to assess how strengths and weaknesses have evolved.

APPENDIX L Recommendations for Using Conducting Plan-Do-Study-Act Cycles With Teachers or Teams

Purpose: This tool presents recommendations for using the Conducting Plan-Do-Study-Act Cycles tool.

Directions:
1. Before using the Conducting Plan-Do-Study-Act Cycles tool, read over these recommendations.
2. Use the recommendations when working through Conducting Plan-Do-Study-Act Cycles with teachers or teams.

Recommendations
❏ The "plan" is a brief description of what the teacher or team will do to address the system weakness. The core of this plan contains the change idea, which articulates precisely what the teacher or team will do, by when, and how.
❏ Be sure that the team or teacher identifies the data that will be collected during the "do" part of the cycle. If the teacher or team does not collect data, then they will not know what transpired as a result of enacting the plan.
❏ Try to keep the plan and data collection process simple. Systems change is an ongoing process, and there is no need to try to change everything all at once. In fact, taking on too much or the most complicated systems change endeavor will likely make the work more difficult. Start with a small change that is likely to be successful and know that each change can build toward the next. Quick wins are important in systems-level changes.

Alliance Assessment

Purpose: This tool can be used to assess alliance between teachers or teams and coaches.

Directions:

1. This form can be completed by the coach as a self-assessment or may be anonymously completed by coaching recipients.
    *   If used by coaching recipients, then first rate the coach in each area of alliance (a 1 reflects a low score while a 5 reflects the highest score). Write down your reasons for each rating and what the coach might do to improve the rating. Return the form to the coach. The coach will use the information to enhance their work with teachers or teams.
    *   If used as a self-assessment, then rate yourself in each column. Use the information to continuously improve as a coach.

Factor of alliance		Rating	Reason for rating	Ideas for improving
Interpersonal skills	Communicating effectively	1 2 3 4 5		
	Building trust	1 2 3 4 5		
Collaboration	Setting goals	1 2 3 4 5		
	Creating a partnership	1 2 3 4 5		
	Setting parameters	1 2 3 4 5		
Expertise	Conveying expertise in content and context	1 2 3 4 5		
	Demonstrating expertise in coaching	1 2 3 4 5		

Coaching Compact

Purpose: This is a negotiated agreement that can be revised at any time based on the needs of the coach or coachee.

Directions:

1. Coach explains the three-phase cycle of coaching and shows teachers or teams the coaching framework of effective coaching practice to clarify what happens in each phase.
2. Coach briefly defines each effective coaching practice, explains the purpose of each practice, and clarifies what the teacher or team can expect when each practice is used. This information is summarized in Coaching Practices at a Glance (Table 6.1) and can be shown to teachers or teams.
3. Coach and teachers or teams discuss each section of the form and use the space provided to take notes as the professionals come to agreement about working together.

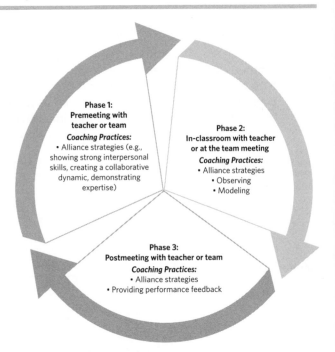

Phase 1:
Premeeting with teacher or team
Coaching Practices:
• Alliance strategies (e.g., showing strong interpersonal skills, creating a collaborative dynamic, demonstrating expertise)

Phase 2:
In-classroom with teacher or at the team meeting
Coaching Practices:
• Alliance strategies
• Observing
• Modeling

Phase 3:
Postmeeting with teacher or team
Coaching Practices:
• Alliance strategies
• Providing performance feedback

Section A. Coming to Agreement on the Use of Coaching Practices (*Note:* Coaches may refer to Chapter 6 for additional information on observing, modeling, and providing performance feedback.)	
Considerations for using coaching practices: What would the teacher or team like the coach to consider when enacting the coaching practices?	**Using alliance strategies:** • How often, if at all, will the coach administer the Alliance Assessment to the teacher or team? • What seemed to make past or current coaching sessions productive?
	Observing: • When coaching teachers: Where can the coach position themself to capture data on teacher practice and students? • When coaching teams: Where can the coach position themself to capture data on all team members during the meeting?
	Modeling: • What is needed for the teacher or team to successfully participate in modeling opportunities when using the "I do, we do, you do" procedure? For example, how will the teacher inform students of what to expect if the coach models?

Considerations for using coaching practices *(continued)*	**Providing performance feedback:** • How will the coach present data to the team (e.g., visually in graphs/charts, verbally, with written notes)? • How can the coach unobtrusively provide performance feedback during an observation? • How can a coach provide performance feedback to teachers or teams to facilitate self-reflection and support teacher or team progress?
Goal(s) of coaching: What will we accomplish?	The purpose of coaching is to assist the teacher or team with:
Considerations for confidentiality	What coaching data, if any, will be shared with others, including leaders responsible for evaluation?
Section B: Logistical Considerations	
Number of coaching cycles per week or month (including premeeting, observation, and postmeeting)	_____ times per _____ (i.e., week, month, quarter, year)
Time commitment per cycle (including premeeting, observation, and postmeeting)	Premeeting: Observation: Postmeeting:
Preferred day of week of coaching	Option 1: Option 2:
Other information	

APPENDIX O

Planning, Conducting, and Reflecting on Coaching Sessions: A Focus on Alliance

Directions:
1. Complete the Planning section of the tool prior to working with teachers or teams.
2. Then, complete the Conducting and Reflecting sections of the tool after working with teachers or teams.

Planning	Imagine that you are planning for upcoming coaching sessions with teachers or teams. 1. What will you do during the **premeeting phase** of the coaching cycle to build alliance? 2. What will you do when observing in the **classroom or at the team meeting** to build alliance? 3. What will you do during the **postmeeting phase** of the coaching cycle to build alliance?
Conducting	1. What did you do during the **premeeting** to build alliance? How did the teacher or team react? 2. What did you do during **the team meeting/when in the teacher's classroom** to build alliance? How did the teacher or team react? 3. What did you do during the **postmeeting** to build alliance? How did the teacher or team react?
Reflecting	1. Think about building alliance across the three phases of the coaching cycle (e.g., premeeting, observation, postmeeting). What worked well for the teacher or team? Why? 2. How could alliance building go better across the three phases? Why? 3. What will you do to enhance alliance building across each phase of the coaching cycle? Why?

Purpose: This guide can be used to reflect on the two scenarios presented in Chapter 5 and discuss reflections with a partner.

Directions:
1. Read the questions that relate to the scenarios included in Chapter 5.
2. Record your responses to each question.
3. Finally, share your responses with a partner.

Scenario 1 Questions
1. Think about Katarina's professional learning options for teachers: participating in bimonthly meetings or participating in one-to-one coaching sessions. Would you offer both types of supports to teachers? Why or why not? 2. How could you use alliance strategies to increase teachers' interest in coaching?

Scenario 2 Questions
1. Why do you think teachers seem reluctant to work with Marta? 2. What do you think about Marta's plan to use the three strategies with Frank? What does and does not make sense to you about the plan? Why? 3. What alliance strategies could Marta use with teachers? Why?

Scenario 3 Questions

1. What are your reactions to the information Esta shared with Carlos?
 	
2a. Read over the requests Esta made of Carlos (shown next).
   • Set goals for the team.
   • Report to Esta what occurs at team meetings.
   • Create and follow an annual plan for what occurs at team meetings.
 	
   What are the pros and cons of meeting each of Esta's requests in relation to building and maintaining alliance?
 	
2b. Should Carlos adhere to each request? Why or why not?
 	
2c. How would you talk with Esta about her requests?
 	
3. How would you begin to work with the team based on what you know from Esta?

Planning, Conducting, and Reflecting on Four Coaching Practices

Purpose: This tool is used by coaches to *plan, conduct,* and *reflect* on coaching cycles.

Directions:
1. Complete the Planning section of the tool prior to working with teachers or teams.
2. Complete the Conducting and Reflecting sections of the tool after working with teachers or teams.

Planning	**Coach:** **Coachee:** 1. What initiated the request for coaching? 2. What will you do during the **premeeting phase** of the coaching cycle to build **alliance**? If the need arises to **model and/or provide performance feedback**, then how will this be accomplished? 3. When working directly **in the classroom or at the team meeting**, how will you build **alliance, observe, and model**? If the need arises to provide in-the-moment teaching/team meeting **performance feedback**, then how will this be accomplished? 4. What will you do during the **postmeeting phase** of the coaching cycle to provide **performance feedback?** If the need arises to model, then how will this be accomplished?
Conducting	1. What did you do during the **premeeting** to build **alliance?** How did the teacher or team react? 2. What did you do during **the team meeting/when in the teacher's classroom** to build **alliance, observe, and model?** How did the teacher or team react? If you provided **performance feedback,** then what did you do, and how did the teacher or team react? 3. What did you do during the **postmeeting** to build **alliance** and provide **performance feedback?** How did the teacher or team react? If you also modeled, what did you do, and how did the team react?
Reflecting	1. What worked well during **each part of the coaching cycle (e.g., premeeting, team meeting/teacher observation, postmeeting)?** Why? 2. What could go better next time during **each phase?** Why? 3. What will you do to enhance **each phase** of the coaching session? Consider how you can improve in each practice: **using alliance strategies, observing, modeling, and providing performance feedback.**

Discussion Guide

Purpose: This discussion guide can be used to reflect on the two scenarios presented in Chapter 6 and discuss reflections with a partner.

Directions:
1. Read the questions.
2. Record your responses to each question in the space provided. Finally, share your responses with a partner.

Scenario 1 Questions
1. Imagine you are Marta. What would you do during the postmeeting session to best support Frank? Consider how you would provide performance feedback and how you would use alliance strategies.
2. What are some things you would avoid doing at the postmeeting if you were Marta? Why?
3. What would you do to prepare for another round of coaching with Frank, assuming the next step would be to conduct a premeeting with him after conducting the postmeeting?

Scenario 2 Questions
1. Imagine you are Carlos. What would you do to help the team become more self-reliant? Be specific by stating how you could begin conducting coaching cycles using the four practices from this book's coaching framework.
2. What do you think is important for you to avoid doing if you were Carlos? Why?
3. How would you work with Esta if you were Carlos? What would you do and why?

Phase 1 Coaching Protocol: The Premeeting

Purpose: Use this protocol to **plan, conduct, and reflect** on a premeeting with a teacher or team. All included prompts are suggestions. Adjust the order of the prompts and/or use only the prompts that work for you and the coachee. Add additional prompts as needed.

Coachee name(s): _____ Coach name: _____ Date: _____

Planning and Conducting the Premeeting
Ask open-ended prompts and use additional alliance strategies.
Open-Ended Prompts
How are you doing today? (Or ask other preliminary questions to kick off the premeeting.)
How has (teaching, leading the school implementation effort) been going lately?
What are you currently working on to improve (teaching, learning, school implementation)?
What concrete action would you like to take to further support improved (teaching, learning, school implementation)? This could be a new action or a continuation of existing actions. Let's refer to this action as your *goal*. **Goal:** _____
Why is this action necessary for supporting improved (teaching, learning, school implementation)? That is, what will happen if you are able to achieve this goal?
How will you measure progress toward your goal?

Coaching for Systems and Teacher Change by Jennifer D. Pierce and Kimberly St. Martin.

Phase 1 Coaching Protocol *(continued)*

Open-Ended Prompts

During an observation, I will collect data by _____. What questions do you have about that?

I may also create a visual that summarizes data I collect. What are your thoughts about that?

I may also model by (describe how modeling may occur). What are your thoughts about that?

Is there anything you would like to discuss prior to observation?

When would it work for me to conduct that observation?

After the observation, we will reconvene to talk about progress toward your goal. When would be a good day and time for us to reconnect?

Other(s):

Phase 1 Coaching Protocol *(continued)*

Additional Alliance Strategies

Showing Strong Interpersonal Skills

- Building trust
  - ☐ Fulfilling responsibilities
  - ☐ Being honest
  - ☐ Showing empathy

- Communicating skillfully
  - ☐ Listen more than you speak
  - ☐ Summarize key ideas from the premeeting
  - ☐ Employ open body language
  - ☐ Ask clarifying and/or open-ended questions

- Nodding your head and/or occasionally verbally confirming you are listening

Using a Collaborative Approach
- ☐ Asking open-ended questions
- ☐ Approaching coaching as a partnership
- ☐ Cocreating a coaching compact
- ☐ Setting one to three actionable and achievable goals with coachee(s) based on needs
- ☐ Coming to agreement about working together and setting parameters

Demonstrating Expertise
- ☐ Sharing knowledge about effective teaching, learning, and/or implementation efforts
- ☐ Showing skill when conducting coaching cycles.

Reflecting on the Premeeting

Respond to the reflection prompts below.

1. How did the premeeting go? What went well? What could go better?

2. What one to three concrete steps will you take to improve the premeeting? Why?

3. How will these steps improve the premeeting?

4. Other reflections and questions:

Phase 2 Coaching Protocol:
The In Class/Meeting Observation

Purpose: Use this protocol to *plan, conduct, and reflect* on the second phase of the coaching cycle when you are observing and/or modeling for the teacher or team. All included data collection tools are suggestions. Adjust the tools so that they work for you and the coachee(s). Add additional data collection tools as needed.

Coachee name(s): _____ Coach name: _____ Date: _____

Planning and Conducting the In Classroom/Meeting Observation

Select data collection source and modeling approach.

See Figure 6.2 for ways to collect data on teacher and team practice.

- List data collection method here:

See Chapter 5 for ways to model for the teacher or team.

- "I do, we do, you do"
- "I do, you do"
- "We do, you do"
- Video exemplars

Collect data.

Teacher/team practice What did the teacher or team do?	Impact How did that affect student learning/ school implementation?	Translation of data into performance feedback? Should I translate this information into performance feedback for the coachee(s)? Yes/No	Time stamp

Phase 2 Coaching Protocol *(continued)*

Construct high-quality performance feedback from data

- The ratio of positive to corrective statements is 4:1 (positive to corrective). If corrective statements are not warranted (e.g., school implementation is not a challenge), then follow the ratio of 4:0 (positive to corrective).
- Positive and corrective statements are specific. Positive statements explicitly link coachee practice to improved student learning or school implementation. Corrective statements explicitly link coachee practice to reduced student learning or school implementation. Both positive and corrective statements contain a rationale why the coachee practice is important. Example: Coachee practice *X* influenced (student learning or school implementation) in *Y* ways. This is important because (research-based rationale for why it is important).
- Performance feedback is provided in a timely fashion (e.g., within 24 hours of conducting Phase 2 of the coaching cycle).
- Verbal feedback can be supported with graphs and/or other visuals.

Performance feedback statement 1 (includes rationale)

Performance feedback statement 2 (includes rationale)

Performance feedback statement 3 (includes rationale)

Performance feedback statement 4 (includes rationale)

Performance feedback statement 5 (includes rationale)

Phase 2 Coaching Protocol *(continued)*

Optional: Create simple visuals (e.g., graphs, charts) to support verbal performance feedback.

- Title for X axis, Y axis, overall visual, and so forth
- Has a legend
- Presentation of data clarifies leader practice and school implementation effort
- Relates to the coachee(s)' goal
- Connects to the verbal performance feedback provided to coachee(s)

Reflecting on the In-Classroom/Meeting Observation

Respond to the reflection prompts below.

1. How did the in-class/in-meeting phase of the cycle go? What went well? What could go better?

2. What one to three concrete steps will you take to improve this phase of the coaching cycle? Why?

3. How will these steps improve this phase of the coaching cycle?

4. Other reflections and questions:

Phase 3 Coaching Protocol: The Postmeeting

Purpose: Use this protocol to **plan, conduct, and reflect** on a postmeeting with a teacher or team. All included prompts are suggestions. Adjust the order of the prompts and/or use only the prompts that work for you and the coachee(s). Add additional prompts as needed.

Coachee name(s): _____ Coach name: _____ Date: _____

Planning and Conducting the Postmeeting
Ask open-ended prompts and use additional alliance strategies.
Open-Ended Prompts
• How are you doing today? (Or other *preliminary questions to kick off the postconference.*)
• During the premeeting, you decided your goal was to _____ (concrete actions) to support (teaching, learning, school implementation). We decided this action necessary for supporting improved (teaching, learning, school implementation) because _____. We also decided to measure progress toward your goal by _____.
• How did it go?
• What helped you make progress toward this goal? How did you know?
• What got in the way of making progress toward this goal? Why?

Phase 3 Coaching Protocol *(continued)*

Additional Alliance Strategies

Showing Strong Interpersonal Skills

- Building trust

  ☐ Fulfilling responsibilities ☐ Being honest ☐ Showing empathy

- Communicating skillfully

  ☐ Listen more than you speak ☐ Employ open body language

  ☐ Summarize key ideas from the preconference ☐ Ask clarifying and/or open-ended questions

- Nodding your head and/or occasionally verbally confirming you are listening

Using a Collaborative Approach

☐ Asking open-ended questions ☐ Setting one to three actionable and achievable goals with coachee(s) based on needs

☐ Approaching coaching as a partnership ☐ Coming to agreement about working together and setting parameters

☐ Cocreating a coaching compact

Demonstrating Expertise

☐ Sharing knowledge about effective teaching, learning, and/or implementation efforts

☐ Showing skill when conducting coaching cycles

Continue to use open-ended questions and provide performance feedback and additional alliance strategies.

- During the second phase of the coaching cycle, I collected data by directly observing you or the team.

- Here is some performance feedback from the data I collected:

  Performance feedback 1:

  Performance feedback 2:

  Performance feedback 3:

  Performance feedback 4:

  Performance feedback 5:

- *Optional: Here is a visual to show links between teacher or team practice and (student learning, school implementation).*

- What are your reactions to this feedback, especially as related to your goal?

- To what degree did (student learning, school implementation effort) improve as a result of what you or the team did? How do you know?

- Thinking ahead to our next coaching session, what can I do to support your efforts to improve?

- Is there anything else you would like to discuss prior to your next coaching cycle?

- When would you like to meet again to begin another coaching cycle?

- Other(s)

Phase 3 Coaching Protocol *(continued)*

Additional Alliance Strategies

Showing Strong Interpersonal Skills

- Building trust
  - ☐ Fulfilling responsibilities
  - ☐ Being honest
  - ☐ Showing empathy
- Communicating skillfully
  - ☐ Listen more than you speak
  - ☐ Summarize key ideas from the preconference
  - ☐ Employ open body language
  - ☐ Ask clarifying and/or open-ended questions
- Nodding your head and/or occasionally verbally confirming you are listening

Using a Collaborative Approach

- ☐ Asking open-ended questions
- ☐ Approaching coaching as a partnership
- ☐ Cocreating a coaching compact
- ☐ Setting one to three actionable and achievable goals with coachee(s) based on needs
- ☐ Coming to agreement about working together and setting parameters

Demonstrating Expertise

- ☐ Sharing knowledge about effective teaching, learning, and/or implementation efforts
- ☐ Showing skill when conducting coaching cycles

Reflecting on the Postmeeting Phase

Respond to the reflection prompts below.

1. How did the postmeeting go? What went well? What could go better?

2. What one to three concrete steps will you take to improve the postmeeting? Why?

3. How will these steps improve the postmeeting?

4. Other reflections and questions:

Readiness Measure

Purpose: Use this assessment to gauge teachers' or teams' readiness to change.

Directions for Administration:

1. Ask individual teachers or each team member to rate themselves on a scale of 1 to 10 for each question (1 = *completely disagree* and 10 = *completely agree*). Coaches may ask the questions verbally and record teacher or team scores. Alternatively, the form can be completed by the teacher or team and then provided to the coach. The Notes column can be used to record any teacher or team comments or questions.
2. Calculate the mean of all the ratings. The mean is the final readiness score. *Note:* For teams, include every score from each person. The total group mean is the final score for the team, which should be used with coaching groups.

Interpretation Guidance: Teachers or teams scoring at 70%–80% can be considered ready to change.

Teacher or team self-rating	Ratings 1 = completely disagree 10 = completely agree	Notes
This change is clearly needed.	1 2 3 4 5 6 7 8 9 10	
I have the skills that are needed to make this change work.	1 2 3 4 5 6 7 8 9 10	
This organization's most senior leader(s) is/are committed to this change.	1 2 3 4 5 6 7 8 9 10	

Purpose: This tool outlines steps for creating and using a communication protocol. A communication protocol provides a process for gathering and sharing information about a change effort. In the protocol, information about the change (why the change is needed, who is affected, the goals of the change effort) is shared with teachers or teams and with leaders working in the system. Just as important, the protocol provides a structured, collaborative process for continually improving the implementation effort.

Directions:
1. Read over the steps, then enact each one.

Steps
1. Work with leaders and teachers or teams to summarize the change effort, including the purpose, the goal, who is involved, what will happen when the change is made, and how supports will be provided to all those affected by the change effort.
2. During the initial meeting, designees involved in the change effort outline the groups, teams, and key individuals involved in the change effort. Outline the types of information that need to be gathered from those involved in the change and disseminated to all parties involved (examples provided in Step 4). Designees from each group or team are identified to be the primary person responsible for gathering and disseminating information.
3. Create a series of virtual or face-to-face meetings where leaders and teachers or teams can convene to talk about the change effort, making sure designees who were identified in the previous step are able to attend. Other people can and should be encouraged to attend the meetings; however, the designees primarily responsible for leading the communication must be present.

4. At each meeting, teachers or teams are asked to share the following:
  a. What is working well
  b. What is not working well
  c. Possible solutions for issues related to the change effort, including who will do what, by when, and how
  d. Any needs they have related to the change effort (e.g., materials, time, other supports)

5. Work with leaders and teachers or teams to ensure that solutions from Step 4c are enacted and needs identified from Step 4d are met.
6. Repeat Steps 3 and 4 so that leaders and teachers or teams continuously communicate about the change effort.

Source: State Implementation and Scaling-up of Evidence-based Practices Center (2013).
Coaching for Systems and Teacher Change by Jennifer D. Pierce and Kimberly St. Martin.

APPENDIX X Tips for Networking Teachers and Teams

Purpose: This document contains tips coaches can use to meaningfully network teachers and teams to other professionals experiencing a similar change.

Directions:
1. Coaches can use these tips when establishing networks of teachers and teams.

Tips
❏ Introduce educators to others who are experiencing similar change efforts.
❏ Facilitate the members in creating an informal purpose statement that describes the focus of the networking community. Research suggests that the most beneficial communities focus on sharing experiences about the change effort, identifying successes and challenges, and offering guidance for the change effort.
❏ Encourage the networked community to create a feasible schedule to interact virtually or face to face about the change effort.
❏ Clarify your role to help the networked community gain access to resources and to listen, rather than guide, the conversations. Encourage members to facilitate the conversation.

Purpose: This resource contains critical questions that coaches can ask teachers and teams when coachees are not ready to make a change. The overarching purpose of motivational interviewing is to offer teachers and teams opportunities for thinking and talking about their own insights about the change effort.

Directions:
1. Familiarize yourself with the questions below.
2. Ask coachees the questions when discussing the change area. The four questions can be asked during a pre- or postmeeting. Coaches may verbally ask the teacher or team to respond to each question and take notes on their responses.
3. It is often helpful to provide the prompts to the teacher or team so that they can reflect on them on their own and then share their responses with you.

Questions
1. Why would you want to make this change?
2. How might you go about it in order to succeed?
3. What are the three best reasons for you to do it?
4. How important is it for you to make this change, and why?

Connecting the Dots:
Readiness for Change, the Coaching
Framework, and Your Coaching Role

Purpose: Use this tool to reflect on what you learned about readiness to change and this text's coaching framework.

Directions:
1. Complete each section of this tool so that you can integrate what you learned from Chapter 7 to your coaching practice.
2. You may find it helpful to discuss your responses with a partner and record any notes.

Questions	
Phase 1: The premeeting	1. What did you learn about readiness that could be applied to Phase 1 of the coaching cycle? 2. What questions remain for you? 3. What are you most excited to apply to your coaching practice? What do you think will be tricky? Why?
Phase 2: In the classroom or at the team meeting	1. What did you learn about readiness that could be applied to Phase 2 of the coaching cycle? 2. What questions remain for you? 3. What are you most excited to apply to your coaching practice? What do you think will be tricky? Why?
Phase 3: The postmeeting	1. What did you learn about readiness that could be applied to Phase 3 of the coaching cycle? 2. What questions remain for you? 3. What are you most excited to apply to your coaching practice? What do you think will be tricky? Why?

Coaching Implementation Checklist

Purpose: This checklist can be used to identify what is and is not in place when implementing coaching. The document also contains suggestions for taking a strategic approach to implementing coaching.

Directions:

1. Go through each bold statement within the Critical Implementation Factors column and ask, "Does this critical implementation factor apply to coaching in our pre-K program/school?" If the answer is yes, then check the box and acknowledge the specific implementation factor is in place. If the answer is no, then do not check the box and then ask, "What can coaches and pre-K/school educators do to achieve this statement?"

2. Then, see the recommendations (shown in italics) to turn unchecked boxes to checked boxes.

System component	Critical implementation factors (bold font) *Recommendations for improving the critical factor (italic font)*
Human resources	☐ **Leaders support coaching by communicating the vision, purpose, and goals of coaching.** *Work with leaders to generate a statement of coaching.* ☐ **Champions voice support for coaching.** *Ask coaches to share coaching success stories with the entire staff. Stories should highlight productive changes in teacher or team practice, systems, and student outcomes.* ☐ **Staff hold positive beliefs about coaching, especially in relation to other professional learning opportunities.** *Anonymously survey staff to determine what forms of professional learning are viewed as most effective and why. If coaching is ranked low, then use the survey information to pinpoint how coaching should change and how it should remain the same. Effective coaching practices should not be omitted.* ☐ **Coach has positive self-efficacy.** *Identify the coach's strengths and how these strengths can continue to develop. Use the self-assessment or direct observation fidelity measure to identify these strengths.* ☐ **Coach demonstrates coaching competencies.** *Use the competencies within this chapter to continually improve coach knowledge and skill.*
Fiscal resources	☐ **Costs (e.g., long-term investment requirements) of coaching are calculated on a regular basis.** *Work with leaders to identify the costs of coaching, including salaries, required technologies and materials (if any), release time, and so forth.* ☐ **Adequate resources are allocated for coaching (e.g., time, funding, personnel) for the role, teachers or teams to participate in coaching, and coaches to participate in their own development opportunities.** *Work with leaders to identify the resources available for coaching and how those resources can be allocated. These resources should take into account the time staff need to participate in coaching, costs for coaches to attend their own development opportunities, and the salaries for coaches. Ideally, these resources should be allocated toward coaching for the long term rather than as a temporary measure.*
Material resources	☐ **Easy-to-use information about coaching that distills current and seminal research is distributed to staff on a regular basis.** *Create one-page informational fliers about the impacts of coaching for staff and distribute the information annually or more frequently as needed.* ☐ **Research-informed professional standards for coaching shape the coaching role.** *Use the coaching competencies within Chapter 9 to create a coaching job description.* ☐ **A research-informed coaching framework shapes coaching practice.** *Incorporate the coaching framework from Chapters 3, 5, and 6 to the coaching job description.* ☐ **The coaching framework is adapted to local contextual needs while retaining the most effective coaching practices.** *Adapt the coaching framework from Chapters 3, 5, and 6 while retaining the four effective practices and overall three-phase coaching cycles.*

Source: Pierce and Ferguson (2014).

Coaching for Systems and Teacher Change by Jennifer D. Pierce and Kimberly St. Martin.

Coaching Implementation Checklist *(continued)*

Policies/regulations	☐ **Policies and regulations support coaches' work with teachers and teams.** *Compile all policies and regulations that relate to coaching. Work with leaders to adjust the documents so that they support coaches' work with teachers and teams.* ☐ **Policies and regulations define coaching as a nonevaluative support mechanism for teachers and teams.** *Compile all policies and regulations that relate to coaching. Work with leaders to ensure that the documents present coaching as a nonevaluative support mechanism for teachers and teams.* ☐ **The written vision and goals of coaching are in alignment with the pre-K/school program's overall values and goals.** *Compile all policies and regulations that relate to coaching. Work with leaders to ensure that the documents present the vision and goals of coaching in alignment with the pre-K/school program's overall values and goals.*
Processes/procedures	☐ **Coaching is implemented with consideration to phases: engaging, planning for coaching, initial implementation, continuous improvement of implementation.** *Before coaching is enacted, staff are asked to provide feedback on the need for coaching, potential benefits and costs, and their willingness to participate in coaching. Feedback gathered from the "engaging" phase is then used to plan for coaching: who will participate, when, why, and how. In addition, during the "plan" phase, coaching job descriptions are developed that are based on competencies and a research-informed coaching framework. Coaches with relevant knowledge and skills are hired, and processes for measuring coach practice are created. During initial implementation, the plan created in the prior phase is enacted. Coaches and leaders work together to understand the impact of coach practice on team or teacher practice, costs, and benefits. Coaches measure their own practice to continuously improve. In the "continuous improvement" phase, the original plan is revisited and improved on based on data on the impact of coach practice, costs, and benefits.* ☐ **There is a process for measuring coach practice, and the process is used on a regular basis.** *Use the self-assessment and the direct observation coaching fidelity measure to collect data on coach practice. These measures are used as often as possible but at least once per year.* ☐ **Plan-Do-Study-Act cycles are used to improve coaching practice.** *Use the self-assessment and the direct observation coaching fidelity measure to conduct Plan-Do-Study-Act cycles at least on an annual basis.* ☐ **Plan-Do-Study-Act cycles are used to identify changes in teacher or team practice, the system, and student outcomes in relation to coaching.** *Follow the steps of a Plan-Do-Study-Act cycle to draw conclusions about the qualitative and quantitative changes found in teacher or team practice, systems, and student outcomes from coaching. Use Figure 4.3 (Appendix I) to support this work.* ☐ **Teachers and teams know how to gain access to coaching.** *Work with leaders to create and share procedures that inform teachers and teams how to gain access to coaching.* ☐ **Teachers and teams can readily access coaching without disrupting typical workflows.** *Work with leaders to ensure that teachers and teams can easily participate in coaching without sacrificing the quality of their primary job responsibilities.*
Next steps	What needs to happen to turn the unchecked boxes to checked boxes?

Calculating the Fiscal Costs of Coaching

Purpose: Use this tool to calculate the costs of coaching. You may need to enlist the help of your school principal or someone from the district finance department.

Directions:
1. Use the top portion of this form to calculate the cost of teacher coaching.
2. Use the bottom half of the form to calculate the costs of coaching teams.

Coaching Teachers			
Column A: Costs	Column B: Salary cost per session	Column C: Number of sessions annually	Column D: Cost per row (for each row, multiply Column B times Column C)
Coach			
Teacher			
Materials			
Other staff (e.g., substitute)			

To calculate the total cost of teacher coaching, add each number from Column D.

Record that cost here:

Coaching Teams			
Column A: Costs	Column B: Salary cost per session	Column C: Number of sessions annually	Column D: Cost per row (for each row, multiply Column B times Column C)
Coach			
Team members (include costs for all team members)			
Leader			
Materials			
Other staff (e.g., include total costs for substitutes for each team member, if required)			

To calculate the total cost of team coaching, add each number from Column D.

Record that cost here:

Connecting the Dots:
Changes in Teacher/Team Practice, System Outcomes, and Student Outcomes

Purpose: Use this tool to identify the impact of coaching.

Directions:
1. Use the top portion of this form to identify the impact of teacher coaching.
2. Use the bottom half of the form to identify the impact of team coaching.

Teacher Coaching			
Data on coaching	*Changes to teacher practice*	*Changes to student outcomes*	*Implications*
Use of coaching framework:			
Information from coaching self-assessment:			
Information from direct observation measure of coach practice:			

Team Coaching				
Data on coaching	*Changes to team practice*	*Changes to system outcomes*	*Changes to student outcomes*	*Implications*
Use of coaching framework:				
Information from coaching self-assessment:				
Information from direct observation measure of coach practice:				

Coaching Self-Assessment

Purpose: Use this tool to assess your coaching practice.

Directions:

1. Think about each area of coaching.
2. Check the boxes that accurately describe how you coach.
3. Rate yourself in each area on the 5 point scale. Provide a rationale for each score and note how you can improve in the future.
4. Calculate your global score by adding up each rating, dividing the total by 3, and multiplying that decimal number by 100 to get a percentage.
5. Record your overall percentage here: _____.
6. Complete this assessment at least annually and compare your results over time.

Area	What did I do?	What is my score? 1 = *Low* 5 = *High* Why? What will I do to continuously improve?

Using coaching practices	☐ I used alliance strategies with teachers or teams.
	
	☐ I observed teachers or teams and collected data on teacher or team practice.
	
	☐ I modeled for teachers or teams (if needed).
	
	☐ I provided performance feedback that was specific, timely, affirmative (positive), and corrective (if warranted).
	  • What went well?
	  • What could go better?
		Circle your score: 1 2 3 4 5
		
		Why?
		
		What will I do to improve?

Planning and reflecting on coaching cycles	☐ I planned coaching cycles.
	
	☐ I reflected on coaching cycles.
	
	Note: The next section self-assesses the act of conducting the coaching cycle.
	  • What went well?
	  • What could go better?
		Circle your score: 1 2 3 4 5
		
		Why?
		
		What will I do to improve?

Using the three-phase coaching cycle	☐ I held a premeeting with teacher or team.
	
	☐ I worked with the teacher in the classroom or I worked with the team in the team meeting.
	
	☐ I held a postmeeting with the teacher or team.
	  • What went well?
	  • What could go better?
		Circle your score: 1 2 3 4 5
		
		Why?
		
		What will I do to improve?

Index

Page numbers followed by *f*, *t*, and *b* indicate figures, tables, and boxes respectively.